Skepticism and the Veil of Perception

Studies in Epistemology and Cognitive Theory
Series Editor: *Paul K. Moser, Loyola University of Chicago*

Metaepistemology and Skepticism
by Richard A. Fumerton, University of Iowa

Warrant in Contemporary Epistemology: Essays in Honor of Plantinga's Theory of Knowledge
edited by Jonathan L. Kvanvig, Texas A&M University

A Defense of the Given
by Evan M. Fales, University of Iowa

Pragmatism and Realism
by Frederick L. Will; edited by Kenneth R. Westphal, University of New Hampshire

Realism/Antirealism and Epistemology
edited by Christopher B. Kulp, Santa Clara University

Belief and Knowledge: Mapping the Cognitive Landscape
by Kenneth M. Sayre, University of Notre Dame

In Defense of Radical Empiricism: Essays and Lectures by Roderick Firth
edited by John Troyer, University of Connecticut, Storrs

Illusions of Paradox: A Feminist Epistemology Naturalized
by Richmond Campbell, Dalhousie University

Rethinking Intuition: The Psychology of Intuition and Its Role in Philosophical Inquiry
edited by Michael R. DePaul, University of Notre Dame, and William Ramsey, University of Notre Dame

Contemporary Theories of Knowledge
by John L. Pollock, University of Arizona, and Joseph Cruz, Hampshire College

The Nature of Meaningfulness: Representing, Powers, and Meaning
by Robert K. Shope, University of Massachusetts, Boston

Knowledge, Belief, and Character: Readings in Virtue Epistemology
edited by Guy Axtell, University of Nevada, Reno

Resurrecting Old-Fashioned Foundationalism
edited by Michael R. DePaul, University of Notre Dame

Reality and Humean Supervenience: Essays on the Philosophy of David Lewis
edited and introduced by Gerhard Preyer, J. W. Goethe University, and Frank Siebelt, J. W. Goethe University, Frankfurt

Skepticism and the Veil of Perception
by Michael Huemer

Skepticism and the Veil of Perception

MICHAEL HUEMER

ROWMAN & LITTLEFIELD PUBLISHERS, INC.
Lanham • Boulder • New York • Toronto • Oxford

ROWMAN & LITTLEFIELD PUBLISHERS, INC.

Published in the United States of America
by Rowman & Littlefield Publishers, Inc.
A wholly owned subsidary of The Rowman & Littlefield Publishing Group, Inc.
4501 Forbes Boulevard, Suite 200, Lanham, Maryland 20706
www.rowmanlittlefield.com

12 Hid's Copse Road
Cumnor Hill, Oxford OX2 9JJ, England

British Library Cataloguing in Publication Information Available

Library of Congress Cataloging-in-Publication Data

Huemer, Michael, 1969–
    Skepticism and the veil of perception / Michael Huemer.
       p. cm.—(Studies in epistemology and cognitive theory)
    Includes bibliographical references (p.) and index.
    ISBN 0-7425-1252-5 (alk. paper)—ISBN 0-7425-1253-3 (pbk. : alk. paper)
       1. Knowledge, Theory of. 2. Realism. 3. Skepticism. I. Title. II. Studies in
    epistemology and cognitive theory (Unnumbered)

    BD161 .H84 2001
    121'.34–dc21   2001019092

Printed in the United States of America

♾ The paper used in this publication meets the minimum requirements of American
National Standard for Information Sciences—Permanence of Paper for Printed Library
Materials, ANSI/NISO Z39.48-1992.

Dedicated to René Descartes,
for obvious reasons

Contents

Analytical Contents

Fumerton argues that the possibility of hallucination shows that perceptual beliefs are not justified by virtue of direct acquaintance with objects. I grant this but maintain instead that they are justified by virtue of the forcefulness of perceptual experience.

Objection: in a case of double vision, you see two of something, but there are not two physical objects; therefore, what you see is something nonphysical. Reply: No, you see a single object, but you see it as being in two different places.

There is always a delay between the time an event happens and the time of your perceptual experience of it. But this does not show that we do not directly perceive the event, in the relevant sense of "direct."

There are causal intermediaries between the distal object and one's perceptual experience. But this does not show that we do not directly perceive the distal object, in the relevant sense of "direct."

Objection: colors do not really exist in the objective, physical world. But since we only see colors and colored objects, it follows that what we see is not physical phenomena. I respond by arguing that colors are in the physical world.

VII. AN OBJECTION TO INDIRECT REALISM: THE PROBLEM OF SPATIAL PROPERTIES
If sense data exist, where are they located? I consider and reject five possible answers.

We may reject this view since the objects of our awareness in perception have shapes, and whatever has shape occupies space.

This would be plausible if sense data were brain states; however, our brain states do not have the right spatial and other properties to be the objects of our awareness in perception.

We have seen the power of direct realism in accounting for perceptual knowledge and have escaped Hume's disheartening conclusion as to the "perplexity and confusion which is inherent in human nature."

Figures

Preface

First, let me say something about the subject matter of this book. It concerns one of the central problems in Western philosophy, the nature of our knowledge of the external world (the world outside the mind). Philosophers who study the nature of knowledge have been beset since ancient times by the arguments of philosophical skeptics. Skepticism, in the sense in which I am using the term here, is the position that it is impossible to know anything about the external world at all. The idea of "the veil of perception" is the idea that all one is ever immediately aware of is one's perceptual *experiences*, or *representations* of external objects, not the objects themselves—an idea which is often supported by the claim that our perception "distorts" the objects we perceive, rather than presenting them as they really are (perceptual illusions and perspective phenomena are often cited in this connection). Thus, our processes of perception are like a "veil" standing between us and the real world, preventing us from ever really perceiving (objective) reality. Evidently, the doctrine of a veil of perception is closely related to skepticism; indeed, I believe the two ideas feed off one another and will stand or fall together—but that is something needing further discussion later.

I oppose both of those ideas. In this book, I explain how we are aware of, and have knowledge of, the character of the external world. I defend a doctrine sometimes called "naive realism," which holds that perception gives us direct awareness of the external world and that it enables us to *know* (some of) what that world is like. Besides giving a positive theory of perceptual awareness, I show the flaws in the major arguments that have been used to motivate skepticism. See chapter I for more elaboration on my aims.

Second, a word about whom this book is for. I have taken the risk of aiming at two different audiences. The first audience consists of professional philosophers (mainly professors). The other audience one might call, for lack of a better term, amateur philosophers; that is, individuals who take an interest in philosophy but are not paid to do so, including undergraduate and graduate students but also any others interested in the subject (I am not, of course, using "amateur" in a negative sense). I say I have taken a risk, because it is difficult to write anything that will satisfy both the specialist and the nonspecialist alike. Nevertheless, I think it can be done.

In consideration of these two audiences: the endnotes are meant mainly for professional philosophers; they contain literature citations, technical qualifications to what is written in the main text, and answers to some possible objections. I use two special symbols that nonprofessionals might not know: "~" for "it is not the case that," and "∴" for "therefore." Apart from that, the text does not presuppose any prior knowledge of the subject. I have tried to explain all of the necessary background before launching into my own solution to the problem with which I am concerned.

Lastly, I would like to thank several other philosophers for the contributions they have made to my philosophical development and to this book in particular. The central ideas of this book grew out of the work I did for my Ph.D. dissertation at Rutgers University; for that reason, I thank the members of my dissertation committee—Peter Klein, Brian McLaughlin, Richard Fumerton, and Richard Foley—for their help in thinking these issues through. I would like to thank Michael Tooley for the conversations in which he tried to convince me of the merits of the representational theory of perception and which led me to the argument of section VII.5. I am also indebted to Bob Pasnau for his many helpful comments on the manuscript, which have led to numerous improvements. Finally, I owe an intellectual debt to René Descartes, not only for initiating the modern era of philosophy, but for inspiring my own interest in the theory of knowledge. I like to think that he would have appreciated my own contribution to the field.

I. Introduction: The Problem of Perceptual Knowledge

Try the following experiment. Hold a finger in front of your face. Focus your eyes on the finger, but attend to a distant object in the background. If you're doing this right, the background object should appear double and blurry. If you now bring the background object into focus, you will see the finger in your visual field split into two, blurry fingers.

There is, of course, a scientific explanation for why this happens. It has to do with the fact that each of your eyes has a different vantage point on the room; one of the finger-images is produced by your left eye, and the other by your right eye. But the scientific explanation is not our concern here. Our concern is with the philosophical implications that may be drawn from this phenomenon, about the relationship between perception and reality. Obviously, there are not really two fingers in the physical world. Nevertheless, you are "seeing" two of something. Therefore, we ask: *What is it that there are two of?*

A number of philosophers have put forward the following answer: There are two *images* of the finger *in your mind*. It is these images—rather than the actual, physical finger—that you are directly aware of; that is why there appear to be two fingers. Now consider the implications of this position. The finger in your visual field can make a continuous transition from being clearly in focus to being clearly out of focus. Therefore, if the blurry "fingers" that you see are really only images in the mind, it seems that the in-focus "finger" is also an image in the mind. In fact, since the same experiment could be performed with any object you see, *all* of the objects you are now seeing are images existing in your mind—which you are in the habit of *mistaking* for real, physical objects.[1]

This idea will probably strike you—it certainly ought to strike you—as quite extraordinary, and perhaps unbelievable. I can see a desk-shaped object in front of me right now; if I reach out with my hand, I seem to feel that same object; it is rectangular, solid; if I sit on it, it will support my weight. Surely this thing is no mere image! Nevertheless, let us pursue the theory to its logical conclusion.

There are similar arguments for the rest of the five senses, to show that what we directly perceive is always an image or "representation" in our minds. Now, if the immediate objects of awareness in perception are always mental images, the question inevitably arises, *What reason have we for believing anything other than the mental images exists?* Your experience *could* be qualitatively the same as it is now without there being a physical finger—that is, if only the image existed.

A common way to illustrate this possibility is through the following scenario. Suppose a group of scientists in a technologically advanced future figure out how to remove a human brain from its body and keep it alive in a vat of nutrients. Furthermore, the scientists have figured out exactly how to electrically stimulate the brain's sensory cortex so as to induce sensory experiences qualitatively identical with the experiences of a normal person, say, reading a book. Theoretically, this is possible; all of the brain's "information" about the world (from which it "constructs" our mental images) comes from electrical signals coming into the brain from various nerves. Imagine the scientists duplicate the normal pattern of electrical stimulation. To the brain, everything would appear normal; the brain would have no way of knowing that it was floating in a vat, and so on. In other words, the brain would be experiencing sensory *images* just like the images you are now experiencing, although there would be no physical objects in the real world corresponding to those images. The brain could "read" a nonexistent book, "walk" down a nonexistent street, and so on. (I use scare quotes because the brain would not really be reading or walking, only seeming to do so.) This sort of scenario is also illustrated in popular movies such as *Total Recall* and *The Matrix*, which the reader may wish to view to make the issues more vivid.

All of this is leading up to the question: *How do you know that you aren't, right now, a brain in a vat?*

Some few philosophers have been led by this kind of consideration to the conclusion that we can never know about the objective world—that is, the world outside of our minds; we can only know, at best, about our mental representations of the world (the "subjective" world). This position is known as "skepticism"—more specifically, it is "skepticism about the external world."

The problem of perceptual knowledge is the problem of how we know that the objects we seem to perceive are real. That is the focus of this book. There are four main positions philosophers have taken on this issue: two forms of realism and two forms of antirealism.

Realists maintain that there is an objective world, existing independent of our perception (a.k.a. "the real world") and that human beings can know about the nature of this world. The two forms of realism are as follows:

1. *Direct realists* maintain—contrary to the argument given above—that we are directly aware of real, physical objects in perception and that this explains how we know about the nature of those objects.
2. *Indirect realists* hold, instead, that our awareness of the real world is indirect. They accept arguments like the one given above, which says that what we are immediately aware of in perception is only mental images;[2] however, they say that we can *infer* the existence of real objects *corresponding* to our images, because that is the best explanation for why we have the sort of mental images we do.

Realism has two kinds of opponents:

3. *Idealists* hold that there is no objective world; there is only the mind and the images, thoughts, feelings, and so on in the mind. (This is called "idealism" because the mental images used to be called "ideas.")[3]
4. *Skeptics* hold that we cannot *know* that there is an objective world nor, if there is one, what it is like.

In the subsequent chapters, I will defend direct realism against all comers. I will argue that perception makes us directly aware of real, physical things, not mental images. I will develop a theory of epistemic justification to show why we are justified in believing in such objects. And I will show that the arguments philosophers have given in favor of our perceiving mental images—including the above argument from the case of double vision, along with several others—are fallacious, as are the arguments used to show that we cannot know about the objective world.

In a way, I am taking up Descartes's project, or at least a part of his project, but I propose an entirely different way of carrying it out. Descartes reflected that there were many beliefs he had accepted, perhaps foolishly, when he was a child and too young to possess sound judgement. He therefore resolved to make a general examination of his beliefs, to root out the false or unjustified ones and to put his whole belief system on a rational foundation.[4] He began with a consideration of the arguments for philosophical skepticism, which, by and by, he tried to refute, in the course of establishing his knowledge of the external world. Descartes also sought a kind of *absolute certainty* with which I do not concern myself here, but the essential point I share with him is the desire to verify the rationality of my overall system of beliefs, particularly in the face of the reasons for doubt raised by philosophical skeptics—the sort of reasons I discuss above and that Descartes discussed at the outset of his famous

Meditations. I have always regarded Descartes's project, since I first learned of it, as both a natural one and one of the foremost intellectual importance. It is what drew me to the discipline of epistemology at first and, ultimately, motivated this book.

This is probably because I took the arguments for skepticism more seriously than Descartes himself did—though I have since come closer to his view of them. Most of those who read Descartes's *Meditations* find the skeptical arguments he presents at the outset far more powerful and convincing than his alleged refutation of them later in the book. Yet Descartes appears to have considered them as little more than an academic exercise, for, referring to his arguments for the existence of the external world, he writes:

> The great benefit of these arguments is not that they prove what they establish—namely that there really is a world, and that human beings have bodies and so on—since no sane person has ever seriously doubted these things. The point is that in considering these arguments we come to realize that they are not as solid or as transparent as the arguments which lead us to knowledge of our own minds and of God, so that the latter are the most certain and evident of all possible objects of knowledge for the human intellect. Indeed, this is the one thing that I set myself to prove in these Meditations.[5]

Yet generations of philosophy students, myself included, have studied Descartes for his discussion of the arguments for skepticism, leaving his arguments about God by the wayside.

When a person first hears about the brain-in-a-vat scenario, he is apt to have one of three reactions. Reaction #1: "That's stupid. I refuse to talk about that." Reaction #2: "Gosh, maybe I *am* a brain in a vat. How would I know?" Reaction #3: "What is wrong with this argument? And what can I learn from that about the nature of knowledge?" I would like to encourage you to cultivate reaction #3. Descartes thought one could learn (not from the brain-in-a-vat scenario, but from others like it) that the knowledge of one's own mind and of God was more fundamental and unquestionable than the knowledge of the physical world and that the latter rested on the former. I think, on the contrary, that Descartes's solution to his skeptical problems failed and that one can learn something else from *that*: that Descartes's theory of perception and perceptual knowledge was fundamentally wrong; that we need to adopt a different theory, a direct realist theory. That is the case I would like to make in this book.

Notes

1. Hume, *Enquiry*, 152; *Treatise*, 202, 210-11.

2. I do not mean that all indirect realists accept the argument from double vision in particular, but just that they accept arguments with similar conclusions. See chapter VI for survey of indirect realist arguments. Also, not *all* indirect realists have sought to rest belief in external objects on inference to the best explanation, as suggested in the text—Descartes did not, but he is the only exception I know of.

3. See Berkeley's *Principles* and *Dialogues*. I do not discuss idealism at any length in this book, because almost no one believes it, but I think that it rests upon the same mistakes as representationalism.

4. *Meditations*, opening paragraph.

5. Synopsis of the *Meditations*, 11.

II. The Lure of Radical Skepticism

Philosophical skeptics hold that one cannot know anything about the external world.[1] The phrase "the external world" (a.k.a. "the objective world") refers to everything that exists outside of one's own mind. So, according to the skeptic, you can not know how many fingers you have, if any. You cannot know whether the book you seem to be reading from really exists, or if it is just a convincing illusion. You also cannot know anything about the minds of other people—you cannot know whether there are any other conscious beings in the world, nor, if there are, what kinds of thoughts they might be having. You can only know, at most, what is going on in your own mind. Every person (assuming there are more than one person) is in the same situation—that is, each person knows only of his own mind.

As an aside, notice that the skeptic does not say you only know what is going on *in your head*. He says you only know what is going on in your *mind*. "Heads," just like fingers and books and brains, are objects in the alleged physical world of whose existence we can never be certain. You think you have a head only because you think you can see and feel it; but what you really, directly experience is only a mental representation of a head (just as, in the case of a finger, you experience a mental representation of the finger), which could be an illusion. For all you know, you might be only a disembodied spirit, subject to a massive hallucination of existing in the physical world.

Notice also that skepticism is not the same thing as idealism. The skeptic need not *deny* the existence of an external world, as the idealist does. Rather, the skeptic maintains that we *do not know* there is an external world. To use an analogy, the skeptic is like the agnostic, whereas the idealist is like the atheist. This puts the skeptic in a stronger position than the idealist, for this reason: the skeptic does not need to prove that our beliefs about physical objects are false or even probably false; the skeptic only needs to create some reasonable doubt about those beliefs.

3. I cannot have an infinitely long chain of reasoning for any of my beliefs.
4. Circular reasoning cannot produce knowledge.
5. Nor can I gain knowledge by structure 2c, for
   (a) I would not know my starting beliefs to be true (from 1), and
   (b) I cannot gain knowledge by deriving it from assumptions that I do not know to be true.
6. Therefore, I cannot know anything.[3]

What is wrong with the above argument? The majority of philosophers and others who hear the argument say that it is premise (1) which is mistaken. They say that there are certain self-evident, or *foundational* propositions. A foundational proposition, by definition, is one that we can know to be true *without* having a reason for it, and the people who believe in such things are called "foundationalists." According to most foundationalists, propositions such as "2 = 2" and "I am now conscious" would be good examples of foundational propositions. I do not have to give an argument, or engage in a process of reasoning, to know that I am conscious, or that the number 2 is equal to itself. I merely think about these propositions and thereupon find their truth immediately obvious.

The skeptic, of course, will deny the existence of self-evident propositions. But why? Obviously, the skeptic cannot say, "It is self-evident that self-evident propositions do not exist." To be consistent, he will have to produce an *argument* against the idea of self-evident propositions. What argument can he give?

Well, the skeptic can argue that the foundationalist has no way of distinguishing *self-evident* propositions from merely *arbitrary* propositions. A self-evident proposition, we have said, is one that we need have no reason for in order to be fully justified (or rational) in accepting it. An arbitrary proposition, on the other hand, is a proposition that we have no reason for and would be wholly unjustified in believing. For instance, suppose I suddenly decide, completely out of the blue, that I think there is a twelve-headed purple dragon living on Venus. This would be an arbitrary belief. The foundationalist must explain what *differentiates* a foundational proposition like "2 = 2" from an arbitrary proposition like "There is a twelve-headed purple dragon on Venus." That is, he must identify some feature of the foundational proposition that the arbitrary proposition lacks, and that explains why the foundational proposition is justified. Let "F" denote this feature.[4]

Assume, then, that I have a belief, A, which is a legitimate foundational belief. And assume that I have another belief, B, which is merely arbitrary. By hypothesis, A has F, while B lacks F. Now, either I am *aware* of feature F, or I am not. But if I were completely unaware of feature F, then how could its presence serve to make it rational for me to accept A? If the presence of F is to explain why I am rational (or justified) in accepting A but not rational in accepting B, it must be something that I am aware of (in the one case, but not in the other). Otherwise, A and B will be, *from my point of view*, equally good (or equally arbitrary) assumptions. In that case, given the information available to me, it would be equally reasonable for me to accept one as to accept the other.

So the foundationalist position will have to be that it is reasonable for me to accept A, because I am aware that A has feature F. But then A is not a foundational proposition after all, because I *do* have a reason for accepting A—namely, that A has F. Thus, foundationalism is reduced to absurdity: from the supposition that A is legitimately foundational, we can derive the conclusion that A is not foundational after all. Therefore, the very idea of a foundational proposition is self-contradictory.[5] Therefore, it appears, the skeptic's argument stands.

2. The Problem of the Criterion[6]

I have on my desk an epistemologically interesting toy called "the Magic Eight Ball." It is a plastic ball painted like an eight ball, and it is meant to be used as follows. You ask the eight ball a yes/no question. Then you turn it over and see an answer float up to a window in the bottom. Answers include the likes of "Yes, definitely," "Very doubtful," and "Cannot predict now."

Now, imagine there were a community in which use of the eight ball was an accepted method of arriving at conclusions.[7] Suppose you meet one of these eight-ball reasoners, and you ask him why he believes that the eight ball is a reliable informant. He swiftly takes out his Magic Eight Ball, says, "Are you reliable?" and turns it over. At this point, if the answer "No" floats up to the window, then the eight-ball reasoner is in trouble. But suppose a definite "Yes" answer appears, and the eight-ball reasoner triumphantly declares that the reliability of the eight ball has been established. Would this be legitimate?[8]

Evidently not. You would no doubt object, rightly, that there is a problem of circularity here. If we already knew the eight ball was reliable, then we would be justified in accepting the answers it produces. But if the eight ball is unreliable, then we should not trust its answers. And if we don't know whether it is reliable, then we likewise should not trust its answers *until* its reliability has been established. The method of eight-ball reasoning presupposes that we know the eight ball to be reliable, in the sense that it would not be reasonable to use the method unless we already knew (or at least had reason to believe) it to be a reliable method. Therefore, we certainly cannot use eight-ball reasoning to establish that the eight ball is reliable.

Now consider an analogous case. Suppose some skeptic comes along and asks you why you believe the senses to be reliable. Why do you think that, when you seem to see, hear, or feel things, this is a reliable indicator of the way things really are, in the external world? How would you respond?

Here is one thing you might try. You go to an eye doctor to have your eyes examined. He gives you a series of tests, and at the end he assures you that your eyesight is perfect. Then you go to another doctor to take some hearing tests. He assures you that you have excellent hearing. (You might have difficulty finding doctors to test your taste, smell, and sense of touch, but let's pass over that difficulty.) You then explain to the skeptic that the reliability of your senses has been established. Would this be legitimate?

Apparently not. You would be engaging in just the same sort of circular reasoning that the benighted eight-ball reasoner used, for you can only collect the results of your tests by using your senses. You may seem to hear the doctors tell you that your hearing and eyesight are normal, but how do you know they are really saying that? Indeed, if you were in doubt as to the reliability of your senses in general, you could not even be sure that the doctors really existed, let alone that they were reliable informants.

So you will have to use some other method to verify the reliability of your senses—you will have to rely on some cognitive faculty other than the senses. But—here is the problem—whatever method you try to use to verify that your senses are reliable, the skeptic can always ask why you believe *that* method to be reliable. For instance, suppose you wanted to prove the reliability of the senses through the exercise of pure reason (though I have no idea how such a proof would go).[9] In that case, the skeptic could ask why you think reason itself is reliable. You could not use reason to establish the reliability of reason, nor could you use the five senses to establish the reliability of reason, again on pain of circularity. So you will need to find yet a third belief-forming method. At which point the skeptic will question the reliability of this third method as well. At some point, and probably sooner rather than later, you will have to either resort to circular reasoning or else give up on answering the skeptic's question. But this means that ultimately you cannot establish the reliability of your cognitive faculties. And all of your beliefs are formed through one or another of your cognitive faculties, whether it be through the five senses, or reason, or memory, or introspection. Since you cannot know whether any of your belief-forming methods is reliable, it seems, you cannot know whether any of your beliefs is true. In short, you are in the same position as the eight-ball reasoner. The eight-ball-generated beliefs were all unjustified since the eight-ball reasoner could not (noncircularly) establish that the eight ball was reliable. Similarly, all of your beliefs are unjustified since you cannot (noncircularly) establish that your belief-forming methods in general are reliable. This argument can be summarized as follows:

1. All my beliefs are formed by some method.
2. I am justified in accepting a belief formed by method M only if I *first* know that M is reliable.
3. I do not have an infinite series of belief-forming methods.
4. Thus, all my beliefs must rest on beliefs formed by methods whose reliability has not first been established. (from 1 and 3)
5. Therefore, none of my beliefs are justified. (from 2 and 4)

This argument is similar to the argument of section II.1. Again we have a threat of infinite regress or circularity, though this time it would be a series of belief-forming methods, rather than a series of beliefs. Once we rule out both the infinite regress and the circularity possibilities, the only remaining possibility is that I have belief-forming methods whose reliability is not established by any method. This is analogous to the beliefs of section II.1 that are not supported by any reasons. I pointed out that even the most impeccable derivation of a conclusion from such assumptions would do nothing to establish the truth of the conclusion, given that we have no reason to accept the starting assumptions. Similarly, even the most scrupulous exercise of method M, whatever that may be, will do nothing whatsoever to establish the truth of any conclusion, given that we have no reason to think M itself is reliable. As a result, it seems, we have no way of knowing anything whatever.

3. How Can You Get outside Your Head?

Most of the things we think we know, including everything we think we know about the physical world, we learn through sensory perception, which includes sight, hearing, taste, touch, and smell. Of course, this does not mean that everything we know about the physical world is something we actually observe. A lot of what we know of the physical world is the result of scientific theorizing or inference, but those theories and inferences are ultimately *based on* observations. For instance, we know of the existence of atoms through inferences from the observed results of experiments. Similarly, I know that the Battle of Hastings took place in 1066, not because I personally observed it, but because I read that in a history book—but I knew what the book said only because I could *see the book*. In that sense, my belief was acquired through the exercise of my senses.

If you think about it, then, you will probably realize that everything you think you know about the external world is dependent on your senses. So in order to determine how much we really know about the physical world, we must first ask what the senses really tell us about the physical world. This question can be separated into two sub-issues: First, what is it that the senses make us *directly aware* of? Second, what can be *inferred* from what we are thus directly aware of?

The skeptical argument we are about to consider seeks to establish, first, that the senses do not make us directly aware of the physical world; and second, that no conclusions about the physical world can be inferred from what we are directly aware of either. It will follow that we can have no knowledge of the physical world.[10]

To put that another way: the skeptic will seek to show, first, that direct realism is false. Second, he will try to show that indirect realism is false as well. It will then be clear that we have no knowledge of the physical world, since we do not know about it directly, and we do not know about it indirectly either.

The first part of the argument—the falsity of direct realism—is supposed to be established by the sort of argument we began with in chapter I. There are, actually, quite a few arguments against direct realism, which we shall consider more fully in chapter VI, but for now, let us stick to the argument from double vision. As you recall, we considered a case in which, though there is only one physical finger in front of you, you seem to see two fingerlike things. This was supposed to show that what you are immediately aware of is mental images, rather than the physical finger.[11] The reasoning can be summarized as follows:

1. As your focus shifts to the background, the fingerlike thing you are seeing splits in two.
2. No physical object splits in two at this time.
3. Therefore, the thing you are seeing is not a physical object.

If the thing you are seeing is not a physical object, the next natural candidate is that it is a mental image (what else could it plausibly be?). These mental images are traditionally called "sense data," so that is what I will call them here.

(Aside: They have also been called "impressions," "ideas," and "percep-tions" by various people at various times. I think those terms are misleading, so I prefer the technical term "sense data." Despite my use above, "mental image" is also misleading, because it suggests that we're talking specifically about visual sense data—in ordinary language, there's no such thing as an 'image' of taste or smell—but in fact, we're talking about mental items that allegedly exist whenever we exercise any of the five senses.)

Now, given that all you ever directly perceive is your own sense data, can you infer anything about the external world? At first glance, this doesn't seem too difficult. Your sense data must come from somewhere, and you know that you didn't create them, since you have no direct control over your sense data. (If you did, you could just decide to stop hearing that horrible music your neighbor is playing.) So they must have been caused by external objects. Suppose you are having a sense datum of a tree. The simplest explanation of why you're having this experience—and normally the correct one—is that there is a tree in front of you, which is causing your experience. Granted, it is possible for a person to hallucinate a tree; however, that is not the normal situation, and there is no special reason for thinking you are hallucinating now.

The great skeptic David Hume neatly exposed the problem with this line of thought:

> It is a question of fact, whether the perceptions of the senses be produced by external objects resembling them. How shall this question be determined? By experience surely, as all other questions of a like nature. But here experience is, and must be entirely silent. The mind has never anything present to it but the perceptions, and cannot possibly reach any experience of their connexion with objects. The supposition of such a connexion is, therefore, without any foundation in reasoning.[12]

Hume believed, plausibly enough, that the only way of knowing that A causes B (where A and B are any two types of events) is by having some experience of A and B—specifically, you must observe A being followed by B on a number of occasions. For instance, suppose there's a light switch on the wall in front of me. In order to find out what the switch does, I'll have to try it out. I flip it a few times, notice the light go on and off, and conclude that flipping the switch causes the light to go on or off. If I never observed the flipping of the switch, I would not have been able to know this. Now, it is true that, when I enter a room I've never been in before, I can often predict that the switch on the wall will turn on the lights. However, this is because I am relying on *past* experience with light switches. If I had never had any experience with any light switches, I would have no idea what it would do.

Now, Hume says, for the reasons given above, that we never actually see physical objects, only our representations of them. Therefore, we have certainly not observed the presence of physical objects being followed by the occurrence of sense data. Therefore, we cannot claim to know that physical objects cause sense data. In particular, we could not claim to know that physical trees cause treelike sense data, because we have never actually had any direct experience of a physical tree; all we have seen is the tree-representing sense data. It is as if I saw the lights go on and off periodically, but I never saw the light switch (suppose the switch was located in another room of which I was unaware). In that case, I would never know what was causing the lights to go on or off.

This argument can be summarized as follows:

1. In order to have knowledge of the physical world, we must be able to know that our sense data are caused by physical objects.
2. In order to know that A causes B, one must have experience of A and B.[13]
3. We have no experience of physical objects.
4. Therefore, we do not know that physical objects cause our sense data. (from 2, 3)
5. Therefore, we have no knowledge of the physical world. (from 1, 4)

4. The Brain in a Vat

Let's discuss the brain-in-a-vat scenario a little more thoroughly than we did in chapter I. The scientists are keeping your brain alive in the vat through artificial means—they have mechanical devices to pump blood to and from your brain, along with machines to add oxygen and nutrients to your blood. They have hundreds of tiny electrodes inserted into your brain to recreate the same pattern of electrical stimulation to your sensory cortex as a normal brain in a human body receives. A giant supercomputer does the calculations necessary to figure out exactly how to stimulate your brain. Of course, the scientists will also need a brain scanner, so they can determine when you are trying to move your body in various ways; then the supercomputer will figure out how to modify the pattern of brain stimulations to make it look as if your body is in fact moving the way it should. Thus, you can exercise your free will (if there is such a thing) within the simulated world. Everything appears normal to you. The scientists decide, for amusement, to throw into the scenario a simulated book talking about the brain-in-a-vat scenario, just to see what you'll think. They have a chuckle when you think to yourself, "That's ridiculous; of course I'm not a brain in a vat."

Let's think about what kind of arguments you might give against the brain-in-a-vat (BIV) scenario. In the first place, you might say, the scenario clearly assumes a level of technology beyond anything we possess. Medical science does not have the ability to keep a disembodied brain alive, nor is current computer technology up to simulating an interactive world with anything like the detail of the real world. But what you don't realize is that it is now actually the year 3440, and the scientists simply chose to program a simulation of life in the twenty-first century—when, of course, human science was very primitive. In the real world, human technology is far beyond where it is in your simulated world.

You might think that even so, it would require an enormous computer to do the sorts of calculations required by the BIV scenario. And why would anyone want to expend the resources to build such a machine? But what you don't realize is that enormous technological and economic advances have occurred in the last 1400 years, making it possible to build computers millions of times more powerful than twenty-first century computers, at a small fraction of the cost.

Is there any evidence to suggest that you are a BIV? No, but if you *were* a BIV there *wouldn't* be any evidence (at least, not that you were aware of). The scientists and their supercomputer control all the "evidence" you receive, which consists in your sensory experiences, and they have chosen not to give you any evidence that you're a BIV. Thus, the lack of evidence supporting the BIV scenario is not evidence *against* it either. That is why, the skeptic says, you simply do not know whether you are a BIV or not.

That is the crux of the matter. Everything you think you know about how the physical world works, about computer technology, about the laws of physics—anything you might try to use to argue against the BIV scenario—depends on sensory experience. All of that information, the skeptic claims, is suspect, since it could have just been fed to you by the scientists who didn't want you to figure out that you are a BIV. No matter what observations you make, a suitably modified BIV scenario can account for them. That is why there cannot, in principle, be any evidence against the BIV scenario.

From this, the skeptic infers that you do not know you are not a brain in a vat. And further, the skeptic infers that you do not know that anything you "observe" is real. And therefore, you do not know anything about the external world at all, since all your beliefs about the external world are based on your alleged observations. In summary:

1. Your sensory experiences are the only evidence you have for propositions about the external world.
2. The BIV scenario predicts that you would be having the same sort of sensory experiences as you are actually having.
3. Therefore, the sensory experiences you are actually having are not evidence that the BIV scenario isn't true. (from 2)
4. Therefore, you have no evidence that the BIV scenario isn't true. (from 1, 3)
5. Therefore, you do not know that you're not a BIV. (from 4)
6. Therefore, you do not know anything about the external world. (from 5)[14]

5. Skepticism and Common Sense

Having just seen four examples of skeptical arguments—what I regard as the four most important skeptical arguments—we are now in a position to define "skepticism" more precisely. I define skepticism as *any philosophical theory that challenges a significant class of common sense beliefs.*[15] Now to explain the terms in that definition.

First, "common sense beliefs." Consider the following propositions, all of which I believe: I am a human being. I have two hands. I have spent my life at or near the surface of the Earth. I have thoughts and feelings. There are other people in the world. They have bodies. They also have thoughts and feelings. The Earth has existed for many years. It generally gets colder in the winter than it is in the summer. 2 is greater than 1. There is a table in front of me now.

I have no serious doubts about any of these propositions. Unless you are either a skeptic or a madman, you have the same or analogous beliefs, and you probably hold them with a similar degree of certainty. I say "analogous" because you may not believe, for example, that there is a table in front of me now. But, when placed in the circumstance of seeing a familiar type of physical object (as I am now), you believe that that object is there. Generally, when you have the same kind of grounds for a proposition that I have for any of the propositions in the list above, you accept that proposition without reservations, as would any normal human being.

I call these things "common sense beliefs." Common sense beliefs generally have these characteristics:

i. They are accepted by almost everyone (except some philosophers and some madmen), regardless of what culture or time period one belongs to.
ii. They tend to be taken for granted in ordinary life. For instance, when I sit down at my table, I *take it for granted* that the table is real; I don't even think about it explicitly, because for me, there is no *issue* about whether the table exists.
iii. If a person believes a contrary of one of these propositions, then it is a sign of insanity. For instance, that I am a human being is, for me, a common sense belief. An example of a *contrary* proposition would be the proposition that I am a chicken. If I thought I was a chicken, that would be a sign of insanity.

The remark in (i) about philosophers and madmen sounds flippant, but it is quite accurate nonetheless. In the context of a philosophical discussion, people will sometimes express doubts about common sense beliefs, but, if sane, this is the *only* time they have such doubts. In real life, philosophical skeptics do not bump into walls because they don't trust their senses, or stick their hands on hot stoves because past experience gives no justification for future predictions, or kick other people because there's no reason to think other people are sentient. A variety of possible explanations for this could be proposed, such as: the skeptic just finds it more fun to *pretend* that there's a real world, that other people are conscious, and so on; or the skeptic is just trying to indirectly modify his own sense data, and he has discovered certain correlations between his own acts of will and changes in his sense data (though this wouldn't work for the inductive skeptic). But in actual fact, the explanation is that in ordinary life, outside of philosophical discussions, the skeptic thinks pretty much like the rest of us, taking for granted the things the rest of us do.[16]

This doesn't prove that skepticism is false; at most it proves that skeptics are hypocritical. But it indicates an interesting characteristic of the beliefs I call "common sense." Most beliefs are not like this; people who question a given opinion do not usually find themselves constantly slipping into taking that opinion for granted. People who think there is no God, for example, do not find themselves praying or planning for the afterlife when they exit philosophical debate. People who think abortion is murder do not find themselves having abortions or in any other way thinking or acting as if abortion were permissible. But the people who say that we have no reason to think physical objects exist do nonetheless, in their everyday lives, take the reality of the physical objects around them for granted. And this marks an interesting difference between, on the one hand, things like the belief that there is a God or the belief that abortion is permissible, and on the other hand, the things I'm calling "common sense beliefs."

Second, what do I mean by a "challenge" to a belief? Where P is some proposition, a "challenge" to P is a claim that could not rationally be accepted in conjunction with P, in that it would be inherently self-defeating to do so. Consider the following propositions, all of which are self-defeating in the sense I intend:

It is raining, but I don't believe it.
It is raining, but that's not true.
It is raining, but I have no reason to think so.
It is raining, but the reasons I have for believing that are false.
It is raining, but I don't know whether it is or not.[17]

It would be *inherently* irrational (independent of what evidence I have) for me to accept any of these propositions, since in order for me to justifiably believe the first half, the second half of each sentence would have to be unjustified. So the second conjunct of each of these five propositions is a "challenge" to my belief that it is raining.[18]

Third, why do I say, "a *significant class* of common sense beliefs"? Suppose someone enters this room and is in doubt about whether there is really a table here. He doesn't have doubts about physical objects in general; he just thinks there is something funny about *this particular* (alleged) table. Well, that is not what we call "skepticism" in philosophy. A philosophical skeptic makes some kind of general claim—for instance, that nothing about the physical world can be known; or that no prediction about any future event can ever be justified.

My definition of "skepticism" differs from those of most philosophers, so I should say a word about that. If asked what skepticism is, most philosophers will say something like "the view that no one can know anything."[19] But my definition fits better with the way philosophers actually use the word when they label various positions "skeptical." Without going into too much detail, I note that my definition applies to inductive skepticism, moral skepticism, and skepticism about the past (none of which says that no one can know *anything*), and it explains why Hume (who spoke mainly about having *reasons* for believing things, rather than about *knowledge*) is considered a skeptic.

6. Skepticism and Internal Justification

There are many possible forms of skepticism under my definition. This is for two reasons: first, because there are different kinds of common sense beliefs that one might be skeptical about (e.g., beliefs about the past, about the physical world, about other people's minds), and second, because there are several different ways to challenge a belief. Some skeptics argue that our common sense beliefs are not true.[20] Others argue that common sense beliefs are not *known* to be true. Others argue that common sense beliefs are *unjustified*.

This last is what I call "radical skepticism." It is important to understand what radical skepticism entails, because it is the form of skepticism the preceding arguments support and the form I will be responding to. To say a proposition is "justified" is to say, roughly, that there is good reason (or good evidence) to believe it, or that it would be rational to believe it.[21] However, justification comes in degrees, so a proposition can be *slightly* justified, *highly* justified, and so on. The radical skeptic I will be confronting holds that (some significant class of) common sense beliefs are *not at all* justified, which is to say: there is no reason to believe they are true; it is no more rational to think they are true than to think they are false. According to one theory of probability, this is the same as to say the beliefs are no more *likely* to be true than false.

There are some skeptics (nonradical ones) who argue *merely* that we cannot be absolutely certain that our common sense beliefs are true, that there is at least *some* chance, however remote, that we could be wrong. This kind of skepticism (if it counts as such) is not very interesting, since it requires at most a minor revision in our beliefs. You could grant this skeptic his point and still hold on to all your common sense beliefs (though not with absolute certainty). In contrast, you could not grant *radical* skepticism and then go on thinking pretty much as you always had. You could not accept that *P* is no more likely to be true than false, but then just go on believing *P*. This would be self-defeating, like saying, "It's raining outside, but it's just as likely that it's not raining as that it is." For this reason, I focus on answering radical skepticism.

The first two skeptical arguments above (sections II.1 and II.2) support radical skepticism *about everything*: if sound, they would show that we have no justification for believing anything. The third and fourth (sections II.3 and II.4) support radical skepticism *about the external world*: that is, if sound, they would show that we have no justification for our beliefs about the external world; they would not show anything about the rest of our beliefs, however—they don't say, for example, that we cannot know about our sense data.

I need to make one more point about what "radical skepticism" is. The radical skeptic is concerned with what philosophers call the "internalist" sense of justification. Internalist justification is justification from one's own point of view, as opposed to justification from (so to speak) the omniscient, third-person perspective.[22] I explain this distinction with an anecdote.

In John Steinbeck's novel, *The Pearl*, the protagonist, a fisherman, discovers an enormous pearl. He thinks that the pearl will bring wealth and comfort to his family for a long time to come, as soon as he sells it. But throughout the rest of the story, the fisherman is beset by people trying to trick or cheat him, highwaymen trying to rob him, and so on. By the end of the novel, it has become clear that the pearl was far more trouble than it was worth.

An English teacher of mine once posed the following essay question about the story: "True or false: When the fisherman discovered the pearl, he should have just thrown it back into the ocean." Many students answered "true," citing the many troubles it would have saved the fisherman and his family. But the teacher claimed the answer was "false," because the fisherman had no way of knowing about those troubles in advance. As far as *he* could tell, the pearl was going to make him and his family rich. It would have been ridiculous to throw it back into the ocean!

What's the right answer? Well, (*pace* the English teacher) the question was ambiguous. *From the fisherman's point of view*—that is, given the information available to *him*—he should have done just as he did, try to sell the pearl. On the other hand, from the point of view of the omniscient observer—that is, given *all* the facts about the case—the fisherman should have thrown the pearl back into the ocean. Throwing the pearl back is the action that would in fact have had the best results; in that sense, he "should" have done that. But taking the pearl and trying to sell it is the course of action that, in the light of his information at the time, it was most reasonable for the fisherman to take; in that sense, he "should" have done that.

The point of this example: When I talk about what beliefs are "justified," I do not mean what things it is reasonable to believe given a total knowledge of all the facts (which would collapse the reasonable into the true). Rather, I mean what things it is reasonable for a person to believe, given their situation at the time. This is what I mean by "justification from the first-person perspective."

Another word for what is justified, or *should* be done or believed, from the first-person perspective, is "rational." If the teacher had asked, "True or false: When the fisherman found the pearl, it would have been rational for him to just throw it back into the ocean," then the question would have been unambiguous, the correct answer being "false."

Justification from the first-person perspective is what matters to us. The reason is that we have only our own perspective from which to decide what to believe. We never have the omniscient point of view, and we never have anyone else's point of view. If I am to decide what to believe, I have to do it on the basis of the information I have; I can't do it on the basis of information *you* have and I don't. Similarly, when *you* want to decide what to believe, you have to do it on the basis of *your* information, not mine.

Radical skepticism, as I define it, holds that our common sense beliefs are not rational, that is, not justified from the first-person point of view. This might seem strange, since surely there is no doubt that we *believe* our common sense beliefs to be justified. But "x is justified from our point of view" does not mean "we believe that x is justified." It means "x is rational for us." The "from our point of view" modifier simply indicates that rationality does not require taking account of things we had no reasonable way of knowing about. If x results from confusion, fallacious reasoning, or arbitrary assumptions, then x is *not* justified, regardless of the fact that we may think it is. As we have seen, the external-world skeptic thinks all our beliefs about the external world rest on mere assumption.

Notes

1. More precisely, that we cannot know any *contingent* truths about the external world; most skeptics do not question our knowledge of necessary truths. Henceforth, my talk of "knowledge of the external world" is to be understood as referring to knowledge of contingent truths about the external world.

2. This illustration, including the Plutonian hypothesis in the following paragraph, is from Fumerton, *Metaphysical and Epistemological Problems*, 39 (I have altered the date of the hypothesized end of the world).

3. Versions of the infinite regress argument for skepticism can be found in Sextus Empiricus, 72-75, and I. T. Oakley.

4. F can be a negative, conjunctive, or disjunctive property if you like; this will not affect the succeeding argument.

5. Essentially this argument appears in BonJour, 30-32.

6. I call the argument of this section "the problem of the criterion" because it is closely related to the ancient skeptical argument in which the skeptic says that one needs a criterion for distinguishing accurate perceptions from illusions, before one can reasonably rely on one's senses. The skeptic goes on to argue that there is no non-circular way of establishing that a given criterion is correct. See Sextus Empiricus, 145-46, and Chisholm, "The Problem of the Criterion."

7. If you are worried about the inconsistencies the eight-ball reasoners would fall into, let the canonical eight-ball method stipulate that the eight ball may only be asked logically independent questions. For instance, if you ask, "Will it rain tomorrow?" and then later ask, "Will there be precipitation tomorrow?" you are misusing the eight ball, and only the first of the eight ball's answers can be accepted.

8. The Magic Eight Ball example is from Fumerton, *Metaepistemology*, 50-51.

9. Descartes attempted such a proof in the *Meditations*, but no one other than Descartes seems to have found his argument convincing. Davidson ("A Coherence Theory of Truth and Knowledge") also gives an argument of this kind, but I think it no better than Descartes's (see Foley and Fumerton for a successful criticism of Davidson).

10. I am assuming here that we have *noninferential knowledge* of something only if we are *directly aware* of it.

11. Some indirect realists say that we don't *see* physical objects but only mental images (Hume, *Enquiry*, 152); others prefer to say that we don't *directly* see physical objects, but we see them indirectly (see Jackson, *Perception*, esp. chapters 1 and 4, though his "immediate perception" is not the same as my "direct awareness"); and still others say that, although we see physical objects, we aren't *directly acquainted* with them (Fumerton, *Metaphysical and Epistemological Problems*, ch. 3, esp. pp. 75-76). The third view sounds most plausible; however, the dispute is a semantic one, and nothing of substance will turn on it. In particular, no part of my defense of direct realism is affected by which way of talking the indirect realist adopts.

12. Hume, *Enquiry*, 153. I have altered the punctuation in the passage to conform to contemporary usage. Although the passage reveals Hume's assumption that the indirect realist must believe external objects "resemble" our mental images of them, this is not essential to Hume's argument. The general problem facing any indirect realist,

Hume might say, is that of determining the nature of the causes of our experiences, which could only be accomplished through some sort of inductive argument. But since induction is simply generalizing from past experience, inductive arguments based upon premises about mental images will only lead us to generalizations about mental images, such as "mental images of type A always have feature F," "images of type A always precede images of type B," and so on.

13. A and B here are types of events (not particular events).

14. The argument has three implicit premises: that if *h* predicts *e*, then *e* is not evidence against *h*; that if we have no evidence against the BIV scenario, then we don't know it isn't true; and that if we don't know the BIV scenario is false, we don't know anything about the external world. I discuss these assumptions in my "The Problem of Defeasible Justification," where I exhibit the similarity between the brain-in-a-vat argument and inductive skepticism. The last assumption, or rather, the more general one known as the closure principle, is discussed below in section VIII.3.

15. This supersedes my earlier characterization of skepticism in chapter I.

16. Hume admitted this in a famous passage:

> I dine, I play a game of back-gammon, I converse, and am merry with my friends; and when after three or four hours' amusement, I wou'd return to these speculations, they appear so cold, and strain'd, and ridiculous, that I cannot find in my heart to enter into them any farther. Here then I find myself absolutely and necessarily determin'd to live, and talk, and act like other people in the common affairs of life. (*Treatise*, 269)

17. G. E. Moore discusses the first of these propositions, wondering why it sounds contradictory even though, formally, it is not (see "Moore's Paradox"). Moore concluded that to assert *P* is to imply that one knows that *P*. The astute reader will notice that the latter conjunct in the first four of these propositions is the denial of one of the necessary conditions on knowledge.

18. Under my definition, ". . . challenges . . ." is a symmetrical relation, so it is also true that the first half of each sentence "challenges" the second half. This doesn't sound right, so the definition should probably be refined such that only the meta-claim counts as a "challenge" to the lower-order claim. However, for our purposes, this refinement is incidental.

19. Stroud, vii; Unger, 1; Lehrer, 284.

20. This is a rare form of skepticism, but it does appear here and there. Unger, ch. VII, is an example. The argument which says that modern science proves that material objects have no color and are not solid is another. Also, idealism is an example of this form of skepticism (although most skeptics are not idealists—see the remarks at the beginning of this chapter).

21. Here I refer to evidential reasons (the sort of reasons that render a belief likely to be true), as opposed to prudential or moral reasons; for instance, even if the argument of Pascal's Wager is correct, I would not consider it to show that belief in God is justified in the relevant sense. Also note that I have said "roughly" in this sentence because the formulation in terms of having reasons applies only to nonfoundational beliefs. A perfectly general definition of internalist, epistemic justification is elusive.

22. "Third-person perspective" is actually an oxymoron, like "the view from nowhere," given what "third-person" means in this context. What I really mean is nonperspectival justification, justification *not* from anyone's point of view, justification in a purely objective sense. This is the sort of thing that externalists in epistemology are interested in. See Goldman for an example of an externalist interpretation of "justification."

III. Easy Answers to Skepticism

1. Is Skepticism Self-Refuting?

Most people, upon hearing the thesis of philosophical skepticism, immediately come up with the following obvious query for the skeptic: *How do you know that skepticism is true?* The skeptic is, after all, a person who believes skepticism. If skepticism is true, it follows (right?) that all beliefs are unjustified; therefore, the belief in skepticism itself is unjustified. And isn't there something wrong with making an assertion and, at the same time, saying that one's own assertion is unjustified? That, after all, was the point of calling radical skepticism a "challenge" to common sense beliefs—that one cannot rationally hold to one's common sense beliefs and embrace radical skepticism at the same time. If radical skepticism is a challenge to our common sense beliefs, it is, in exactly the same way, a challenge to itself. This being the case, it cannot rationally be accepted at the same time that *it itself* is accepted; that is, it cannot rationally be accepted.

Well, matters are not *quite* that simple. We need to distinguish the skeptic *about everything* (the "universal skeptic" as we might call him) from the skeptic *about the external world*. The universal skeptic is indeed subject to the charge of the preceding paragraph. But the external-world skeptic is not. The reason is that external-world skepticism is not a claim about the external world (in the relevant sense). The external-world skeptic holds that beliefs about the properties and arrangement of physical objects are one and all unjustified. That statement—"beliefs about the properties and arrangement of physical objects are one and all unjustified"—is not a claim about the properties and arrangement of physical objects; it is, rather, an evaluative claim about our beliefs. Hence, it does not defeat itself. Another way to put the point is this: the thesis of external world skepticism does not entail the existence of any external objects, so it does not apply to itself.[1] Since the first two skeptical arguments in the last chapter defended universal skepticism, while the last two defended external-world skepticism, we can conclude that the latter two arguments remain undamaged.

What if we restrict our attention to the universal skeptic? The radical, universal skeptic actually has two problems. The first problem is that, when he asserts the premises of his argument, he must, in order to be consistent, admit that no one has any justification for accepting those premises; if that's so, why are we listening to his argument? The second problem is that, as we mentioned, the skeptic will have to admit that his conclusion is unjustified as well. What would a skeptic say to this?

We don't have to guess; there have been a few (albeit very few) universal skeptics in the twentieth century, and they have recognized the self-refutation issue. First, let's hear from one-time skeptic Keith Lehrer:

> The form of scepticism that concerns me does not embody the thesis that we know that we do not know anything. That thesis is obviously self-refuting. Rather, the contention is that no one knows anything, not even that no one knows anything. You might feel a surge of confidence . . . because the sceptic has admitted that he does not know that he is correct, and hence, that he does not know that you are incorrect when you affirm that you do know something. But this confidence is misplaced because scepticism entails that, just as the sceptic does not know that we do not know anything, so we do not know that we do know anything, and, moreover, that we do not know anything.[2]

Lehrer does not seem to see the real problem. It appears that Lehrer is only aware of the issue of whether skepticism is a formal contradiction—that is, a statement whose truth would entail its own falsity. But that's not the problem. The problem is that skepticism is self-defeating, in that its truth would entail our *lack of justification* for asserting it. To illustrate the distinction: The sentence "It is raining, but it is not raining" is a contradiction; that is, it entails its own falsity, since the truth of the first half of it entails the falsity of the second half, and vice versa. But the sentence "It is raining, but I have no reason to think it is" is not contradictory; after all, there are possible situations in which it could be raining while at the same time I lacked a reason for thinking that it was (of course, I would never know such a situation obtained at the time). The statement is nevertheless an illogical one, because there is no way I could be justified in believing what it asserts. Similarly, universal, radical skepticism faces the problem, not that it is necessarily false, but that it is necessarily irrational to accept it.

Lehrer goes on:

> The sceptic is not prevented by his agnoiology from believing most of the

same things that we believe; indeed, all his position debars him from is believing in such things as would entail that we have knowledge.[3]

Again, Lehrer is addressing only the need for consistency, not the need for justification. The skeptic, to the extent that he presents an argument for his view, is apparently trying to *justify* it. If he admits that he cannot justify it, then what is the point of the whole exercise?

A similar blindness afflicts radical skeptic I. T. Oakley, who attempts to fend off the self-refutation charge as follows:

> [T]he above discussion provides the basis for a suitable rejoinder to the critic who would turn the conclusion [radical, universal skepticism] against itself, remarking that if it is true, we cannot be justified in believing it, or indeed the premises from which it is drawn. The convinced skeptic will of course embrace this conclusion, kicking away his ladder along with everything else. But in any case, I will regard my current purpose as fulfilled if my reader accepts that the conclusion is derivable from the currently unquestioned.[4]

The first sentence above is merely explaining the antiskeptic's objection. The second sentence, incredibly, grants the objection straight out, whereupon the author proceeds as if nothing has happened. In the third sentence, Oakley is saying that, although the premises of his argument (Oakley gives a version of the infinite regress argument, as in section II.1) are not really *justified*, they are nevertheless things that the nonskeptics believe. (The "currently unquestioned" remark alludes to Oakley's distinction between what is, at a given point in a discussion, under question, and what is being granted by the parties to the discussion. The important point for our purposes is that Oakley does not regard things that are "currently unquestioned" as being genuinely justified.) Somehow, that is supposed to be sufficient for his purposes. But Oakley does not explain how the skeptic can be rational in accepting either the premises or the conclusion of the skeptical argument, given that skepticism is true. By definition, one cannot rationally accept an argument whose premises and conclusion are all unjustified. The fact that one's dialectical *opponent* accepts the premises of said argument is irrelevant; that does not make it more rational for oneself to accept them. Likewise for the putative fact that no one is presently calling the premises of the argument into question (which in itself would be an overgenerous concession to Oakley); that would no more show that one is justified in accepting the argument. At best, Oakley is offering a tu quoque response. (Tu quoque is the fallacy of attempting to rebut a criticism by arguing that the person making the criticism is guilty of the same failing.)

Against some sorts of self-refutation charges, the skeptic may appeal to the method of *reductio ad absurdum*. This is the form of argument in which one starts by assuming the opposite of what one wants to prove and derives a contradiction or an absurdity from that assumption. One then is entitled to reject the assumption. For example, it is possible to prove that there is no largest prime number, because if one assumes that n is the largest prime number, one can construct a prime number larger than n by multiplying all the prime numbers up to n and adding 1. Since this results in the contradiction that there is a prime number larger than the largest prime number, we must reject the assumption leading to this conclusion.

The interesting feature of the reductio ad absurdum type of argument is that one need not have justification for the "assumption" with which one starts, because one is not really asserting it. One is only assuming it hypothetically or "for the sake of argument." So, in the prime number example above, it would be out of place for someone to object that since we have no justification for believing that n is the largest prime number, the argument fails.

Similarly, a skeptic might say that he is merely trying to construct a reductio ad absurdum of our common beliefs about knowledge. For this purpose, it is not necessary that the skeptic himself accept those beliefs; in fact, he does not accept them. He is merely trying to refute us by showing that our own beliefs lead to a contradiction.

Does this reply work on the skeptic's behalf? Obviously, it assumes that the premises of the skeptical arguments are indeed among our common beliefs about knowledge, but let's grant that. The universal, radical skeptic still cannot take this line. The reason is that reductio ad absurdum—even when it does not require us to have any genuine premises (premises that we are really asserting)—is still an (alleged) method for *justifying* conclusions. It is a kind of *argument*, after all, and arguments are attempts to justify conclusions. Returning to the prime number example, the proof, obviously, is supposed to justify, to prove, the conclusion that there is no largest prime number. If, as this form of skepticism implies, nothing can ever be justified, then reductio ad absurdum cannot justify skepticism.

What if the skeptic tries rephrasing his thesis as follows: No person can ever be justified in believing anything, *except* this very proposition. Does this escape the problem? It would, if skeptical arguments could be devised that would lead to that conclusion. But the arguments we considered in chapter II do not support that conclusion with the exception built into it. The arguments of sections II.1 and II.2 support universal, radical skepticism: that no one can ever be justified in believing anything, period. The only way to get a special exception in the conclusion would be to build the exception into the premises. For instance, you could change the first premise of the regress argument from "In order to know something, one must have a reason for believing it" to "In order to know something, one must have a reason for believing it, unless that something is the proposition 'No person can ever be justified in believing anything, except this very proposition,' in which case one does *not* need a reason for believing it." But then, to include such an exception would be purely arbitrary. Why shouldn't skeptical claims be subject to the same standards of justification as all other claims?

I think, therefore, that the universal skeptics have no defense against the charge of self-refutation. Yet this victory seems somehow too easy; in what sense, I will explain in section 4.

2. The G. E. Moore Shift

G. E. Moore famously claimed that he could "perfectly rigorously" prove the existence of external objects. How did he do it? He held up one of his hands, saying as he did so, "Here is one hand." Then, making a certain gesture with the other hand, he said, "And here is another." Hands, as Moore took great pains to explain, are the sort of thing meant by "external objects." Therefore, he concluded, external objects (at least two of them) exist.[5] Moore, by the way, was a guileless and serious philosopher. He did not intend his "proof" as any sort of joke, nor as a way of making fun of skeptics, nor as a way of making some subtle point that is not apparent on the surface. He seriously and simply meant that his performance was a proof of the existence of external objects.[6]

Now, if the external-world skeptic were simply a person who says, out of the blue, "Prove to me that there are external objects," then Moore's reply would be appropriate. But Moore's proof does not seem like much of a response in the light of the specific *arguments* given by skeptics to show why we cannot know about the external world. How would Moore respond to those arguments?

In fact, he discusses Hume's skeptical argument (the argument of section II.3, although Moore formulates it differently) in "Hume's Theory Examined," where he identifies two general principles that Hume's skepticism rests on. Conceding that, if Hume's premises were true, then it would be impossible for anyone to know of the existence of any external object, Moore proposes to *prove* that Hume's premises are false. How?

> I *do* know that this pencil exists; but I could not know this, if Hume's principles were true; *therefore*, Hume's principles, one or both of them, are false. I think this argument really is as strong and good a one as any that could be used: and I think it really is conclusive. In other words, I think that the fact that, if Hume's principles were true, I could not know of the existence of this pencil, is a *reductio ad absurdum* of those principles.[7]

Moore's view is that skepticism is so obviously false that any theory leading to skepticism should be rejected for that very reason.

Philosophical skeptics are unlikely to be impressed by this reasoning. They think skepticism is true, not absurd. But *that* fact would not impress G. E. Moore either, nor should it. The question is whether the skeptics have given *us* any good reasons to accept skepticism. They have presented some arguments purporting to do so. These arguments are *logically* sound—meaning just that their conclusions follow from their premises.[8] But that is not enough. If someone presents a logically sound argument for a given conclusion, this does not automatically mean that you should accept their conclusion. What it means is that, *if you accept the premises of the argument*, then, in order to be consistent, you must accept the conclusion. Or, more precisely, the conjunction of the premises of the argument with the denial of the conclusion is a contradiction.

So let's say you have a skeptical argument with two premises, A and B. Let K be the proposition denied by the skeptic, that we have a certain kind of knowledge (so, in the case of an argument for universal skepticism, K would be the proposition that at least someone knows something; in the case of an argument for external world skepticism, K would be the proposition that someone knows something about the external world). And now consider the following three arguments which can be constructed using these propositions:

A	A	K
B	K	B
$\therefore$ ~K	$\therefore$ ~B	$\therefore$ ~A

In the first argument, the falsity of K is deduced from A and B; in the second, the falsity of B is deduced from A and K; and in the third, the falsity of A is deduced from B and K. What is required for each of these arguments to be logically sound? Each of them is logically sound under exactly the same condition: namely, that A, B, and K are jointly incompatible (that is, "A & B & K" is a contradiction). For, provided that A, B, and K are incompatible, if any two of them are true, it follows that the third must be false; whereas this does not follow if they are compatible. This is a general point about all arguments: whenever you have a logically sound argument, you can also construct a logically sound argument with the negation of the first argument's conclusion as a premise, and the negation of one of the first argument's premises as its conclusion (keeping the other premises the same). In the present case, the philosophical skeptic endorses the first argument above. Moore says that either of the other two arguments would be better (though he is noncommittal on which of Hume's premises is false).

How could we determine which of the three arguments above, if any, is *best*? We grant that, in all three cases, the conclusion follows from the premises. Therefore, the issue comes down to which of them has the more plausible premises. That is, which argument has the premises that seem to you most likely to be true? Moore thought that a statement like, "I know this pencil exists" would always be more plausible than any philosophical theory about the nature of knowledge, or the nature of perception, etc., that the skeptic might rely on. Prior to argument, he was more certain that he knew about the pencil, than he was that any given philosophical theory was true. It would therefore be irrational to reject the proposition, "I know this pencil exists" because it conflicts with such a theory; it would make much more sense to reject the theory.

We can say something stronger, and this will be a general response to any kind of skeptical argument. Recall that we defined skepticism as any theory that challenges a significant class of common sense beliefs. This means that we cannot, rationally, accept such a theory and also accept those common sense beliefs; we have to choose between them. This being the case, we will, rationally, choose whichever we find more initially plausible. (The "initial plausibility" of a belief is the degree to which it seems true, prior to argument; in other words, how obvious it is.)

But the nature of common sense beliefs, as such, is that they have the highest initial plausibility of all beliefs. This, in fact, may serve as a useful definition of common sense beliefs; it explains the other features of common sense beliefs that we noted in section II.5. Common sense beliefs are almost universally accepted, regardless of time or place, *because* they are the most obvious propositions. We take them for granted, usually not bothering to state them explicitly, because they are so obvious. Their denial is a sign of insanity, because they are the most obvious truths, and therefore it would require a very serious mental disorder for a person to disbelieve one of them. This also explains why even skeptics find it difficult to shed their common sense beliefs. Psychologically, skeptical arguments prove impotent to supplant common sense beliefs *because* common sense beliefs are so much more plausible than the premises of those arguments.

To gauge the plausibility of common sense beliefs, imagine the following scenario. You know the Pythagorean Theorem. Let's assume that you have seen a proof of it. You thus have a high degree of (justified) certainty that the Theorem is true, a degree of certainty that should rival that of your common sense beliefs, if anything does. Now imagine that you are watching the news tonight, and the reporter mentions that the Pythagorean Theorem has been disproved. Of course, this only merits a very brief news story before they move on to other current events, and the details of the refutation are not provided.

What would you think?

Your first reaction might be that this reporter doesn't know what she is talking about. But let us suppose that the news story is corroborated by every other major news source that you know of. An article in *Science* discusses the well-respected Harvard mathematics professor who just refuted the Pythagorean "Theorem" and who discovered flaws in all the hitherto known "proofs" of it. Suppose that the rest of the community of mathematicians has reviewed this mathematician's work and has agreed that it is sound, and that the Pythagorean "Theorem" is false after all. Unfortunately, the details of this work are too complicated to be reported in the news stories, and you don't have the time (or the inclination) to read the 600-page book that has been published on the subject.

(To those who consider my scenario outlandish, you may substitute this one: the community of mathematical physicists announce that the "theorem" which says the interior angles of a triangle must add up to 180 degrees has been refuted. This latter has actually happened, and most people who hear of it accept the word of the physicists.)

Assume that you are a reasonable and cognitively normal person. What would you think about the Pythagorean Theorem at this point? Would you still believe it?

I don't think so. At this point, surely you would at least *doubt* the PT, if not accept its denial. The evidence that you would have against the PT would be solely testimonial, whereas in favor of the PT you have what appears to you to be a valid mathematical proof. But you can be wrong about what constitutes a valid proof, and in this situation the evidence that you are wrong—mere second-hand evidence though it is—seems to outweigh, or at least rival, the evidence that you were right.

Now contrast this hypothetical case. Tonight, on the news, it is announced that rocks do not exist. All other news sources corroborate this. *Science* magazine publishes an article about the team of Princeton physicists who recently proved scientifically that, contrary to popular opinion, there are no rocks in the world. All of the experts who have reviewed this work have agreed that it is sound and that the existence of rocks has indeed been refuted. Unfortunately, the work is too complicated to describe briefly, and you haven't had a chance to read the 600-page book that has been published on the subject.

What would you think this time? Would you accept that rocks don't exist? I think not. You might wonder, as improbable as it seems, if this is some kind of massive joke orchestrated by the scientific community. Or you might conclude that the scientists have collectively gone mad. Or, perhaps the most likely explanation, you might conjecture that the scientists have taken up some strange new, technical meaning of "rock" or "exist" which is different from the ordinary meaning. But even if you can't think of any plausible explanation for why the physicists speak as they do, the one alternative that, I think, you would not seriously consider is that all those rocks you seem to see every day really don't exist. You might let the physicists tell you some pretty surprising things about the properties of those things, but I do not think you would take seriously their assertion that there are no such things at all.

The moral of this story: the degree of plausibility of a common sense belief such as "there are rocks" is greater even than that of a proven mathematical theorem, since expert testimony could outweigh the latter, but otherwise similar expert testimony could not outweigh the former. This may come as a surprise to some; traditionally philosophers have held that necessary truths like the Pythagorean Theorem, when known, were known more perfectly and with greater certainty than contingent propositions about the external world. But that is simply wrong; necessity should not be confused with certainty.

If, then, common sense beliefs have the highest level of initial plausibility, it follows that a common sense belief could not be refuted by another, non-common-sense belief; the effect of a conflict between two such beliefs would be that the non-common-sense belief would be refuted instead. I now assert, as I think most of my audience will agree, that no philosophical theory has the status of a common sense belief. Far from it, in fact; it is far more likely, prima facie, that you would be mistaken in an abstract, philosophical judgement (such as "In order to gain knowledge of the external world, we must be able to know that our sense data are caused by external objects") than it is that you would be mistaken in a common sense belief (such as "There are rocks"). Further confirmation of this assessment can be found in the notorious disagreements among philosophers about most matters of philosophical significance. Given that the experts in the field of philosophy contradict one another so often, we can conclude, at the least, that human philosophical judgement is highly fallible. On the other hand, common sense beliefs, by definition, are things about which there is virtually no controversy. Therefore, when philosophical theory contradicts common sense, which should you choose? The eighteenth-century philosopher Thomas Reid answered this question, and his answer is one that many contemporary thinkers might profit from:

> In this unequal contest betwixt Common Sense and Philosophy, the latter will always come off both with dishonour and loss; nor can she ever thrive till this rivalship is dropt, these encroachments given up, and a cordial friendship restored: for, in reality, Common Sense holds nothing of Philosophy, nor needs her aid. But, on the other hand, Philosophy . . . has no other root but the principles of Common Sense; it grows out of them, and draws its nourishment from them. Severed from this root, its honours wither, its sap is dried up, it dies and rots.[9]

The argument of this section can be summarized as follows:

1. Given a conflict between two beliefs, it is rational to reject the less initially plausible one, rather than the more plausible one.
2. Common sense beliefs have the highest level of initial plausibility.
3. Philosophical theories do not.
4. Therefore, given a conflict between a philosophical theory and common sense, it is rational to reject the philosophical theory, rather than common sense.

A corollary of the conclusion is that, given an argument for skepticism, it is more rational to reject one of the premises of that argument than to accept the conclusion, since the conclusion conflicts with common sense. No skeptic has ever devised an argument whose premises were not more controversial than the common sense beliefs the skeptic seeks to challenge.

Now, some may think that I am equivocating on the word "conflict." They may say that skepticism doesn't necessarily *conflict* with common sense: the skeptic need not *deny* our common sense beliefs (he need not say they are false); he merely says we do not *know* they are true. So what the skeptic says is compatible with their being, in actual fact, true. Moore's argument was that, if two propositions *logically contradict* each other, then we should prefer to give up the one that we find less plausible. His claim was then that it is more plausible that *I know that this is a pencil* than it is that Hume's premises about the nature of perception and knowledge are true. I think Moore is right about that. But I also think something stronger: I think that if one proposition *challenges* another (even if they don't contradict), then we should prefer to give up the one we find less plausible. This is because even if the two propositions do not logically contradict, the relation between them is still such as to force us to choose between them, and this choice should be guided by our general epistemic goal of believing truths and avoiding error. Therefore, this comparison is relevant: it is more plausible that *this is a pencil* than it is that Hume's premises about perception and knowledge are true. Since that is the case, we should give up Hume's premises about perception and knowledge (that means, in the argument at the end of section II.3, we should reject proposition (1), (2), or (3)). And of course, a similar lesson applies to all of the skeptical arguments we have considered.

3. Stroud's Defense

But skeptics do not see the matter this way. Those who are initially moved by skeptical arguments usually see Moore's response as some variant on the fallacy of begging the question.[10] Contemporary skeptic Barry Stroud uses an analogy to show what he thinks Moore is *trying* to do, and also what he thinks is wrong with Moore's response to skepticism:

> Suppose a murder has just been committed in a country house during a weekend party. The young duke is found stabbed on the far side of the large table in the hall, although the butler was with him the whole time except for a few seconds when he left to answer the telephone in the foyer where there were many people. An experienced detective and his younger assistant are among the guests and are trying to determine how it could have happened.[11]

First stage of the investigation: the assistant decides that someone must have rushed in and stabbed the duke to death while the butler was out. "No," the detective replies, "we know that this table is here and is so large that no one could have come through that door and got around to this side of the table and stabbed the victim and got back out again before the butler returned."

Here, the detective makes a successful objection to his assistant's theory. The detective simply reminds him of something they both know which conflicts with that theory. The theory must therefore be rejected. Moore apparently thinks of himself as doing just this sort of thing: David Hume has put forward some theories about the nature of perception and about how one knows of cause-and-effect relationships. Moore then reminds us of something we all know, our knowing which conflicts with those theories. Hume's theories must therefore be rejected. If we are right to see Moore's response to the skeptic as analogous to the detective's response to his assistant, then Moore's response succeeds straightforwardly.

But Stroud proceeds to a later stage in the story. The assistant, having given up his first theory of the crime, has obtained a list of all the party-goers from the duke's secretary. Further, let's suppose, the assistant proves that none of those people, other than the butler, could have killed the duke. He concludes that the butler did it. Again the master corrects him: "No, that list was simply given to you by the secretary; it could be that someone whose name is not on the list was in the house at the time and committed the murder. We still don't know who did it."

Now, what if at this point the assistant responds, "No. You're wrong, because I know the butler did it."[12] We may even imagine that the assistant bolsters his response, G. E. Moore style, by reporting: "I find myself more certain that I know the butler did it, than that your argument is correct. Therefore, the rational thing for me to do is to reject the premises (one or more of them) of your argument." And let us suppose that the first statement is true: suppose the assistant is, psychologically, more certain (that is, more strongly convinced) that he knows the butler did it, than he is that the detective's objection is sound. Still, the assistant's response seems irrational. It would be absurd to call that a good and conclusive refutation of the detective's objection.

Why? Why can't the apprentice plead that he is just doing the same thing the detective did earlier, and the same thing Moore does? The detective made a claim, "We still don't know who did it." The apprentice now simply reminds him of something they (allegedly) know, their knowing which conflicts with the detective's "theory."

According to Stroud, the assistant's response fails because the detective's assertion, "We don't know who did it," was backed up by a specific objection to the justification the assistant offered. The detective did not merely gainsay his assistant; rather, he identified a specific flaw in the reasoning leading to the conclusion that the butler did it. One cannot show that there was no such flaw by simply repeating the conclusion thereby under challenge. Nor, again, is the assistant's high degree of psychological certainty in the claim "the butler did it" relevant, for if the assistant does not know that the list he obtained from the secretary is complete, then his certainty that the butler did it is unwarranted.

Although I ultimately wish to side with Moore, I do think Stroud is on to something important here. Stroud does not say this, but I think the following considerations are what make his response to Moore seem plausible: Knowledge is hierarchical, in that some things we know depend (in a logical, or justificatory sense) on others. For instance, I may know that my car has a full tank of gas, *because* I see the fuel gauge pointing to "F." The "because" indicates a certain asymmetrical relation, a dependence relation.[13] To put it another way, my knowledge that the car has a full tank of gas is *based on* my knowledge that the fuel gauge is pointing to "F." The latter can therefore be called "more basic" than the former. Now, once we realize that knowledge is structured in this sense, we can identify further, relevant considerations that Moore overlooked. Moore thought—or argued as if he thought—that if two initially plausible claims come into conflict, the only relevant consideration in deciding how to resolve the conflict is the level of plausibility of the respective beliefs (which we have so far understood in a purely psychological sense). Moore did not think to ask where the two claims fit into the logical hierarchy of beliefs.

Now in the case of the apprentice, the claim that the butler did it is not epistemologically basic. It is based on an argument. The senior detective has raised an objection to that argument. So, in order for the apprentice to (legitimately) use his belief "the butler did it" to prove anything, he must *first* answer that objection; that is, defending the soundness of his argument comes prior, epistemologically speaking, to the use of that argument's conclusion to infer further consequences. Otherwise, you could get away with adopting extremely confident beliefs on the basis of fallacious arguments and then "refuting" any attempt to demonstrate those fallacies by appeal to the great certainty of your beliefs—and according to Moore's logic, we would have to describe your procedure as perfectly rational.

Here is another illustration, which I think is even better for Stroud's case. Suppose that you go through a mathematical proof, or something that you take to be a mathematical proof, coming to conclusion C. Since (you think) you have just *proved* C mathematically, you come to accept C with a very high degree of confidence, bordering on absolute certainty. Then a mathematician comes along, reads through your proof, and says, "There is a division-by-zero error in step sixteen." How should you respond? Should you compare your degree of certainty (prior to the mathematician's claim) in C with your degree of certainty that (1) the mathematician is telling the truth, and (2) division by zero is an error? Further, if there is a division by zero in line sixteen, then should you take your degree of certainty (prior to learning this) that you *know* C as evidence that division by zero is not a fallacy?

Obviously not. Keeping in mind the logical hierarchy of beliefs, you realize that your conclusion, C, cannot be used to prove that the argument for C was sound. It goes the other way around. If you cannot defend the soundness of the argument independently of your belief in its conclusion, then your psychological certainty in C counts for nothing, as that certainty was never justified to begin with. That is why, when our mistakes in reasoning are pointed out to us, we do not thereupon acquire evidence that they weren't really mistakes.

Now notice two things about this argument. First, I am not saying that "my argument for C was sound" is one of the *premises* on the basis of which I believe C. (I had better not be saying that, because that's a simple confusion.) Still, it seems that the soundness of the argument is at least presupposed, at least *implicitly* assumed, when I conclude that C; at any rate, it certainly seems that the soundness of the argument cannot be proven by citing the alleged fact that I know C, when that argument is my only basis for believing C. Granted, in doing so, I would not *exactly* be using the statement "my argument for C was sound" to justify itself, but there clearly is some sort of circularity problem.

Second, I am not *merely* saying that your confidence in C (or in the proposition that you know C) fails to *refute* the belief that division by zero is a fallacy. G. E. Moore could perhaps accommodate that fact by claiming that it is more certain that division by zero is a fallacy than it is that C (or that you know C). But in addition, I am observing that your confidence in C does not even constitute any substantial *evidence* that division by zero isn't a fallacy. I do not see how Moore could explain that fact.

It seems that these considerations vitiate Moore's response to skepticism, to the extent that the skeptic is able to identify specific deficiencies, or alleged deficiencies, in the justification for our common sense beliefs. Just as I cannot prove that my argument for C was valid by appealing to my "knowledge" that C, Moore cannot prove that beliefs about the external world are justified, in the face of the skeptic's objections, by simply appealing to his "knowledge" that this is a pencil.

So how can I possibly side with Moore against Stroud?

Well, although I grant that Moore's view is oversimplified, I think the position described above (which may be Stroud's position) is also oversimplified. Our belief systems do have logical structure, but it is overly simplistic to think that this structure consists purely of unidirectional, "upward" relations from justifiers to the justified—the sort of structure you find in a mathematical system such as Euclid's *Elements* (the "simple foundationalist" structure, figure 3.1). Our beliefs interact in complex ways, which can include sideways and downward-pointing justification relations (the "foundherentist" structure,[14] figure 3.1); or perhaps it would be more accurate to say that there is no distinction between up and down in logical space. This sounds esoteric, but the sort of phenomenon I have in mind is one that I think everyone is familiar with. Consider a few examples.

First example: You are working on a crossword puzzle. On the basis of one clue, you tentatively fill in 4 across. Later, you think you have the answer to 3 down, on the basis of the clue for 3 down. When you find that your answers to 3 down and 4 across "fit" (have the same letter where they overlap), this

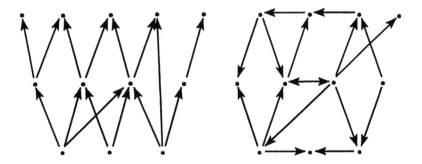

Figure 3.1. The simple foundationalist structure (left) and the foundherentist structure (right). Dots represent beliefs. Arrows are logical relations between them.

strengthens your confidence in *both* answers. This is an example of what I called "sideways" justification. The clues to the crossword puzzle are the basic data, at the bottom of your "belief system" about the puzzle. The tentative answers to 3 down and 4 across are each supported by separate clues, but, in addition, they support *each other*. Crossword puzzles are designed to work this way, so that, ideally, you only know you've done it correctly when the whole thing is filled in.[15]

Consider a second example, more relevant to our present concerns. Suppose you are working out a problem in your physics class. You've been given certain data and asked to figure out the circumference of the Earth on the basis of it. You go through a series of careful calculations, every part of which seems correct to you at the time, and eventually come up with the answer: 32 miles. This scenario is not at all unrealistic; if you have any experience with working out mathematical problems, you know what I'm talking about. Now, if you are very naive, you might write "32 miles" on your paper, perhaps with a feeling of astonishment that the Earth is so much smaller than you thought, and move on to the next problem. But a good student—a *rational* student—would realize, upon reaching the conclusion that the Earth is only 32 miles around, that he must have made a mistake. The rational student, upon reaching a result, at least checks it by asking himself, "Is this a reasonable answer?" Now, what if you check your work over, and you cannot find any mistake? *Then* should you conclude that the Earth is 32 miles in circumference? I think not. Again, this is not at all unrealistic; I have myself more than once made mistakes in problems of this sort that I did not detect, even after reviewing my reasoning several times, and even when I knew there had to be a mistake somewhere.

In this case, the unreasonableness of a conclusion calls into question the reasoning leading to it. This is the sort of thing I had in mind when I mentioned "downward-pointing" justification relations.[16] Notice that this need not be because you independently know what the circumference of the Earth *is*. It is just that you can recognize that *some* answers to that question are unreasonable.

Take a similar example. The Greek philosopher Zeno of Elea famously argued that motion is impossible; nothing can ever go anywhere. For suppose an object wanted to move from point A to point B. It would first have to go half the distance. After that, it would still have to go half the remaining distance (3/4 of the total distance). And after that, it would have to go half the remaining distance, again (bringing it to 7/8 of the total distance). And so on. Thus:

1. In order to get from A to B, the object must complete the series {½, ¾, ⅞, . . .}.
2. {½, ¾, ⅞, . . .} is a series with no end.

3.   A series with no end cannot be completed.
4.   Therefore, the series {½, ¾, ⅞, . . .} cannot be completed. (from 2, 3)
5.   Therefore, the object cannot get to point B. (from 1, 4)

Since point B may be chosen arbitrarily, no object can get anywhere. Unless you have studied this argument pretty seriously, you probably cannot say what is wrong with it. But does that mean that you should accept that nothing ever moves? Would that be the conclusion of a *rational* person? (Zeno apparently accepted it, and he thought that all the observations, using the five senses, that appear to reveal motion must therefore be mere illusions.) Of course, in theory, it must be possible to say what is wrong with the argument, if there is something wrong with it, other than just saying the conclusion is false. But, in the real world, where human beings have limited reasoning capacities, where our thinking is susceptible to subtle errors and confusions, a dose of common sense is often a necessary corrective to sophistical arguments whose errors are most cleverly hidden.

I do not think that my assessment of these examples should be controversial. And the lesson for philosophical skeptics seems clear. The conclusion that no one ever knows anything, or that no one ever knows anything about the physical world, is no more plausible prima facie than the conclusion that nothing ever moves, or that the Earth is only 32 miles in circumference. If taken literally, the thesis would invite such questions as: If Sue really doesn't know her own name, then how come she answers when you call "Sue"? If no one knows the positions of physical objects in their environment, how come we aren't constantly walking into walls, off cliffs, and so on? If the skeptic doesn't know that I exist, or that I'm talking, or what my words mean *if* I'm talking, then how can he hold a conversation with me? The skeptic might try explaining these things by appeal to our many *true beliefs* (not knowledge) about the world. But from the skeptic's point of view, our beliefs are nothing but completely unjustified *guesses* about the world, so there remains the question of how such guesses keep turning out to be accurate. Moore's rejection of skepticism follows the same eminently and uncontroversially rational procedure as that involved in the cases of the calculation of the Earth's circumference and Zeno's Paradox. If the procedure is rational when confronting those arguments, it is hard to see why Stroud feels it becomes irrational when the topic turns to epistemology.

I have yet to analyze Stroud's example of the assistant detective. Stroud would want to know in what respect Moore's response to the skeptic is different from the assistant detective's declaration, "No, you're wrong, because I know the butler did it." There are several important differences.

First, the belief that the butler did it is not close to being a common sense belief according to the standards we've laid down. It would not be nearly universally accepted, it would not be taken for granted in ordinary life, and it would not be a sign of insanity to accept an alternative theory of the crime. It is essential to the Moorean response that the position one responds to be one that is *absurd*, the sort of thing that would not be taken seriously in ordinary life. The detective's statement, "We still don't know who killed the duke," is very far from being absurd.

Second, the detective is challenging an isolated belief of his assistant's. A relatively minor adjustment to the assistant's belief system will accommodate the challenge (namely, remove the belief, "the butler did it"). In contrast, the skeptic is challenging a vast range of our beliefs—possibly all of them, depending on what kind of skeptic we're talking to. To accommodate the skeptic, one would have to throw out almost one's entire belief system. This, again, is a relevant consideration from Moore's point of view. That an isolated belief of one's own would be the result of an error is not so implausible. In most cases, it would make more sense to revise the one belief than to revise one's general standards of justification just to maintain that one belief. But when you have standards of justification that impugn practically every belief you have, *then* it becomes more reasonable to think that the standards of justification are in error than to think that almost all of your other beliefs are the product of error. After all, there is no reason why beliefs in epistemological standards should be any more immune from error than other kinds of beliefs, and one symptom of such an error is that the belief would fail to cohere with the rest of our beliefs about what is known/justified.

Stroud never explicitly addresses the question of how we know that an epistemological standard, or a criterion of justification, is correct. He might think we just know this intuitively. But even that intuition should be checked by our judgements, in particular cases, about what we know and are justified in believing. If a principle about what conditions are required for knowledge turns out to conflict with our judgements in almost all the cases when we normally say someone "knows" something, the principle should be revised. To take just one example, in section II.1 we employed a premise that, in order to know something, one must have a good reason for believing it. This seems plausible. However, if it turned out that almost all of the things people normally call "knowledge" are things they lack reasons for, then we should revise the principle. The skeptics, of course, would say, "No, then we should stop calling those things knowledge." But then, I think, the skeptics are treating their general epistemological principles as if they were infallible, immune from testing by reference to our other beliefs—an attitude peculiarly incongruous with their generally skeptical nature. The skeptic trumpets certain remote possibilities of error (brains in vats, hallucinations, and so on), while averting his gaze from certain other, much closer possibilities of error—those involving his, the skeptic's, making a mistake in intellectual judgement or reasoning.

Third, the premises the detective relies on to criticize his assistant's conclusion would be uncontroversial in the circumstances: that the assistant got the list of names from the secretary; that he did not verify that the list was complete; that it is possible that someone whose name is not on the list was present and committed the crime. Surely the assistant would not deny either of the first two facts; he is not amnesic. Suppose he tried denying the third: "No, it isn't possible that someone whose name is not on the list committed the crime." What could he have in mind? Surely he would be asked why it isn't possible. And if he gave a plausible answer to this, he would in effect be verifying that the list was complete (contrary to our hypothesis that he didn't do this).[17] So it seems that, if the assistant tries to *elaborate* his position, beyond the mere "I know the butler did it," he cannot do so in any at all plausible way. Of course, this is what Stroud is relying on when Stroud calls the assistant's position "ludicrous." But in contrast, the premises used in skeptical arguments are not uncontroversial. I grant that the premises of the skeptical arguments considered in chapter II seem at least plausible on their face, but at least one of them in each argument is still controversial—competent and reasonable epistemologists disagree with them. Some epistemologists offer alternative theories about knowledge that, considered in themselves, seem at least plausible—not obviously unreasonable—and that explain how we could gain knowledge of the external world. The point is that the assistant in Stroud's example doesn't seem to have available any serious theory of what is wrong with the detective's argument (or if he does, perhaps we should change our assessment of him), whereas there are many serious epistemological theories that offer alternatives to skepticism.

I think Stroud would accept that, when such a theory is put forward, it becomes the basis for a legitimate objection to the skeptic—indeed, Stroud's major complaint against Moore seems to be that Moore declined to do any such thing; Moore has nothing more to say than that skepticism is wrong because he, Moore, knows "this is a pencil." The point I want to make here is that the Moorean argument, or something very much like it, can supplement and strengthen the presentation of an alternative, nonskeptical theory of knowledge. Once we have two alternative, initially plausible epistemological theories before us, if one of them is consistent with our everyday, prephilosophical beliefs about what people know, while the other one is radically revisionary, this fact becomes a strong argument in favor of the former. In the following chapters of this book, I present precisely such a theory—a theory that maintains our common sense beliefs about perception, knowledge, and justification to a greater extent even than most nonskeptical philosophers would think possible.

4. Why Study Skepticism?

I have observed that universal skepticism of the sort raised in chapter II is self-refuting and that both universal skepticism and external-world skepticism are absurd theses that should be rejected for that reason. There are some who would think this is enough said about skepticism—perhaps too much said. Some readers will ask, if indeed I regard skepticism as an irrational position—comparable to the belief that the earth is 32 miles in circumference, or that nothing ever moves, as my use of examples in section 3 suggests—then how much needs to be said about this theory?

I do not think that a theory needs to be plausible or reasonable in order to be *important* in philosophy, so let me now explain why.

The responses to skepticism in the first two sections of this chapter are well and good, if you were seriously wondering whether to become a skeptic. But on another level, those responses are disappointing, because they enable us to dismiss skepticism without learning anything positive from the encounter (or anyway, not learning very much). If all I had to say about skepticism was what I have said so far, then I would be endeavoring to leave you essentially in the same state of mind you were in before you ever heard of skepticism. And that isn't what I want. I want you to keep your common sense knowledge, since I think it is knowledge, not merely belief, but I also want you to come to a clearer and fuller understanding of the nature of that knowledge.

Notice that in sections III.1 and III.2, we did not have to address the specifics of any of the skeptical arguments. I did not identify a specific mistake in any of these arguments, or a specific premise that I thought was false. Even Moore, when he had only two of "Hume's principles" to choose from, said only that "one or both of them" was false. He declined to specify which one was false, let alone why it was false. His argument did not require him to do so. But that is what is disappointing about it: from a theoretical point of view (and that is certainly our point of view here), we want to know not merely *that* skepticism is mistaken, but why; what is the nature of the mistake or mistakes that make it seem plausible?

The interesting thing about the skeptic's arguments is that they start from premises that are widely accepted, or that when introduced, seem perfectly reasonable—for instance, that in order to know something, you at least need a good reason for believing it, or that knowledge cannot be gained through circular reasoning, etc. You would probably accept any of these premises, if it was presented in a context where it wasn't being used to support skepticism. Yet you probably reject skepticism. If this is true, then you have contradictory epistemological views—you hold principles that lead to skepticism while rejecting skepticism itself.

And what's so bad about that? One of the things that's bad about it is that, if you have contradictory premises, you can derive any conclusions whatsoever from them. This is a well-known principle of logic; here is a brief proof of it: Let P and Q be any two propositions. To prove: that from P and $\sim P$, you can derive Q.

    1. P and $\sim P$.   (premise)
    2. P.   (from 1)
    3. P or Q.   (from 2)
    4. $\sim P$.   (from 1)
    5. $\therefore Q$.   (from 3, 4)

(The "or" in step 3 is inclusive; that is, (3) means that P is true, or Q is true, or they both are.) Of course, there is little danger that a person inadvertently holding contradictory beliefs would go through a reasoning process quite like that above. But what is more relevant to the present context is that, if one has false or contradictory epistemological standards, then one can derive all sorts of conclusions—in some cases, one can derive whichever epistemological conclusion one wants—about particular propositions.

To state the problem more clearly: The fact that skeptical arguments seem plausible to us—or anyway, their premises do, when considered in isolation—suggests that we hold a set of very stringent criteria for justified belief—criteria so strict, in fact, that they can be used to rule out any proposition whatsoever from being considered justified. But the fact that we reject skepticism and accept common sense beliefs indicates that, at the same time, we hold a much looser set of criteria for justified belief—criteria that allow lots of propositions to be considered justified. Now, suppose there are a number of claims, about which it is controversial which of them, if any, are justified. Here's something that might happen: I come upon claim A, which I happen to like. So I apply my loose standards of justification, and find A to be justified, whereupon I accept it. Then, some time later, I come upon claim B, which I don't like. So I apply my strict (skeptical) standards of justification, and find B to be unjustified. In reality, it may be that both claims are equally justified (or equally unjustified), but my inconsistent standards enable me to believe whatever I like. This is a prescription for intellectual chaos. This is a danger not only for epistemology, but for every field of inquiry wherein claims need to be assessed as justified or unjustified—which is every field of inquiry.

I believe that this sort of thing happens fairly frequently in our thinking about matters of controversy. You might hope that intellectual honesty and self-awareness would be sufficient to prevent people from switching justificatory standards in the way I have described. But my experience is that the human capacity for self-deception is both vast and subtle. It enables us to seize upon any available tools for maintaining the beliefs—particularly about philosophy, religion, and politics—that we prefer, while avoiding full consciousness of its own operation. In fact, it takes a concerted, conscious effort *not* to engage this otherwise automatic faculty.

Detailed discussion of this problem, as it applies to various areas of inquiry outside of epistemology, is beyond the scope of this book. Here I will mention just one example. Our present-day society seems to have an animus against morality: we don't like moral judgements. Many people have theories about the nature of morality, almost all of which are skeptical. That is, almost everyone who has any views about the nature of morals denies that there is such a thing as *knowing moral facts* (typically, people say things like, "Morality is all subjective"). This denial is often rationalized by skeptical arguments not unlike some of the ones we considered in chapter II, except that the premises and conclusion are restricted to speak only about moral knowledge; the people offering such arguments do not reject knowledge of the physical world. In other words, we apply stringent standards of knowledge to rule out moral knowledge while applying more liberal standards to let in all of the (other) common sense knowledge that we like. (Of course, if I am right to regard at least some moral judgements as common sense beliefs, then it is *also* true that almost everyone *accepts* some moral judgements. We think that morality is all subjective, but that doesn't stop us from condemning all those people who behave immorally!)

Be that as it may, I stipulate that our interest here is in forming a correct conception of human knowledge, particularly knowledge based on perception. Such a conception will enable us to see what is wrong with the skeptical arguments of chapter II, in the sense of identifying precisely which premises are mistaken and why. In my view, this is a test to which any theory of perceptual knowledge must be subjected: if the theory does not enable us to identify the flaws in the arguments against the existence of perceptual knowledge, then it doesn't really explain perceptual knowledge.

Notice that, on my understanding of the significance of skepticism, the challenge for epistemologists exists independently of the existence of *skeptics*. It does not matter whether anyone believes skepticism, whether anyone could believe skepticism, what might be going on in the mind of someone who advocates skepticism, and so on. The problem is not one of refuting *the skeptic*. The problem is that principles pertaining to knowledge and justified belief that we, nonskeptical people accept or feel inclined to accept, entail a conclusion that we cannot accept. This problem, and the intellectual responsibility of understanding and repudiating the errors in our own thinking that give rise to it, would exist even if there were no skeptics in the history of philosophy.

Notes

1. As mentioned in footnote 1 from the preceding chapter, the external-world skeptic really only denies knowledge of *contingent* truths about the external world. You might think that the proposition, *no person knows any contingent truth about the world external to his mind,* is a claim about the world external to your own mind, since it applies to other people, and other people are external to your mind. However, the skeptic would say the proposition is necessarily true, not contingent (note that it is true even if there are no other people). Hence, it escapes self-reference.

2. Lehrer, 284. Lehrer goes on to explain that we lack knowledge because we can never be "completely justified" in any belief. The intended function of the modifier "completely" is unclear, since Lehrer seems to be claiming that there is no reason at all to reject the sort of skeptical scenario he discusses on pp. 292-93.

3. Lehrer, 284. "Agnoiology" means "theory of ignorance."

4. Oakley, 228.

5. Moore, "Proof of an External World."

6. See Moore, "Proof of an External World," 297, where he compares his proof to an analogous proof that there are three typos on a certain page; and "A Reply to My Critics" in Schilpp, 668-75, where he disavows other, less straightforward interpretations of his argument.

7. Moore, "Hume's Theory Examined," 119-20 (emphasis Moore's). The principles in question are as follows. (1) "Nobody can ever know of the existence of anything which he has not directly apprehended, unless he knows that something which he has directly apprehended is *a sign* of its existence." (2) "Nobody can ever know that the existence of any one thing A is a *sign* of the *existence* of another thing B, unless he . . . has experienced a *general conjunction* between *things like* A and *things like* B" (109; emphasis Moore's).

8. I use "logical soundness" for validity in the logicians' sense and "factual soundness" for the property of having true premises. Thus, an argument is sound *tout court* iff it is both logically and factually sound.

9. Reid, 7.

10. As Malcolm notes in Schilpp, 348.

11. Stroud, 102-3.

12. Stroud, 108.

13. Cf. Oakley's discussion (221-22) of justificatory dependence.

14. The term "foundherentism," referring to a position that is midway between extreme versions of foundationalism and coherentism, is from Susan Haack (see "Theories of Knowledge" and *Evidence and Inquiry*, esp. 19)—but note that I do not mean by my use of the term to imply a view according to which *all* foundational beliefs are fallible (contrast Haack, "Theories of Knowledge," 145, 149). The point I am making here is only the relatively weak one that an initially plausible belief can be undermined by its failure to cohere with the rest of one's beliefs, including beliefs that are not in any clear sense epistemically prior to it. This point is related to, but not exactly the same as, Haack's "Up-and-Backism" ("Theories of Knowledge," 149;

Evidence and Inquiry, 31-32).

15. Compare Haack, *Evidence and Inquiry*, 81-89.

16. This is actually a *defeater* relation, rather than a *justification* relation, since the result is to remove justification rather than produce it. In this case, it removes your justification for believing that your calculations were correct. It is "downward" pointing if, as may very well be the case, your belief that the Earth is not 32 miles in circumference is more derivative than your belief that you performed the calculations correctly. The latter might even be foundational, if the calculation is short and you can hold it all in your mind at once.

17. The assistant might try claiming—by analogy to my own response to brain-in-a-vat type scenarios in section VIII.3—that we lack evidence that it *is* possible that someone whose name was not on the list committed the crime. But this would be belied by our background knowledge about human nature, about some people's ability to get into places where they aren't invited, and so on.

IV. A Version of Direct Realism

This chapter and the next form the core of my positive theory of perceptual knowledge. They explain exactly what form of direct realism I am defending. My direct realism embodies two main theses: first, the thesis that perception is direct awareness of external reality; second, the thesis that we have noninferential knowledge of the external world as a result of perception. The present chapter deals with the former issue, the issue of *direct awareness*. Chapter V will consider the latter issue, that of noninferential, or *foundational knowledge*.

This might seem redundant—you might wonder what is the difference between having "direct awareness" of something and having "foundational knowledge" of it. But this will be made clear in due course.

1. The Concept of Awareness

What is awareness? First, let's distinguish my use of "awareness" from another common use of the term. The term "awareness" could be used in a very broad sense, such that to have any mental state at all (or perhaps, any *conscious* mental state) is to be "aware." In this usage, thinking, imagining, having a tickling sensation, desiring, and many other mental states and processes would count as species of "awareness."

That is not how I use the term herein. In my usage, awareness is always awareness *of something*. Logically, awareness is a *relation* between a being who is aware (the "subject of awareness") and that of which he is aware (the "object of awareness").[1] Notice two logical implications of this: First, if S is aware of x, it follows that x exists. For one cannot stand in a relation to what does not exist. The existence of a relationship always depends on the existence of the things related. Second, "S is aware of x" and "$x = y$" together entail "S is aware of y." For if one stands in a certain relation to x, and x is y, then one stands in that relation to y.[2]

Although not every mental state counts as awareness, all awareness involves a certain kind of mental state. But in order to talk about this, I will need to introduce some technical terminology. The kind of mental state involved in awareness I call an *apprehension*. Note that this is a technical use of "apprehension," which does not exactly correspond to the way the word is used in ordinary English. Also notice that having an apprehension is not the same as having awareness; having an apprehension is only *one* of the things required for awareness (the rest to be described below).

Next, we need to explain the notion of "representational content."[3] This is best done with examples. Suppose I say that the cat is on the mat. My statement, "The cat is on the mat," is a kind of representation: it represents a certain possible state of affairs, a state consisting in the cat's being on the mat. That possible situation—the cat's being on the mat—is called the "content" of the representation. Similarly, suppose I draw a picture of a cat on a mat. The picture is another kind of representation: it represents a similar situation. (The picture, by its nature, must contain more information than the statement. For instance, the picture will have to show the mat being rectangular, or round, or some other specific shape, whereas the statement says nothing about the shape of the mat. If done in color, the picture will represent the cat as being some specific color, and so on. For this reason, the picture cannot have *the same* content as the statement. It has a richer content. Hence the saying, "A picture is worth a thousand words.") For another example, suppose I *believe* that the cat is on the mat. This, too, is a kind of representation, albeit of a very different kind. It too, has a content, the same as the content of the statement: it is *about* the cat's being on the mat, just as the statement was about the cat's being on the mat. Finally, suppose I *see* that the cat is on the mat. In this case, I would maintain, there is another kind of representation, the visual experience that I am having, that is about the cat, the mat, and the cat's being on the mat. The content of the visual experience, by the way, is similar to the content of the pictorial representation, but not exactly the same, since no picture looks exactly like the real thing.

Notice one important difference between the pictorial representation and the others: the picture represents a certain state of affairs by resembling it. What does that mean? Perhaps it means that the picture of the cat on the mat shares some of the same characteristics (for instance, shape and color) as the actual cat on the mat? Well, I don't think this is quite right, since the actual cat is three-dimensional, while the picture is flat, so they are not the same shape. Rather, to say the picture "resembles" the object is to say the picture *looks like* the object, that is, the two produce similar visual experiences in human observers. (A decoy duck is said to "resemble" a real duck because they produce similar visual experiences, not because they are objectively similar.) Notice that none of the other kinds of representations mentioned in the preceding paragraph represent through resemblance—not the statement, not the belief, and not the visual experience either (visual experiences of cats don't look like cats, or like anything else, because you can't see a visual experience; that would require having a visual experience of a visual experience).

Some mental states are representational, but not all are. Thoughts, desires, and the states one has when imagining and perceiving are representational. (The content of a desire is the state one wants to come about.) On the other hand, a tickling sensation, say, does not appear to be representational—there is nothing the tickle is *of* or *about*, or that it represents.[4] This is why a tickle does not count as a form of "awareness" in my terminology.

"Representations" as such (unlike states of "awareness") need not have actually existing objects.[5] For instance, I can imagine a unicorn, even though unicorns do not actually exist. I can make statements about God, even if there is no God (of course, the nonexistence of God would make most statements about Him *false*, but the statements nonetheless exist as representations). This is one sense in which the content of a representation is *abstract*: the representation has content, even if there is no object (or event, state, etc.) in reality that corresponds to the representation.[6]

There is another sense in which the content of a representation is abstract: Two distinct representations can have *the same* content. Suppose you believe the cat is on the mat, I believe the cat is on the mat, and you say, "The cat is on the mat." All three representations—your belief, my belief, and your statement—have the same content. Notice also that contents are not language-specific. If you say, "Le chat est sur la natte," this statement has the same content as the statement, "The cat is on the mat," even though the two statements have no words in common.

Apprehensions are a particular species of representation, just as states of awareness are a particular species of apprehension. Apprehensions are *mental* representations—they exist in the mind, unlike pictures and statements, which exist in the publicly observable, physical world. They also have another interesting, defining feature: apprehensions represent their contents *as actualized*. This feature I refer to as their "assertiveness," based on the following analogy to sentences. Consider the sentences, "Please close the door," "Will you close the door?" and "You will close the door." These sentences have a common content—they are all about your closing the door. The first sentence requests or commands that the state be actualized, while the second asks whether it will be actualized. Only the third is assertive: it represents that state of affairs "as actual," that is, as what is actually going to happen.[7]

Analogously, in the life of a conscious being, different kinds of representations serve different functions. Desires represent the world as one would like it to be (this is a tautology, of course, but a useful tautology in this context), and one usually aims at *making* those states of affairs actual. Imagination represents ways the world might be (this is useful in deliberation and in anticipating future events). Apprehensions have the function of representing the world as it actually is.[8] Of course, apprehensions do not always *fulfill* their function—sometimes the world is not really the way they represent it. But they always purport to represent reality. That is why there is something wrong with an apprehension that fails to correspond to reality. For example, if you *believe* that you are immortal, you are wrong. But if you *wish* that you were immortal, you are not thereby "wrong."[9]

In sum, we can define an apprehension as an assertive mental representation. Beliefs are a kind of apprehension, as are the experiences we have when perceiving things. There may also be other kinds of apprehensions, such as intuitions, but we need not concern ourselves with them here. However, desires, emotions, and exercises of imagination are not apprehensions, because they do not represent their contents assertively.

Now, in order for one to be aware of *x*, one must have an apprehension that is related to *x* in the right way. What is the right way? Well, for one thing, the nature of *x* must correspond, at least roughly, to the content of the apprehension. In order to be aware, for instance, of the cat's being on the mat, one must have an apprehension representing the cat as being on the mat; one could not be aware of the cat's being on the mat by having an apprehension of, say, a tree, or a bucket of linguine. A further condition is that this correspondence between the content of the apprehension and reality must not be due to mere chance (must not be "accidental"). The apprehension must have been formed in such a way, and under such conditions, as to make its correspondence with reality probable. This last condition is somewhat vaguely stated, nor do I plan to give a precise elaboration of it here.[10] However, I will give two examples to illustrate what I mean, and I will discuss further how the condition applies to the forms of awareness we are mainly concerned with—namely, perception and perceptual knowledge—in later sections. The first example, then: suppose that I am presently sitting in my apartment, but, as a result of a dose of LSD, I am having sensory experiences as if I were in a jungle, watching a purple elephant walk by. Suppose further that, as chance would have it, there happens to be a purple elephant of exactly the sort I seem to be seeing, walking through a jungle in South America. There is no causal connection between the elephant in South America and my present experience; it's just a coincidence. In this case, am I seeing that elephant in South America? Am I perceiving it? Am I aware of it? I take it that the answer to all these questions is "No." Why?

Because it is just an accident that there is a correspondence between the content of my experience and an actual elephant in South America.

Second example: Suppose that a gambler has the feeling that the ball on the roulette wheel is going to land on red. Assume he has no good reason to believe that he actually possesses ESP and that, in fact, he does not possess ESP. Nevertheless, he believes that the ball will land on red, so he bets a lot of money on it. As it happens, the ball does in fact land on red, and the gambler collects. In this case, did the gambler *know* that the ball was going to land on red? Was he aware of the fact that the ball was going to land on red? Again, the answer to both of these questions is "No," because it was just an accident that the gambler's belief was correct. It could just as easily have been wrong, given the way he formed the belief.

To summarize the conditions required for awareness:

S is aware of *x* if and only if:
i.   *S* has an assertive mental representation (an apprehension),
ii. *x* exists and at least roughly satisfies the content of that representation, and
iii. it is not accidental (not due to chance) that the content of the representation is satisfied.

There are at least two different *forms* of awareness, which we will have occasion to discuss in more detail later: there is perceptual awareness (a.k.a., "perception"), and there is cognitive awareness (a.k.a., "knowledge"). But first, we must attend to another distinction.

2. Direct and Indirect Awareness

Sometimes, our awareness of one thing leads us to be aware of something else. In that case, the latter awareness is "indirect." In general, you are indirectly aware of *x* if you are aware of *x*, but your awareness of *x* is based on your awareness of something else. You are directly aware of *x* if you are aware of *x*, and your awareness of *x* is *not* based on your awareness of anything else.

What about this "based on" relation? It is a relation that can hold between two apprehensions. The paradigm (but not the sole) example is inference. Suppose I call up my friend Liz on the telephone. The phone rings eight times (I am counting) with no answer. I conclude that she is not home and hang up. In this case, I have two beliefs—I believe that the phone rang eight times with no answer, and I believe that Liz is not home—and the second belief is *based on* the first.[11] From this example, we can see several things about the basing relation.

First, the basing relation is causal. If I hadn't thought that the phone rang eight times with no answer, I would not have thought that Liz wasn't home. That is because my belief that the phone rang eight times with no answer *caused* me to accept the further belief that Liz wasn't home.

Second, the basing relation is also logical. The content of my first belief is *relevant to* the content of my second belief. More specifically, my belief that the phone rang eight times with no answer appears to me to *support* the belief that Liz isn't home (in the context of my background knowledge), in the sense that if the (content of the) former belief is true, it would be for that reason highly probable that the (content of the) latter belief would be true.

The above two features of the basing relation are connected. When one apprehension, B, is based on another, A, A causes B *because* A (apparently) logically supports B. In the example at hand, I am disposed to infer that Liz isn't home from the fact that her phone rang eight times with no answer, only because the latter fact appears to me logically relevant to that conclusion. (I insert the qualifier "apparently" because there are cases in which I base one belief on another, even though the latter is not genuinely supported by the former; this is known as committing a fallacy.)

Third, notice that the function of the basing relation is to transmit awareness: we start out with awareness of certain things, and by basing further apprehensions on that initial awareness—if everything goes well—we expand the scope of our awareness. Thus, for instance, starting from awareness of the observable properties of middle-sized physical objects, we can ultimately become aware of things like electric fields and quarks, by basing theoretical beliefs on that initial awareness. But what happens if one's initial apprehensions are not awareness? This can happen either because they fail to correspond to reality, or because their correspondence to reality is merely accidental. In that case, the *failure*, the defectiveness, of the initial apprehensions will be transmitted to any further apprehensions based on them. In other words, suppose B is based on A. Then it follows that, if A is not genuine awareness (meaning A fails condition (ii) or (iii) in the definition of awareness), B is not genuine awareness either (B must fail condition (ii) or (iii) also).

To apply this point to our example: suppose that I am mistaken in my belief that Liz's phone rang eight times with no answer. Unbeknownst to me, let's say, I misdialed, and it was someone else's phone that I was ringing. Well, it follows that I do not *know* (and am not *aware* of the fact) that Liz is not home. Even if Liz really is not home, my belief doesn't constitute awareness of that fact. Why? Because—given my misdialing—it would be merely accidental, merely a matter of chance, if my conclusion that Liz is not home was correct.

I maintain, as we will see in chapter V, that there are other examples of the basing relation, besides inference. Inference is just the special case in which one *belief* is based on another belief. But there are other, nonbelief apprehensions, and they may instantiate the basing relation as well. The above observations about the basing relation apply equally to noninferential basings as they do to inference (indeed, if they did not, I would have no right to speak of noninferential basings). Obviously, a nonbelief apprehension can cause or be caused by another apprehension. But some philosophers will feel that my second observation—that basing is a logical relation—causes trouble. "Can a mental state other than a belief be logically related to anything?" they will wonder. But I see no difficulty in this. All apprehensions have representational content. Either there exists something in reality that satisfies that content, or not. In some cases, the satisfaction of the content of one apprehension renders it probable that the content of another apprehension is satisfied.[12] This is what I mean by saying that one apprehension "logically supports" another.

Now we are in a position, finally, to understand the first part of my direct realist theory, which we had left at an intuitive level in chapter I: the thesis that perception is *direct awareness* of the external world. This means that in perception, we are aware of (some parts or aspects of) the external world, and this awareness is not based on the awareness of anything else.

3. The Analysis of Perception

Literally, "analysis" means the process of taking something apart. An analysis of perception is an account of the elements involved in perception—an account, that is, of the conditions that, when combined, constitute a person's perceiving something. The traditional analysis of perception, which I endorse, says that when you perceive an object, three things happen:

i.   You have a purely internal mental state called a "perceptual experience" or "sensory experience."
ii. There is something in the external world that at least roughly satisfies the content of that experience. This thing is called the "object of perception." (Note: The object of perception need not actually be a physical object; it could be an event, or a quality, etc., as when one perceives a thunderclap, which is not really an "object" in the usual sense of that word. "Object of perception" just means whatever it is that is perceived.)
iii. There is a causal relation between the experience and the object; that is, the object is causing you to have the experience.

These are defining characteristics of perception, so if any of these conditions does not obtain, you are not perceiving. If (i) is satisfied but (ii) or (iii) is violated (that is, your experience is not caused by anything even roughly satisfying its content) then you are *hallucinating*, rather than perceiving.

Each of these conditions requires some defense, to which I now turn.

3.1. The Existence of Perceptual Experiences

Perceptual experiences (also called "sensory experiences") are defined as the purely internal, mental components of perception. In calling them "purely internal," I mean that the existence of such a state does not logically imply the existence of an external object. When I see the cup on my desk, something goes on in the physical world (the cup reflects light towards my eyes, and so on), and something also goes on in my mind (I have a certain sort of experience, an experience in which it looks to me as if there is a cup before me). The latter is the perceptual experience. Notice that *perceptual experience* is not equivalent to *perception*, since my perceptual experience could exist as such even if there were no cup before me, but if there were no cup my experience would not count as *perception* (due to the failure of condition (ii) in the above analysis); instead, it would be a *hallucination*. Thus, the existence of a perception implies the existence of a perceptual experience, but the existence of a perceptual experience only implies the existence of *either* a perception or a hallucination.

Some philosophers question the existence of perceptual experiences in this sense.[13] They do not question that people perceive things, however. What they question is that perception can be analyzed into a purely internal state, plus something else. Instead, they think that when you perceive an object, the only relevant mental state you are in is the state of *perceiving that object*, and this state logically could not exist unless the object existed. This view (often called "the disjunctive conception of experience") is an extreme form of direct realism. Unfortunately, it is not true.

You might think that the question could be settled by introspection, together with a little imagination: I contemplate the experience I am now having as I look at, and perceive, the cup on my desk. I then imagine a possible situation in which I have an extremely vivid hallucination of a cup of just that sort on my desk—so vivid that I would erroneously take there to be a cup there. The fact that I have never (as far as I know!) actually had such a hallucination is irrelevant; it is enough that it is logically possible to have such a hallucination. It seems obvious that in the hallucination scenario, I would be having the same experience as in the actual case of normal perception.[14] And in the hallucination case, I would be having a purely internal mental state. Therefore, such a purely internal mental state also occurs in the case of normal perception.

Those who deny the existence of perceptual experiences point out that the preceding argument is inconclusive. The imagined hallucination would *seem* just like a normal perception—introspection would reveal no difference. However, it does not follow from this that the two experiences are really of the same type.[15] (Compare this case: A decoy duck might *seem* just like a real duck, but it does not follow from this that they are objects of the same type.) I think this observation is correct as far as it goes—from the fact that the hallucination would seem exactly like a normal perception, it does not follow deductively that they are the same kind of experience. It is not inconsistent to say that our introspection would be deceived. But I think the fact that the two experiences would seem exactly alike introspectively, no matter how acute and careful one's introspective observation was, is at least a strong reason for thinking that they are in fact of the same type. This consideration at least shifts the burden of proof onto those who doubt the existence of perceptual experience—a burden which they have not discharged.[16] Compare this case: You and I see what appears to be a cow grazing in a field. I hypothesize that it is actually not a cow, but an incredibly realistic cow-decoy. I present no evidence that this is true; I merely point out that from the fact that the object seems to be a cow, it does not follow that it really is one. Have I provided rational grounds for doubting that the object we are seeing is a cow?

But I think there is a clearer and more conclusive argument to be made. Imagine the following two situations:

Case 1: John sees an apple on a table in front of him. (The case of normal perception.)

Case 2: Sue is in a dark room, with no table and no apple in it. Sue, however, is the subject of a brain experiment, in which scientists have inserted electrodes into her head. The electrodes directly stimulate her visual cortex, in exactly the same way that John's visual cortex is being stimulated by the signals from his optic nerves. As a result, Sue has a visual hallucination of an apple on a table.

Sue's hallucination, presumably, is a purely internal mental state. Its existence does not entail the existence of any object of which she is aware (in fact there is no relevant object of which she is aware), and there is no reason for holding that it entails the existence of any other external object. This internal mental state is caused by a certain brain state. Now, John is having precisely the same brain state. Therefore, John must also be having that same internal mental state: if you duplicate the causes, you duplicate the effect. In other words:

1. In general, if A causes B, then any event qualitatively identical with A would cause an effect qualitatively identical with B.
2. It is possible to have a hallucination induced by brain events qualitatively identical to the brain events that occur during normal perception.
3. In such a case, the brain events cause a purely internal mental state.
4. Therefore, during normal perception, one's brain events cause a qualitatively identical effect—that is, a mental state of the same kind.[17]

This establishes that the mental state you have when you have a hallucination of the kind described is also present during normal perception. It would be implausible (and contrary to introspection, not to mention Ockham's razor) to suppose that there are *two separate* mental states going on during normal perception; therefore, we must conclude that that purely internal mental state is part of the perception.

3.2. Content-Satisfaction

We turn to the second condition in my analysis of perception, which requires that the content of the perceptual experience be at least approximately satisfied.

Sometimes the objects you perceive are not quite as they appear, so the content of your experience is not quite satisfied, but this does not prevent you from perceiving them. There is the famous example of the straight stick, which, while half-submerged in water, appears bent. It would be silly to conclude, just because the stick isn't really bent, that you aren't even seeing the stick.[18] This is why I include the qualifier "roughly" or "approximately"—of course, you can still see the stick, even though it does not *exactly* correspond to the content of your visual experience.

But what if the nature of external reality were to diverge radically from the content of your experience? What if that stick were somehow causing you to have an experience such that it looked to you as if there was a fluffy, green kitten, floating on the water? Are you then, by having that experience, seeing the stick? I think not. This is the sort of case that motivates the content-satisfaction condition.

There is a similar condition for other kinds of awareness, and indeed for other kinds of representation (though it applies less strongly to nonmental representations, where conventions and intentions can come in to help determine reference). To take one illustration: suppose that an anthropologist has recently returned from a study of a remote, primitive tribe. He reports that the natives, like us, have an idea of the sun. But unlike us, they happen to have a lot of erroneous beliefs about the sun. They don't realize that the sun is round and yellow, nor that it gives off light and warmth. Actually, they think that the sun is a large plant, with branches and leaves, living on a distant mountainside. What would you think of this story? You would probably think that the anthropologist must be confused. The natives might be mistaken about the sun, but they could not be *that* mistaken. The natives might have an idea of *something* (a tree, perhaps) about which they believe those things, but whatever it is, it is not an idea *of the sun*. A similar point applies to words as applies to ideas—we could also tell the anthropologist that whatever word the natives are using that he has translated as "sun," does not mean "sun." Notice that this is not merely an epistemological point. The point is not merely that there could be no reason for attributing to the natives the belief that the sun is a tree. The point is that what, in reality, an idea is an idea of is determined at least in part by what in reality best matches the content of the idea. An idea that figures in the sorts of beliefs described does not count as an idea of the sun. There is a general condition that a representation must be at least minimally adequate to its object.

To take another illustration, suppose you have contracted an artist to paint a picture of you. After several days' work, he shows you the finished product, which turns out to look something like figure 4.1. At this point, I think you would have cause to complain that the contract has not been fulfilled—that the picture he painted is not a picture *of you*, regardless of what the artist may say

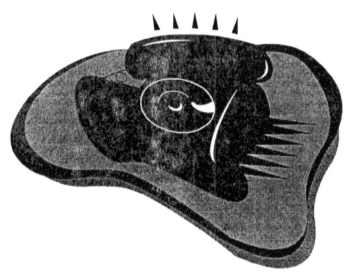

Figure 4.1. Not a picture of you. (Image ©1996 by Corel Corporation.)

or what he may have been thinking when he painted it.[19]

Note that in laying down this content-satisfaction condition on representations in general, I am not implying that every representation must correspond to something in reality. I am only saying that *in order* for there to be a specific thing in reality that a representation represents, that thing must roughly correspond to the representation (that is, it must be roughly as it is represented as being). There always remains the possibility of representations that have no real objects, like the representation of a unicorn.

The content-satisfaction condition also helps to explain what we consider the object of perception in normal cases. I'm looking at the cup on my desk: Why is that particular cup the thing that I'm seeing, and not something else? If we consider just the first and third conditions on perception, we might say: because that particular cup is the thing that is causing my perceptual experience. But the problem is that there is a complex chain of cause and effect leading up to my perceptual experience, in which the presence of the cup is only one link. My perceptual experience is just as much caused by the light rays traveling from the cup to my eyes, by the images on my retinas, by the electrical impulses on my optic nerves, and by the brain processes in my visual cortex. But we don't say that I am seeing the light rays, retinal images, optic nerve impulses, or brain processes. The last three things I have never seen in my life. (People sometimes see light rays—as, for instance, when someone shines a flashlight in your face. But I do not think that we normally see light rays, when looking at material objects; we just see the material objects. Light *enables* us to see material objects, but that is far from saying that light is what we see.) The causal chain also extends in the other direction: my present visual experience is also caused by the light rays *incident* on the surface of the cup, but I am not seeing those either.[20] Why not? What necessary condition on perception do I fail to satisfy with respect to, say, my optic nerve impulses, that I do satisfy with respect to the cup?

The answer is that the optic nerve impulses do not come anywhere close to satisfying the content of my visual experience, whereas the cup does. My visual experience represents there to be a yellow, cup-shaped thing on the desk. My optic nerve impulses are not anything like a yellow, cup-shaped thing on the desk, so they cannot count as the object of my perception. The retinal images come closer to satisfying the content of my experience, but nevertheless, the cup itself clearly satisfies that content better. The retinal images are very small and oriented upside down, relative to my body,[21] they are located inside my head, and there are two of them. But my visual experience represents a single, larger thing, located outside of me, and oriented right-side up.[22]

There is one important objection to the content-satisfaction condition that we must deal with before moving on.[23] It seems that there is a certain family of counter-examples to this condition:

Example 1: I walk into a dark room and see something in the corner that looks like a snake. In fact, suppose, there is no snake in the room. What is in the corner is a coil of rope, which I (incorrectly) *see as* a snake. Seeing something *as* a snake is not the same as seeing a snake, of course, and I am not seeing a snake since there is no snake there to be seen. The coil of rope is what I see. But the coil of rope, arguably, does not roughly satisfy the content of my perceptual experience, since that experience represents there to be a snake in the corner, and a snake is not objectively very similar to a coil of rope.

Example 2: My next-door neighbor, let's say, has a clock that marks the hour with sounds of bird calls. When 12:00 comes, I hear the clock through the wall. My auditory experience is not representing there to be a clock though. It may represent there to be a bird, or simply certain sounds, but not a clock. Nor is the clock similar either to a sound or to a bird. But I am still hearing the clock.

Example 3: I look out the window and see John Smith walking by. But only his head is above the level of the window pane. In fact, it is only the facing surface of his head that actually reflects any light to my eyes. So my visual experience, arguably, just represents there to be a surface of a certain shape and color there (nor, by the way, *need* it be the case that I see this *as* the surface of John's head). John himself is not approximately the same as that surface. But it is still quite proper to say that I have seen John.

Each of these cases seems to be one in which I perceive something even though that thing does not satisfy condition (ii) in my analysis of perception. Therefore, there seems to be something wrong with the analysis.

The analysis needs to be qualified. We need to distinguish between what I shall call "perception in the primary sense" (or "primary perception") and "perception in the secondary sense" ("secondary perception"). You perceive A in the secondary sense when there is some other thing, B, such that you perceive A *by virtue of* perceiving B; that is, perceiving B *counts as* perceiving A, in the circumstances.[24] You perceive A in the primary sense when you perceive A, and there is no other thing by virtue of perceiving which you perceive A. A distinction between primary and secondary awareness can be defined analogously. And the qualification to our definitions of awareness and perception required to meet the objection is this: that those definitions must be understood only as applying to the primary senses of "awareness" and "perception."

This naturally raises the question of how to define secondary perception, which comes down to the question *When does perceiving A "count as" perceiving B?* I do not have a complete answer to this question (which seems to depend heavily on conventional and pragmatic factors that are not very interesting philosophically), but there seem to be three general sorts of cases in which this happens. First, sometimes perceiving certain attributes of a thing counts as perceiving the thing itself. Example 1 illustrates this. I see the rope by virtue of seeing certain of its attributes, particularly its size, shape, and location (perhaps also its color, depending on how dark it is). Notice that those attributes do roughly correspond to the content of my visual experience, so my analysis of perception, with the new qualification, accommodates the example.

Second, sometimes perceiving something counts as perceiving its cause, as in example 2: I hear the clock, but only by virtue of the fact that I hear the *sound* emitted by the clock. And again, notice that that sound satisfies the content of my auditory experience (having the appropriate tonal qualities), so we again escape counter-example.

Third, sometimes perceiving a part of something (including perceiving the surface or part of the surface of it) counts as perceiving the thing itself. We see this in example 3, in which I count as seeing John by virtue of seeing the facing surface of his head. The facing surface of John's head satisfies the content of my visual experience, as per our analysis of (primary) perception.

In visual perception, what we are primarily aware of is the shapes and colors of surfaces, specifically the portions facing us of the surfaces of physical objects. Both example 1 and example 3 are consistent with this.

3.3. The Causal Condition

The motivation for the final condition in my analysis of perception—

iii. There is a causal relation between the experience and the object, that is, the object is causing you to have the experience.

—is straightforward and uncontroversial. Return to my visual experience of the cup on my desk. Suppose, as is in fact the case, that there are thousands of cups in existence that have the same observable properties as the cup that is on my desk. One of these other cups happens to be in the kitchen cabinet, in fact. (I would not be able to tell them apart just by looking.) Still, I am not perceiving any of those other cups. The only one I am seeing is the particular cup that happens to be on the desk now. Why? Because that is the one that is actually causing my present visual experience.

Consider another case: nefarious brain scientists have gotten electrodes into my brain again and are stimulating it so as to artificially induce in me a visual experience representing a yellow cup on my desk. As it happens, there is a yellow cup on my desk, but it doesn't have anything to do with why I am having the experience; it's just a coincidence. Again, we wouldn't consider this to be a case of my seeing the actual cup that's on the desk.

So we see that some sort of causal connection between the object and one's experience is necessary for perceiving an object. But not just any causal connection will do. Imagine that the brain scientists have chosen to induce in me the visual experience of a yellow cup *because* they, the scientists, are aware of the cup that is actually there—whatever was on the desk, they would have stimulated my brain to have a corresponding visual experience. So the presence of the cup has indeed caused my visual experience of a cup (albeit indirectly). But it still isn't right to say I am *seeing the cup*. This is what is known as a "deviant causal chain." (Roughly, the term connotes a causal chain that is convoluted and abnormal.) I shan't enter into the question of how exactly one might define "deviant causal chain," although we can see here at least one rule: a causal chain that works through another conscious being's inducing experiences in me will probably always count as "deviant."

Nevertheless, the lack of a precise definition of deviant causal chains should not be thought to impugn the truth of my analysis of perception. For there is a problem of deviant causal chains in many other cases, possibly all cases where a causal connection is part of the analysis of some everyday concept.[25] For instance, no one doubts that to *break* an object is to (in a certain way) cause the object to be in the state of brokenness. But not just any causal connection will do. Suppose I tell you to break the vase, which induces you to throw it on the ground, whereupon it breaks. Well, I have (indirectly) caused the vase to break, but *I* did not actually break it. This is a deviant causal chain. The fact that I don't know exactly how to define deviant causal chains does not cause me to doubt the causal theory of "breaking." Similarly, I do not think there is any ground for doubt about the causal theory of perception—that is, that perceiving an object is having the object cause (in a certain way) one to have a perceptual experience representing it. And the question of how to define deviant causal chains is not a task specifically for the theory of perception.

4. The Nature of Perceptual Experience

Perceptual experiences are the purely internal states that are involved in all perception. There is quite a lot that might be said about the nature of our perceptual experiences, including observations about the ways that the experiences of the different senses differ from one another, but here I shall confine myself to the most general and fundamental characteristics of perceptual experience. Perceptual experiences typically have three aspects:

i.   their sensory qualia,
ii. their representational content, and
iii. their forcefulness.

(ii) and (iii) are essential aspects of perceptual experience, and so must be present in all cases, but there are rare cases of perceptual experiences lacking (i). I will explain each of these presently.

4.1. Sensory Qualia

A *quale* (plural: "qualia") is a kind of property of an experience. The quale of an experience is *what the experience is like*, from the subject's point of view; in other words, what it is like for the person who is having the experience.[26] In the case of emotions and tactile sensations, this can be rephrased as *how it feels when you have this experience*. For instance, there is a certain way it feels to be tickled; there is a certain way it feels to be in love; there is something it is like to smell a rose.[27] These are examples of qualia—specifically, the quale of tickling sensations, the quale of love, and the quale of the experience of smelling a rose. *Sensory* qualia are simply the qualia that sensory experiences have (as opposed to the qualia of emotions or other sorts of nonperceptual experiences).

Qualia are ineffable, in a certain sense. Suppose a deaf person asks you what it is like to hear a bell ringing. Well, there isn't much you can tell him. Pretty much the only way you could answer the question would be if you could induce the experience in him, and then you could say, "It's like *that*." Nevertheless, there is no doubt that you know what it's like to hear the ringing of a bell (assuming you're not deaf), even though you cannot describe it for the benefit of someone who has not had any auditory experiences. You know, for instance, how that experience differs qualitatively from, say, the experience of smelling a rose.

Some readers may be feeling uncomfortable, now, at my positing of "ineffable" qualities. There are those who would consider talk about such things a resort to obscurantism and mysticism, unfit for an analytic philosopher.[28] But on further reflection, the sort of ineffability that I ascribe to qualia is not so mysterious. It results from the facts (a) that you cannot describe a phenomenon to someone who does not have the concepts required to grasp it, and (b) that the concept of a given quale can be gained only by experience of that quale or other, similar ones. Fact (a) is a truism that applies to all phenomena. Similarly, you could not explain what a "computer" is to someone who did not have the concept of a calculation (unless, of course, you first induced him to form that concept). Fact (b) is an empirical observation—when it comes to taste, smell, sound, and other experiences, we come to understand what they are like only by actually having them. There is nothing inherently strange about that, and so there is nothing particularly strange or puzzling about the limited sort of ineffability I ascribe to qualia. ("Limited," because you *can* describe a quale to the satisfaction of people who have had the relevant experience: e.g., "the way tickling sensations feel" describes a quale, to the satisfaction of people who have been tickled.)

I view qualia as something over and above the representational contents of experience. It is possible to have perceptual experiences that lack qualia, and this provides one way to illustrate what qualia are and how they differ from representational contents. The only actual example I can think of is awareness of the position of one's body (proprioception).[29,30] Even in the dark, and when it is not touching another part of your body, you are aware of how your arm is positioned—whether it is pointing up, or straight out, whether it is bent, and so forth. This is a sense over and above the five senses, although most people are unaware of it (they are aware of their body position, but they are not aware that they have a special sense of body position). The reason they are not aware of it is that proprioception has no qualia. It represents one's body as being positioned a certain way, but there is no special feeling or other "what-it's-like" to it—the only noticeable manifestation of proprioceptive "experiences" is that one is inclined to think one's body is positioned a certain way. For this reason, it is strained to even call these states of awareness "experiences," but it is convenient for my purposes to construe "perceptual experiences" broadly, since this sort of qualia-lacking awareness plays the same sort of role in our knowledge of the external world as the more typical perceptual experiences.

There is another way to demonstrate the difference between qualia and representational content—more precisely, to demonstrate that qualia are something over and above representational content.[31] It involves the "inverted color spectrum" thought experiment. Consider the sensory experiences you normally have when viewing things that are, respectively, red, orange, yellow, green, blue, or violet (those are the colors of the rainbow, arranged from longest to shortest wavelength). I shall call the qualia of these experiences, respectively, red*, orange*, yellow*, and so on.[32] So red* is a property of an *experience*, whereas red, of course, is a property of physical objects. When I see a tomato, the tomato itself, the physical object, is red, and my *experience* is a red* experience.

Imagine a person who has his qualia reversed. He has an experience qualitatively identical with your experience of red, when he looks at the objects reflecting the *shortest* wavelength in the visible spectrum. In other words, he has a red* experience when looking at violet things. When he looks at blue objects, he has an orange* visual experience. When looking at green objects, he has a yellow* experience. And so on. The causal relations between wavelengths of light and the qualia he experiences are inverted, relative to your way of perceiving.[33]

Once you have entertained this possibility, you might start to wonder how you know there aren't really people with such inverted qualia. You couldn't tell by asking them: the person with the inverted qualia would have learned to use the word "red" in the same way you did, by observing people referring to objects such as tomatoes, apples, and fire engines as "red," even though he experiences them differently from you. You could try asking him if he has red* experiences when he looks at red things. But how could you explain to him what a red* experience is? Saying, "Red* experiences are the sort of experiences we normally have when looking at red things" fails for obvious reasons. In fact, you might wonder if you yourself might have abnormal qualia (relative to the rest of humanity). Those questions are not really germane to the point I want to make with the thought experiment, but I will make two brief remarks about how you might be able to verify that a particular person does not have inverted qualia. First, the phenomenon would probably mess up the person's aesthetic sense, including their judgements about such things as what colors go together, what is a "warm" color, and what is a "melancholy" color.[34] Second, since the same cause must produce the same effect, in principle you could examine their brain processes to determine whether there was any difference between their brain processes and yours during the perception of color. If no significant physical difference could be found, it would be reasonable to conclude that there was no significant difference between their qualia and yours.

But now, imagine that there were a race of beings (whether people, animals, or space aliens does not matter) with inverted (relative to us) color qualia. Would those beings (call them "the Inverts") be *misperceiving* the world? Would their sensory experiences be *illusions*, in respect of the apparent colors of things? Any reason we might have for saying such a thing would seem to be a reason they would have for saying the same about us. Apart from the temptation of arbitrarily privileging our own way of perceiving, if one set of experiences is to be deemed deceptive, there is no reason for thinking that our experiences are the "right" ones. Note that I am not merely saying that, if we were to encounter the Inverts, then, in that situation, we would have no reason for thinking our experiences to be more veridical than theirs. I am saying that we *now* have no reason to regard our experiences as more veridical than the Inverts' would be. There is no reason to regard the quale we experience when looking at red things as the uniquely right way of perceiving those objects.

I assume that when I, a normal human, look at a ripe tomato and have a red* experience, my experience is not an illusion or hallucination—that is, my experience does not *misrepresent* that object. But if I were to look at a violet object and if, due to some abnormal conditions, I were to have the red* experience, *then* I would be suffering an illusion. We would describe the situation thus: It looks to me as if the object is red, but in fact it is violet. As a related point, consider the fact that, when lighting conditions are abnormal, it is easy to misperceive the colors of things. Therefore, my red* visual experiences have a content that is normally satisfied by red things, but that is not satisfied by violet (or yellow, green, etc.) things.

Notice that what I have said in the preceding paragraph is pretty weak. I have not offered a theory of what colors are, though I have assumed at least that physical objects are often colored.[35] I also have not specified what the content of a red* experience is. I have only said that, whatever that content is, and whatever redness is, the latter satisfies the former, while violet does not. This abstract statement will be enough for the argument I want to make.

Now, we agreed above (I hope) that it would be unacceptably arbitrary to declare the Inverts' experiences of color to be illusions while ours are not. Therefore, what we say about the Inverts' experiences should mirror what we just said above about the normal humans' experiences; that is, when the Inverts look at a red object and have a violet* experience (which is normal for them), their experience is veridical (nonillusory, nondeceptive). If an Invert looks at a violet object and, due to some abnormal (for him) conditions, has a violet* experience, *then* he is subject to an illusion. That is just how the Inverts would describe the matter. So an Invert's violet* experience has a content that is satisfied by *red* objects and not satisfied by violet objects. In other words, the Invert's violet* experiences have the same representational content as *our* red* experiences, since they are satisfied by precisely the same kinds of things.

But by definition, their violet* experiences do not have the same qualia as our red* experiences. So qualia are not a function of representational contents.[36] So qualia are something over and above representational contents. To sum up my argument:

1. The content of my red* experience is satisfied by red things and only red things.
2. The content of the Invert's violet* experience is satisfied by red things and

only red things.
3. So the content of my experience and the content of the Invert's experience are satisfied under the same conditions. (from 1, 2)
4. So my experience and the Invert's experience have the same content. (from 3)
5. My experience and the Invert's experience do not have the same qualia. (One of them has the red* quale, while the other has the violet* quale.)
6. Therefore, the quale of an experience is something over and above its content. (from 4, 5)[37]

Once we accept this conclusion, another interesting question arises. If indeed the quale of a perceptual experience is something beyond its representational content, and if the function of perceptual experiences is purely assertive (that is, their function is just to give us information about the world), what, if anything, are qualia good for? Is there any biological reason why we should have experiences with qualia, rather than just having experiences with representational contents and no qualia? I do not know the answer to this, but I can suggest two possible sorts of answer. The first is that the particular information that we get from perceptual experiences would be difficult or impossible to represent without qualia. For instance, how might we perceive something as red, without having any qualia? It seems impossible. *Maybe* we could perceive the object as reflecting a certain wavelength of light, without having any special qualia associated with that perception, but it seems as if that would be giving us too much information. It also may be impossible to represent that sort of content nonconceptually.

My second speculation is that perceptual experiences do not *merely* have an information-gathering function. That is their main function, but they also have a conative function. Consider the perception of warmth, which has a certain quale. When you have this sort of perceptual experience, one thing you get is information about whatever it is that feels warm. But the experience is also *pleasant*. Likewise, the experiences by which we perceive extreme heat and cold are painful.[38] Thus, we are motivated to seek out places that are mildly warm and to avoid places that are extremely hot or cold. This motivation would not be generated by experiences that *merely* conveyed information about the physical properties of things; it is generated by the particular quale of our experiences when we detect those properties. Or consider the perception of red. As everyone knows, red is the most *striking* color; it is used to get people's attention. I suspect this is because it is the color of blood (or rather, red* is the quale associated with the color of blood, because red* is the most striking quale). But again, mere information, without qualia, would not have the property of strikingness, nor any other aesthetic quality.

It seems that the qualia of our perceptual experiences function to simultaneously give us information about the world and give us emotional reactions or desires. Those two functions are integrated into the same experience, rather than being functions of two separate states or events.

4.2. The Representational Content of Experience

Why do I say that perceptual experiences have "representational content"? Well, when you are having such an experience, there is a way that things *thereby* appear to you to be. That "thereby" is important—things appearing to be a certain way is not some further consequence of your experience; things appear a certain way by virtue of your having the perceptual experience itself.

To see what I mean by this, consider a contrasting theory: one might hold the view that, when you say, "It looks to me as if *P*," you are stating a conclusion, or tentative conclusion, that you draw from your experience—that you are placing an "interpretation" on the experience, which is extraneous to it, rather than describing the intrinsic character of the experience. For instance, take the famous example of the straight stick that appears bent when half-submerged in water. When we say the stick appears to be bent, according to this view, we are saying that one would be tempted to judge the stick to be bent, as a result of the sort of visual experience we are having.

The important issue here is not the semantic one of how "appears" is used in English. As far as that goes, I would be content to grant that there is a use of "appears," "seems," and "looks" in which these terms are used to express tentative judgements or report dispositions to make judgements.[39] The significant issue, rather, is whether our experiences are representing the stick as bent, or whether that content is something contributed by our faculty of judgement. To invoke an obvious metaphor, the question is whether the senses are telling us that the stick is bent or whether they are simply giving us certain qualia that we interpret (or are inclined to interpret) as being caused by a bent stick.[40]

My view is that the sensory experience you have is, of its own nature, representing the object to be bent. There are two important considerations supporting this, as against the alternative, judgement-based theory.

The first consideration is the observed independence of sensory appearances from our beliefs.[41] When I experience this particular illusion, I certainly do not judge, and am not even tempted to judge, that the stick is bent. I know very well that the stick is straight. But this knowledge has no effect on how it looks. However much I know about the optical phenomena and the actual properties of sticks, I still cannot *see* the stick as straight. A defender of the judgement theory might reply that, although I do not for a moment think that the stick is bent, I have at least a *disposition*, perhaps a suppressed disposition, to think that.[42] Now, perhaps it is correct that I have at least some sort of disposition to think that—as I might say, if I didn't know better, I would think the stick was bent—but I have a stronger disposition to think that the stick is straight; therefore, why would it be less apt to say that the stick appears straight?

But the second consideration shows more fundamentally what is wrong with the judgement theory. Assuming that I judge, or have a disposition to judge, that the stick is bent, we have to ask *why* I am disposed to judge that. Do I just spontaneously find myself inclined to believe that, for no reason? Well, no, the disposition, if there is one, is due to the nature of the experience I have: if I didn't know better, I would think the stick was bent, *because it looks that way*. Its looking that way must, therefore, be a fact existing independently of my belief or belief-disposition. Notice that the way the stick looks can explain the belief I am inclined to form only when *how the stick looks* is understood as a matter of how the senses are "telling me" the stick is, and not if it is understood as a matter of how I am inclined to think the stick is.

Some would reject my thesis that perceptual experiences are representational, in the hopes of stalling a certain kind of skeptical argument. Skeptics frequently point to cases in which your senses deceive you; they then ask how you know that you can ever trust the information the senses provide. If one denies that sensory experiences have representational content, then one can avoid this skeptical challenge altogether: one will find the idea of the senses "deceiving" oneself to be nonsensical—for that would imply that the senses are "telling" us things that are false. If the senses don't tell us anything at all, then it follows that they cannot possibly *deceive* us. All that can happen is that we can make incorrect judgements about the causes of our experiences. Furthermore, it would make no sense, on this view, to ask, "How can we know the information the senses provide us is accurate?" If experience is nonrepresentational, then it can be neither accurate nor inaccurate.[43]

But this would be a shortsighted way of responding to the skeptic. For just as it implies that the senses cannot provide us with *false* information, it also implies that they cannot provide us with *correct* information either—they simply do not provide us with information. And surely this does not enhance our position for gaining knowledge of the external world.

Consider an analogy. Suppose I have something that you take to be a letter written by George, which apparently asserts that it is going to rain next Tuesday. Upon viewing the letter, I announce that I think it is going to rain on Tuesday (assume my viewing of the letter caused me to adopt that belief). You then ask, "How do you know that what George is telling you in that letter is true? How do you know George is trustworthy?" Now suppose I reply that your question is based on faulty assumptions, because in fact George wasn't telling me anything in that so-called letter. It is just a meaningless series of words. Therefore, although I admit that my belief was caused by my viewing of the letter, I need not provide any evidence that the letter is "accurate." It is neither accurate nor inaccurate.

Am I now in a good position to know that it is going to rain on Tuesday, since I have fended off your skeptical challenge? I think not. If anything, I have worsened my epistemic position by declaring that I take the letter to have no content. If that is the case, then it is all the more mysterious how I can justifiably say that it is going to rain on Tuesday as a result of viewing the letter.

Similarly, suppose the skeptic believes that a certain kind of perceptual experience represents there to be a tomato in front of oneself. The skeptic notices that, when I have that kind of experience, I accept that there is a tomato in front of me. The skeptic asks me how I know my perceptual experience is trustworthy. I reply by saying that my perceptual experience is neither accurate nor inaccurate, since it has no representational content at all. Haven't I just made my belief all the more mysterious and seemingly arbitrary? The skeptic should have a field day with this. I have not averted the responsibility of explaining how my belief is justified; I have merely repudiated one way in which one might have thought it to be justified.

Now, I might wish to argue that my experiences need not have representational content in order for them to give me information, in a certain sense of "give information." Maybe I experience certain qualia, and I know that those qualia are correlated with certain sorts of events in the external world; so I can thereby make conclusions about what is going on in the external world. But Hume's problem returns here with a vengeance.[44] How could I ever find out what sorts of qualia are correlated with which sorts of external phenomena? Hume, of course, thought that you could not know what sorts of external events were correlated with what sorts of experiences, *even if* your experiences have representational content. But getting rid of the content seems to make Hume's conclusion more clearly inevitable. If we just have a series of intrinsically meaningless states going through our minds, how could that make us justified in believing propositions about external objects? It would seem that the experiences would just be completely unrelated (logically) to the beliefs.

Of course, if you are a skeptic, you would not be impressed with the foregoing reasoning as a reason for attributing representational content to experiences. But here is a reason even a skeptic could appreciate: if we do not attribute representational content to perceptual experiences, it becomes not only impossible to *justify* the beliefs we form about the external world, but impossible even to account for why we form those beliefs. When I see a tomato on the table, if my experience is not representing there to be a tomato (or at least something tomato-like), then it is a mystery why I come to believe there is a tomato there, rather than, say, a rock, or an elephant. Worse, it would be hard to see how I could even form concepts of various kinds of external objects, if the experiences on the basis of which I was to form them did not represent kinds or qualities of external objects.

The foregoing reasons for accepting that a perceptual experience has content also support the thesis that this content is *propositional*. By that, I mean it is something that is either true or false—a perceptual experience represents something *to be the case*. A perceptual experience might have as its content a proposition like [that there is a red, round thing in front of me]. (That is not quite an accurate description, for reasons we shall discuss shortly, but it conveys the general idea of the propositional content of experience.) If experiences did not have propositional content, it would be difficult to understand how a perceptual experience could be the basis for a belief, which does have propositional content, for there would be no logical relations between them.[45]

In spite of this, I do not say that experiences have *conceptual* content. Their content is propositional but (at least part of it is) nonconceptual. What I mean by this is that experiences have (at least some) content independent of the concepts that the subject of the experiences has. Nonconceptual content is content that does not depend upon one's having concepts adequate for grasping that content.

Conceptuality is not an intrinsic property of a content. Rather, it is a way that a content can be entertained. One can entertain a content conceptually (by means of concepts) or nonconceptually (not by means of concepts). A person might even entertain the same content both conceptually and nonconceptually at the same time. For instance, it is logically possible to have a perceptual experience that (nonconceptually) has a certain content and at the same time to have a belief that (conceptually) has that same content.

This would not normally happen, however, and the reason it would not happen is also the main reason for affirming that perceptual experiences have nonconceptual content. The reason is that the content of our experiences is typically much more *fine-grained* than our concepts. Gareth Evans illustrates this point by comparing our visual experiences of color with our color concepts.[46] It is estimated that the human eye (meaning, really, human beings, by means of their visual experiences) can distinguish two million different colors. But we have only a handful of color concepts—certainly my conceptual scheme does not contain concepts for two million different colors. Many of these different colors I would, conceptually, classify as the same—for example, as fitting under the category "red." But that doesn't mean I do not *perceive* the differences among them. Thus, my concepts are inadequate to fully capture the content of my experiences of color. A similar point can be made about shapes, or smells, tastes, and so on.

Now I need to distance myself from certain things I am not saying here. First, I am not denying that the concepts one has may influence the way one perceives things. Consider the duck-rabbit picture made famous by Wittgenstein (figure 4.2).[47] This can be seen either as a duck with its bill pointing to the left or as a rabbit with its ears pointing to the left. You can shift from the one way of seeing it to the other, and something about your visual experience (not your beliefs or other mental states) changes, depending on which way you are seeing the picture—*in a sense*, the picture will look different (it can go from looking like a duck to looking like a rabbit), although there is another sense in which it always looks the same (after all, the black lines on the page don't shift their locations in the visual field). Now suppose you showed the drawing to someone who had no concept of a duck, having never encountered one. This person would be unable to have the experience of seeing the picture as a picture of a duck. Similarly, if he had no concept of a rabbit, he could not see it as depicting a rabbit. This shows, then, that the content of at least some experiences is at least partly conceptual—that is, the way things actually look to you is to some extent dependent on what concepts you have. What I am saying,

Figure 4.2. The duck-rabbit.

however, is that there is a nonconceptual element to experience as well. Everyone with normal vision will *at least* see the picture as a certain black shape on a white background, regardless of what concepts they have (even a dog would presumably see that much). And in addition to that, if they have the appropriate concepts, they may also see it as a picture of a rabbit or a picture of a duck. Thus, the visual representation of specific shapes and colors is nonconceptual. (By "specific colors" I mean the colors of which there are two million, the colors that are too fine-grained for our concepts. "Specific shapes" should be understood analogously.)

Notice that my view leaves room for a broadly empiricist account of (some of) our concepts. The empiricist view of concept-formation has traditionally been that concepts are in some sense derived from, or "abstracted" from, experiences. In order to say this, we need not hold that experiences never have any conceptual content. But we need to hold that experiences at least have *some* content that is nonconceptual.

The second thing I am not saying is that experiences have a kind of content that is intrinsically ineffable. I am not saying, that is, that the content of a typical perceptual experience is something that one could not, in principle, entertain conceptually, nor am I saying it could not, in principle, be described in words. I see no reason in principle why one could not have separate concepts for all the two million colors we can visually discriminate, in which case the content of a visual experience, at least in respect of color, could be conceptualized. Similarly, there is no reason, apart from pragmatic constraints, why one could not have words for stating that content. Apropos of this, consider McDowell's objection to the notion of nonconceptual content:

> It is possible to acquire the concept of a shade of colour, and most of us have done so. Why not say that one is thereby equipped to embrace shades of colour within one's conceptual thinking with the very same determinateness with which they are presented in one's visual experience . . . ? In the throes of an experience of the kind that putatively transcends one's conceptual powers . . . one can give linguistic expression to a concept that is exactly as fine-grained as the experience, by uttering a phrase like "that shade," in which the demonstrative exploits the presence of the sample.[48]

McDowell's effort here seems to be to show that people have (or can acquire—notice the "possible" in the first sentence) the ability to conceptually entertain the same contents as their perceptual experiences have. I doubt that he has shown this, since I do not think the term "that shade" expresses a concept, but the important point is that even if McDowell is right, it poses no threat to the notion of nonconceptual content that I have defended. My view is not that the content of perceptual experiences *cannot* be conceptualized. It is that (some of) the content of perceptual experiences *need not* be able to be conceptualized, in order for the experiences to have that content. A state has content nonconceptually when its having the content it has *does not depend upon* one's having concepts for expressing that content. If one should happen to have concepts for expressing that content anyway, that's all right.

But perhaps McDowell was not attempting to show that experiences have conceptual content in that passage. Perhaps he was only trying to show that Evans's argument for nonconceptual content is invalid. But the problem is that, as long as it is *possible* for a person to have an experience with a certain content while lacking the resources to conceptualize that content, that is sufficient to show that the experience has its content nonconceptually. McDowell's observation that "most of us" have the concept of a shade of color would seem to be an implicit recognition that not everyone necessarily has the cognitive wherewithal to grasp the contents of their experiences conceptually.

4.3. The Forcefulness of Perceptual Experience

This last characteristic of perceptual experience is one about which I have little to say, apart from explaining what it is. Consider the difference between imagining a tomato and perceiving a tomato. Both mental states have approximately the same content—both are about a tomato.

One difference would typically be that the perceptual experience has a more specific and detailed content; it includes a representation of an (almost) exact shape and an (almost) exact shade of red, which your imagination need not. To make this difference more obvious, change the example: imagine a newspaper. There is no difficulty in doing this. However, your "image" of a newspaper in this case is not as detailed as a visual experience of a newspaper. If you are having a visual experience of a newspaper, you can thereby read said newspaper. But I doubt you will find yourself able to read the newspaper you are merely imagining. The mental image is too indeterminate in its representational content.

But there is another, more interesting difference between imagination and perception. Even if you have a very vivid, very detailed imagination, or if you have very poor eyesight, you still would never confuse seeing a tomato with imagining one.[49] The reason lies in what I call the "forcefulness" of perceptual experiences: perceptual experiences represent their contents as actualized; states of merely imagining do not. When you have a visual experience of a tomato, it thereby seems to you as if a tomato is actually present, then and there. When you merely imagine a tomato, it does not thereby seem to you as if a tomato is actually present.

David Hume spoke of the "vivacity" of "perceptions" (under the term "perceptions," unfortunately, Hume included all mental states, including what I call perceptual experiences, exercises of imagination, beliefs, sensations, and even emotions). He held that perceptual experiences (he called them "impressions") had the highest level of vivacity, while memories were a little fainter, and exercises of imagination were the faintest of all.

> [T]he ideas of the memory are much more lively and strong than those of the imagination, and . . . the former faculty paints its objects in more distinct colours, than any which are employed by the latter. . . . [I]n the imagination the perception is faint and languid, and cannot without difficulty be preserved by the mind steady and uniform for any considerable time.[50]

He seems to have thought that the differences in vivacity were the *only* intrinsic differences among perceptual experiences, memories, and exercises of imagination (unless being voluntary counts as an intrinsic property of an exercise of imagination). It is worth taking note of how my position differs from that of Hume. Hume was mistaken both about memory and about imagination. A memory experience is distinguished from a perceptual experience chiefly by the fact that the object of a memory experience seems to the subject to be something that happened in the past, and this has nothing to do with how colorful or faint the memory may be. There is no reason why a faint image should *thereby* (that is, by virtue of its faintness) appear to be of something existing in the past.

An exercise of imagination is distinguished from a perceptual experience chiefly by the fact that the object of the latter seems to the subject to be present then and there, while the object of the former does not seem to exist at all. Again, this has nothing to do with how strong or faint the image is.[51] My "forcefulness" is therefore not equivalent to Hume's "vivacity," insofar as I understand the latter.

Suppose that you take a series of photographs of a tomato on a black background. The first photograph comes out very nicely, with the red color of the tomato quite rich and distinct. The second photo comes out a little fainter, a little less colorful. The third, due to insufficient exposure, comes out very faint, and you can only just see the tomato image in it. In Hume's view, it seems that these three pictures would be related in the same way that a perceptual experience, a memory, and an exercise of imagination are related. In fact, when you look at the first photograph, your experience should be roughly like seeing a tomato (which is true); when you look at the second, you should have an experience roughly like remembering a tomato (since the experience will be less vivid); and when you look at the third, you should have an experience roughly like imagining a tomato. But of course, the latter two implications are false. The second photo no more seems to be of something in the past than the first does, merely because it is less vivid. Nor does the third any the less seem to be real than the first or second, merely because of its faintness. When you look at the third photograph, you will not have any temptation to think you are instead imagining a tomato.

This shows what forcefulness is not. It is not a matter of how faint or vivid an experience is, and it is not a matter of how detailed and specific its content is. Forcefulness is not a matter of either the qualia or the representational content of an experience; it is a third aspect of experience. As to what that aspect is, I have no more to say than what has been said above: it is the fact that, in the experience, it seems to one that something satisfying the content of the experience actually exists, here and now.

5. Is This Direct Realism?

At a casual glance, one might think that my theory of perception is a version of representationalism, also known as "the representational theory of perception" or "indirect realism." After all, I am claiming that in perception, we have certain states that exist purely in our minds and that "represent" external objects. That is just what the representationalists think, is it not? The answer is yes and no. Representationalists do believe that, but they also believe something more: they believe that those mental states *are the only things that we can be directly aware of.* It is the latter thesis that defines indirect realism, and it is the latter that I reject.

A "version of direct realism" would be any theory of perception which implies that in perception, we are directly aware of something external to the mind. To see whether I have presented a version of direct realism, we therefore need to ask, in terms of my theory, *What (if anything) are we aware of in perception, and is this awareness direct or indirect?* That "in terms of my theory" includes my account of what awareness is, what the difference between direct and indirect awareness is, and what is the nature of perception. On my account, awareness involves three elements.

First: one must have an apprehension, which is an assertive mental representation. This condition is satisfied by episodes of perception, for I have argued that perception involves the occurrence of certain mental states (perceptual experiences), that these mental states have representational content, and that they have an attribute, which I call their forcefulness, that qualifies them as being assertive. Thus, perception involves the having of apprehensions.

Second: there must exist an object (the so-called "object of awareness") that at least roughly satisfies the content of the aforementioned apprehension. This condition is also satisfied in cases of genuine perception (as opposed to hallucination), since in perception, the content of the perceptual experience must be at least roughly satisfied.

Third: it must be nonaccidental that the content of the apprehension is satisfied. This is true in perception, since there is a (nondeviant) causal chain between the object satisfying the perceptual experience and the experience itself.

We see, then, that on my account perception is a species of awareness. The next question is, what is it the awareness of? The object of awareness (that of which one is aware), in general, is the object that satisfies the content of the apprehension. What phenomena satisfy the contents of our perceptual experiences? Normally, physical facts do. The content of a visual experience might be, for instance, that there is an object of a certain specific shape and color in front of me. Assuming there is in front of me a physical object of the appropriate shape and color (which there normally is), that fact is what I am aware of, since that fact is what corresponds to the content of my experience. Notice that my perceptual experience does not count as the awareness of any mental state or event, since no mental state or event has any shape or color.

Finally, is this awareness of facts in the external world direct or indirect? This boils down to the question of whether perceptual experiences are based on some other sort of apprehension. I have not addressed this question before now, but I think it is clear that the answer is no. When one sees a tomato, one's visual experience of a tomato is not caused and logically supported by any other apprehension. I cannot even think of a plausible candidate for a state it might be said to be based on. One might try citing the brain states involved in the visual system's "information processing" preceding the visual experience of the tomato. But I think this would be a mistake, for those brain states are not apprehensions. There is nothing, nor does there even appear to be anything, that one is aware of in having those brain states, other than the tomato. One is not aware of, not even seemingly aware of, the brain states themselves, nor of the information they are supposed to be processing; the first thing one is actually aware of is the tomato, as a red, roughly spherical thing.

In sum, we have perceptual experiences which at least represent there to be objects having certain specific shapes and colors (a similar point can be made using tastes, smells, and other observable properties). These experiences are caused by physical objects having those very properties, and there are no other mental states on which the experiences are based. In the primary sense of "aware," then, we are directly aware of the fact that there are objects with those colors and shapes. We might also be said to be aware (directly and primarily) of the colors and shapes of the (facing surfaces of) physical objects around us, since that could also be described as what satisfies the content of a state representing there to be objects of those colors and shapes. We must therefore conclude that direct realism is true.

6. The Mistake of Representationalism

In my view, perception is *essentially* the direct awareness of external particulars. That is, the truth of direct realism follows from the existence of perception. Indirect realism is not merely a mistaken view of how perception works, but moreover (like most false philosophical views), it is *confused.*

The fundamental mistake that seems to make indirect realism plausible (apart from the alleged refutations of direct realism that we will consider in chapter VI) is a confusion between an *object* of awareness and a *vehicle* of awareness. An object of awareness is that *of which* one is aware. A vehicle of awareness is that *by which* one is aware of it.[52]

Here is a very loose analogy. Suppose that a man is chopping a block of wood with an axe. The wood is the object of the chopping—it is that which is chopped. The axe is not being chopped; it is, instead, the means by which the chopping of the wood is carried out. No one would be tempted to argue that because the man needs to use an axe to chop his wood, therefore it is not truly the wood that he chops—or that he is only "indirectly" chopping the wood, and there must be some other thing that he is "directly" chopping. In the case of the wood-cutting, we are unlikely to confuse the object on which the action is performed with the tool with which the action is performed.

The indirect realist recognizes, correctly, that we cannot perceive external objects without having perceptual experiences that represent them. But then he mistakenly concludes that we are not really, or not directly, perceiving external objects at all, but only our representations. In fact, perceptual experiences are the "tool" with which we perceive external objects. Their existence no more precludes us from perceiving those objects than the use of an axe precludes the woodcutter from chopping his wood. And just as it would be a mistake to conclude that the man is really chopping his axe, so it is a mistake to conclude that we are really perceiving (or otherwise enjoying awareness of) our perceptual experiences.[53] We perceive external objects by *having* perceptual experiences—in the sense that those experiences partly constitute our perceiving of external objects; we do not perceive external objects by *perceiving* perceptual experiences. The same thing may be said with awareness substituted for perception: Our awareness of external things *consists of* our having apprehensions that are appropriately related to those things; this does not mean we *are aware of* those apprehensions. To be aware of an apprehension would be to have a second apprehension that was appropriately related to the first—that is, a representation of a representation.

I am not claiming that one can never be aware of a perceptual experience or other apprehension (as distinct from merely having it). Indeed, if I were to say that, I would defeat my own position, for it would follow that I myself was not aware of perceptual experiences, in which case how could I be justified in claiming they exist? One can be aware of a perceptual experience, by reflecting, introspectively, in which case one has a second-order apprehension. What I am claiming, however, is that our awareness of external things does not depend upon awareness of perceptual experiences, nor of any other mental phenomena. As an illustration of this lack of dependence, the average dog is aware of lots of things in his environment, but I doubt that the dog is aware that he has perceptual experiences. The dog simply goes around paying attention to the physical objects around him, never taking notice of the mental processes by which he is able to do this. We humans, of course, periodically take notice of our experiences as such, but this reflective awareness is not inherent in the nature of perception.

The error I am describing seems easy enough to avoid, and yet I think it has really been committed by a number of modern philosophers, with great adverse effects on their philosophical systems. I briefly mention a few examples to explain what I mean.

In the introduction to his *Essay Concerning Human Understanding*, John Locke explains how he intends to use the word "idea":

> It being that term which, I think, serves best to stand for whatsoever is the object of the understanding when a man thinks, I have used it to express whatever is meant by *phantasm, notion, species*, or whatever it is which the mind can be employed about in thinking. . . . I presume it will be easily granted me that there are such *ideas* in men's minds.[54]

Locke seems to be unaware that he is making two different stipulations here—on one hand, "ideas" are supposed to be things existing in the mind; on the other hand, they are supposed to be the *objects* of the understanding, and the things we think *about*. The implicit assumption, then, is that mental states or objects are the only things we can be aware of; object and vehicle of awareness are one. But what if external objects are among the things we think about and understand? I am thinking about Mount Everest now. Is the mountain, then, to be called an "idea"? Notice that Locke does not so much as consider the alternative view (namely, that ideas are vehicles of awareness, not objects of awareness). He does not argue against it; he simply rules it out by definition, and he thinks it will be immediately granted to him that "ideas" in his sense exist.

Bishop Berkeley's philosophy was the inevitable result of this confusion. Berkeley was to argue from Locke's assumptions to the conclusion that there are no external objects, but only ideas in the mind. He begins with the following statement:

> It is evident to anyone who takes a survey of the *objects* of human knowledge that they are either ideas actually imprinted on the senses, or else such as are perceived by attending to the passions and operations of the mind, or lastly, ideas formed by help of memory and imagination.[55]

This is the very first sentence following the introduction in his *Principles of Human Knowledge*. No argument precedes it, and the argument following presupposes it. Berkeley just takes it as "evident" that all objects of awareness are ideas. If he had even conceived of the possibility of holding ideas to be vehicles of awareness rather than objects of awareness, he surely would have realized that the assumption needed argument.

Consider Berkeley's argument for why heat cannot exist external to the mind. In his dialogues, the argument begins thus:

> *Philonous*: But is not the most vehement and intense degree of heat a very great pain?
> *Hylas*: No one can deny it.[56]

Well, the *experience by which we perceive* great heat is a kind of pain. Philonous simply assumes that this is the same as saying the heat is a pain. Hylas never challenges him on this point because his author was oblivious to the distinction. Hylas does try suggesting a bit later (correctly) that the heat is not identical with, but rather a cause of, the pain. But he is too easily satisfied with Philonous's response that they must be identical since we only "perceive" a single sensation:

> *Philonous*: Seeing therefore [that the heat and the pain] are both immediately perceived at the same time, and the fire affects you only with one simple, or uncompounded idea, it follows that this same simple idea is both the intense heat immediately perceived, and the pain; and consequently, that the intense heat immediately perceived, is nothing distinct from a particular sort of pain.[57]

From hence, Philonous infers that heat cannot exist in an inanimate object, since pain cannot exist in an inanimate object. Hylas should have replied: "We do not perceive a single sensation, nor a single idea, because we do not perceive sensations or ideas at all; that is a category error. The sensation that we have is the *way* in which we perceive the heat, and the sensation is, at the same time, painful. The sensation (and hence the pain) can only exist in the mind. But the thing sensed is a property of the external object. There is no conflict in this." Alas, almost all of Berkeley's arguments depend upon similar confusions, and Hylas, restricted as he is by his creator's conceptual abilities, never has the presence of mind to distinguish that which we perceive from that *by* which we perceive, nor to question the assumption that we perceive sensations. The fact that none of his contemporaries, apart from Thomas Reid, were able to refute Berkeley—and that philosophy students even today are often confounded by his arguments—attests to our deep-seated tendency to make this confusion.

The same confusion infects Immanuel Kant's distinction between "phenomena" (or "appearances") and "noumena" (or "things in themselves"). Kant, famously, argued that the only things that we can ever perceive (or have knowledge of) are "appearances"; we can never perceive "things in themselves." This thesis was tied to his theories of space and time (roughly, he thought that space and time have no objective existence and only exist as ways in which we perceive things; so things in themselves have no spatiotemporal properties).[58] But what did Kant *mean* by "appearances"? Commentators have wrestled with this question,[59] but I think the truth is that Kant had no single, coherent idea in mind. Rather, the Kantian concept, "appearance," is a confusion between two things: On the one hand, Kant characterizes appearances as "objects of a possible experience."[60] On the other hand, appearances are supposed to be representations in us (meaning in the mind) of things:

> [T]hings as objects of our senses existing outside us are given, but we know nothing of what they may be in themselves, knowing only their appearances, that is, the representations which they cause in us by affecting our senses.[61]

> [N]othing intuited in space is a thing in itself . . . what we call outer objects are nothing but mere representations of our sensibility, the form of which is space. The true correlate of sensibility, the thing in itself, is not known, and cannot be known, through these representations; and in experience no question is ever asked in regard to it.[62]

These remarks show the dual role of "appearances": they are both *representations* and *things represented*, both the mental states by which we are aware of things and the things of which we are aware.

It is easy to see why—even apart from Kant's special views about the nature of space and time—if one makes this confusion, and one is otherwise consistent, one must be led to some form of idealism or at least representationalism, that is, some form of the doctrine that the things we perceive exist only in our minds. For consider the following logically (but not factually) sound inference:

1. We only perceive by means of mental representations.
2. The means by which we perceive is the same thing as the object we perceive.
3. Hence, we only perceive mental representations.

From here we would be forced to conclude that external objects, if they exist, must be imperceptible (invisible, inaudible, intangible, etc.), and from there it is but a short step to the conclusion that the nature of external objects is beyond our ken. Berkeley and Kant each reached this conclusion by their separate routes; Berkeley did, and Kant did not, consider this a sufficient reason for rejecting the existence of such objects altogether.

Of course, I do not say that the little syllogism above precisely represents either Kant's or Berkeley's reasoning, nor that of the indirect realists. No philosopher (I hope) would explicitly endorse premise (2). It is the nature of conceptual confusions to be only implicit; once they are explicitly stated, their falsity is apparent. What I suggest is not that Berkeley and Kant *believed that* the object of awareness is the same as the means of awareness, but that they simply did not notice the distinction, and consequently that it was easy for them, and almost inevitable, to reach the conclusion in (3). And I think that this oversight is most fundamentally what makes both indirect realism and idealism seem right, prima facie, to those for whom it does seem that way.

Notes

1. In a strict sense, awareness of *x* is not itself a relationship, but rather a *state that is related* to *x* in a certain way. The formal logic sense of "relation" is as referring to whatever can be ascribed by an open sentence with two or more free variables, though this does not correspond to the ordinary English use of the word.

2. In other words: "*S* is aware of _____ " is an extensional context, and this follows from the fact that "is aware of" is a relation-ascribing predicate. Philosophers of language will object: "believes" also attributes a relationship (between the believer and a proposition), but we all know that "believes" generates intensional contexts; doesn't this falsify my logical claim? No, because "*S* believes _____ " is an extensional context; if one fills in the blank with expressions denoting the same proposition, one necessarily gets sentences with the same truth value. For instance, the following inferences are valid: "Sue believes that in a right triangle, the square on the hypotenuse equals the sum of the squares on the other two sides. That proposition is the Pythagorean Theorem. Therefore, Sue believes the Pythagorean Theorem." "Sue believes that the sky is blue.

That the sky is blue is the proposition I was just thinking about. Therefore, Sue believes the proposition I was just thinking about." What we all know is that "*S* believes that _____ is *F*" is intensional, but that is just because substitution of coreferential expressions into "that _____ is *F*" does not guarantee reference to the same proposition. It does not falsify my claim that "*S* believes _____" is referentially transparent.

3. See Searle for detailed discussion of this property of being representational, also known as "intentionality." I follow Searle's account fairly closely.

4. Unfortunately for my example, this is not exactly right. Tickles are associated with particular parts of one's body; the tickle feels as if it is on one's foot, say. Thus, a representation of some part of one's body seems to be inseparable from the tickling sensation. And this, by the way, requires us to say *either* that there is some sort of physical property or event that the sensation represents as going on in that part of one's body, *or* that one has the (necessarily false) impression that a sensation, a mental event, is located on one's foot, so that tickling sensations always involve a kind of illusion. I cannot convince myself of either of these things, so I leave this question about the nature of tickles unanswered. A similar question arises for sensory pleasures, pains, and other tactile sensations.

5. As I use the phrase, "*S* has a representation of _____" is intensional. What goes in the blank specifies the content of the representation, not an object that is represented. Hence, "*S* represents *x*" does not entail "*x* exists," nor do "*S* represents *x*" and "*x* = *y*" entail "*S* represents *y*." Contrast note 2 above.

6. For those interested in the ontology of representational contents, there are (at least) two ways of thinking about how this works. On the one hand, we might think of the "content" of a representation as a sort of abstract object existing independently of the representation but related to it in a certain way. Variants on this idea include the views that the content of a representation is a *proposition*, that it is a *possible* individual (or possible event, possible fact, etc.), and that it is a universal (or collection of universals).

On the other hand, it is possible to view mental representations as having an intrinsic (nonrelational) property, called "having content," where *having the content that P* is a species of *having content*. In this view, there is no such entity as a "content," in much the same way as there is no such person as "the average man"; the right question is not, "what is a 'content'?" but "what is it to 'have content'?" In this view, there is an internal relation between some representations and some facts or states in reality (a relation that might be called "correspondence" or "truth")—that relation supervenes on the intrinsic character of the representation plus the character of the world. A representation is said to have the content that *P*, then, when it has that intrinsic character such that, if and only if *P*, the fact that *P* corresponds to the representation (or: when it has that intrinsic character such that the representation is true if and only if *P*). The notion of having a certain content can thus be defined in terms of the notion of truth.

I do not know which of these views is better, but here is one thing to be said in favor of the latter, unconventional view: it seems to me that there are certain mental states such that, from their having the intrinsic character they do, it follows that they have content. For instance, consider a visual experience of a red square. It seems to me that it is impossible for a state qualitatively like that to occur, without its having content. The latter view about content, of course, makes perfect sense of this. The former view about content, however, implies that for the state to have content, there must exist, in addition to the state itself, another, abstract entity for the state to be related to. And I am wary about saying that, from the existence of a particular state with some intrinsic property, the existence of anything else follows. But this consideration is far from conclusive, particularly as the abstract objects may be held to have necessary existence.

7. Compare Searle's notions of "illocutionary force" and "psychological mode" (6).

8. I use "the world as it is" broadly, so it includes how the world 'is' at all times, past, present, and future. For example, the belief that the Battle of Hastings happened in 1066 counts as a representation of "the world as it actually is."

9. Searle expresses this point by saying that beliefs have "mind-to-world direction of fit" whereas desires have "world-to-mind direction of fit" (7-9).

10. The precise elaboration of this notion of nonaccidentality is a generalized form of the Gettier problem (generalized because it applies to awareness in general, not just knowledge). See the voluminous literature on the definition of "knowledge" for various ways that "not due to chance" might be interpreted. Shope provides a useful summary of most of this literature.

11. I also have a host of background, dispositional beliefs, including that Liz would have answered the phone before the eighth ring if she were home, and all the background beliefs on which *that*, in turn, is based.

12. This sentence is ambiguous. One interpretation is this: "That $[(\exists x)(\exists y)(x$ is the content of the first apprehension, and y satisfies $x)]$ renders it probable that $[(\exists x)(\exists y)(x$ is the content of the second apprehension, and y satisfies $x)]$." Another interpretation is this: "$(\exists x)(\exists y)(x$ is the content of the first apprehension, and y is the content of the second apprehension, and [that x is satisfied] renders it probable [that y is satisfied])." I intend the second interpretation.

13. See McDowell; Hyman; Langsam; and Dancy. Their position is called "the disjunctive conception of experience" because it holds that there is no mental state common to both hallucination and perception, other than the disjunction of the two (that is, the "state" of "either hallucinating or perceiving").

14. Perhaps the experiences could not be token identical, due to their having different causes. But at least they seem to be type identical, which is sufficient for the present point.

15. See Dancy.

16. The authors mentioned in note 13 have not presented arguments designed to *refute* the existence of perceptual experiences; they seem only to be arguing that the existence of perceptual experiences has not been proven.

17. Langsam (46-47) tries to avoid this argument by hypothesizing that hallucinations are not purely internal states, but rather are relations to something, but he is entirely noncommittal about the nature of these relations or what their relata are. I shall not pursue this suggestion here, other than to note that it would be the burden of the disjunctivist to provide a plausible account of what we are related to when we hallucinate and of what the relationship in question is.

18. Austin, 29-30.

19. One could probably imagine a context which would enable figure 4.1 to count as a picture of you. For instance, suppose this artist frequently does what he calls portraits of people, in which he uses a person's most-prized possession to represent that person. He often paints pictures in which the inanimate objects are depicted doing things that the person would normally do (e.g., a picture of a watch talking to a computer, when a person who prizes his watch highly often talks to a person who prizes his computer highly). It happens that your most prized possession is your telephone. Thus, in a (somewhat strained) sense figure 4.1 would be a picture of you. For purposes of the example, assume no such special context is present (note that the special context involves other forms of intentionality, such as the artist's beliefs and intentions, and the intentionality of other pictures, which will not apply in the case we're really interested in, that of the intentionality of perceptual experience); in that case, the content of the image in figure 4.1 would be as representing a telephone-shaped object, and then it could not be a picture of you.

It is natural to wonder what is the difference between my position here, and Davidson's view in "A Coherence Theory of Truth and Knowledge" that it is impossible for a person to have radically mistaken beliefs. There are two main differences. First, Davidson's thesis concerns belief systems as a whole, whereas my thesis applies to any individual representation. Second, Davidson's thesis concerns beliefs in general, whereas mine applies only to *de re* representations, as indicated in the paragraph following in the text. Thus, I believe, in opposition to Davidson, that it is metaphysically possible for a person to have a radically false system of beliefs, but I say that in such a case, he would be having only *de dicto* beliefs, rather than *de re* beliefs, at least with respect to those subjects where he was radically misguided.

20. Notice also that these other causes of my experience cannot be said to be involved in a *deviant* causal chain (like those discussed in section IV.3.3), so as to exclude them as objects of perception. We can be sure of this even without an analysis of deviant causal chains, simply because these events are members of the same causal chain as the object I am uncontroversially perceiving. They are part of the causal chain in all normal cases of visual perception. (I assume only that if a causal chain is deviant, then any larger chain which includes it is also deviant.)

21. This point depends on the assumption that we have a nonvisual awareness of our bodies, and that it represents our bodies as in the same space as the things we see.

22. Here is an alternative theory, attempting to analyze perception purely in terms of the causal relation: The object of perception is the earliest member of the causal chain leading to my perceptual experience such that that type of phenomenon is reliably correlated with this sort of experience. The pattern of optic nerve impulses is reliably correlated with the visual experience—when you have this pattern of optic nerve impulses, you regularly get this sort of experience—but it is not the earliest member of the chain that is so correlated. The cup itself is reliably correlated with the experience, and the cup comes before the optic nerve impulses. The light rays incident on the surface of the cup are even earlier in the causal chain, but they are not reliable causes of the experience (light rays of that sort do not usually lead to this particular sort of visual experience, since light rays of that sort are present whenever the room is lighted like this, whether any cups are around or not, whereas I only have the experience when a cup is present). But here is a problem with this account: suppose I happen to be in the

dark a lot—in fact, 70% of the time, when there is a cup in front of me, it is too dark to see it. In that case, the presence of a cup would not be a reliable cause of the sort of visual experience in question. Still, it would be wrong to conclude that, on those occasions when the lights are on and a cup is in front of me, I don't see it.

23. I owe both the objection and the response to it to Brian McLaughlin (in conversation), although I do not know whether he would endorse either.

24. My definitions of "primary" and "secondary perception" derive from Jackson's definitions of "immediate" and "mediate perception" (*Perception*, 15-20).

25. I owe this point to Brian McLaughlin (in conversation).

26. Jackson, "Epiphenomenal Qualia."

27. The reader may be curious why, in the case of tactile sensations, I refer to their qualia as "how they feel" (or "what they feel like"), but I do not refer to the quale of an olfactory experience as "how it smells" (nor as "what it smells like"). The reason is that the latter expressions would imply that we can smell experiences—meaning we can perceive experiences by the sense of smell—whereas, in my view, we can only smell things in the external world (particularly, chemicals). But talk of how a tactile sensation "feels" does not imply that we can perceive tactile sensations by the sense of touch. "To feel" has more than one sense: to feel a material object is to perceive it by the sense of touch, but to "feel" a sensation just means to have it. "To smell" does not similarly have two senses.

28. One gets this impression from Dennett, "Quining Qualia" and *Consciousness Explained*, esp. 33-39, 385-86.

29. The importance of this sense is made clear in Sacks, 43-54, which discusses the case of a woman who lacks proprioception, this lack causing her great difficulties.

30. Another possible, but nonactual, case illustrating the same point is the hypothetical case of "super blindsight," in which a person would find himself able to identify objects in a part of his visual field even though, as it would seem to him, he does not see them (Block, 385-86).

31. Michael Tye has challenged this thesis, rendering the following argument necessary. Qualia also seem to be left out of Armstrong's and Pitcher's theories of perception. I am not giving an argument for the *existence* of qualia, however; I take that to be established directly by introspection. I am giving an argument—assuming experiences have qualia (there is something it is like to have them)—that these qualia cannot be accounted for merely by appealing to the representational contents of experiences.

32. Note that the term "red*" is a rigid designator whose reference is fixed by, but which is not synonymous with, the description, "the quale exemplified by the sort of experiences that red objects normally cause in us." See Kripke, 48-49, 53-60, on rigid designators and reference-fixing descriptions.

33. Dennett denies that this scenario is even logically possible, but this denial rests upon verificationist assumptions (*Consciousness Explained*, 115-26, 390). Dennett also criticizes the notion of an intrapersonal qualia inversion that would have no behavioral effects (*Consciousness Explained*, 390-98). More persuasively, Hardin argues from asymmetries in the subjective color space against the possibility of an undetectable spectrum inversion ("Reinverting the Spectrum"). However, these objections do not concern the sort of scenario I am stipulating here; see also note 37 below.

34. Cf. my remarks at the end of this section about the conative function of qualia.

35. What I have said so far, I think, is consistent with any theory of color, provided that theory allows that physical objects are colored. It is not consistent with the view that nothing is colored, nor with the view that only mental things are colored. If you are an eliminativist about color, I have not given an argument against your position, so you need not, and probably should not, accept my conclusion about qualia. If you think colors are only properties of mental things (as in Russell, *The Problems of Philosophy*, 9-10, 28-29), I also have not given an argument against that view yet, but I will argue against the existence of sense data in general in chapter VII.

36. In other words, qualia do not supervene on representational contents.

37. This argument is similar to Shoemaker's in "The Inverted Spectrum," although Shoemaker is attempting to refute functionalism, as well as to establish the distinction between qualia and intentional content, whereas I only want to do the latter. As a result, I do not need to argue that the Invert's violet* experience would be functionally identical to my red* experience.

Someone with Searle's view of intentionality (see his chapter 8), to which I am sympathetic, might object to either (3) or (4) in the argument, saying that the content of my red* experience is something along the lines of, "That object has the surface property that normally causes in *me* experiences of the red* variety." The Invert's red* experience will have the same content, except that it will make reference to what causes those experiences in *him*. The Invert's violet* experience will have a similar content, but with "violet*" substituted for "red*." It therefore will not be the same as the content of my red* experience, contrary to (4) and perhaps to (3), depending on how the latter is interpreted. My response, however, is that a philosopher who takes this view is immediately committed to a distinction between qualia and contents, since the occurrence of "red*" used in specifying the content of my red* experience cannot without circularity be taken to be referring to a certain content; that is, the view cannot be that the content of the experience is "that object has the property that causes in me experiences with the content *x*," where *x* then has to be replaced with the entire quoted phrase.

38. Berkeley makes this point (*Dialogues*, 113-16), except that he misstates it by saying that extreme heat *is* a kind of pain, thence falsely concluding that extreme heat can only exist in the mind.

39. See Chisholm, *Perceiving*, 43-53. I do not believe that there is more than one *sense* of "appear" in English, even though Chisholm is right to distinguish different purposes for which "appear" words are used. I think "appear" words always refer to apprehensions and, in some manner, report their contents. The distinction between "comparative" and "noncomparative" uses of "appear," in my view, arises from the existence of two levels of content to our experiences. For instance, when the lighting conditions in the room change, there is a level on which my experience represents the colors of the material objects as being different. At the same time, there is a further level of content which represents the material objects as being the same color (hence the phenomenon of "color constancy"), this second level of content depending on my past experiences and being produced by my visual system's automatic "correction" for lighting conditions. The so-called "comparative" use of "appear" reports this second level of content.

The so-called "epistemic" use of "appear" arises out of conversational implicature: normally, if one were certain that *p*, one would choose to assert *p*, rather than merely to report that one has a mental state representing it as being the case that *p*. If one does the latter, I think, one indicates that one has a certain sort of justification for *p* (see chapter V below), but that the justification is not conclusive. This has the effect of a tentative assertion of *p*. Compare the effect of saying, "There are good arguments that *p*," rather than simply saying "*p*." As indicated in the text, however, I do not think it important to examine these semantic questions in great detail.

40. The metaphor is potentially misleading in its apparent implication that the senses are something separate from you, and that first the senses determine what they "think" is the case, and then they report it to you. I do not intend either of these implications. The senses are simply a part or aspect of you, and there are different ways in which you can entertain a given content: perceptually (by having a sensory experience) or cognitively (by having a belief).

41. Evans, 123-24.

42. Armstrong, 84-87, makes this reply, though not in defense of the view discussed here; rather, he uses it to defend his view that perceptual experiences consist of nothing but beliefs or inclinations to believe. I think my reply in the text equally well refutes Armstrong's theory as it does the theory that perceptual experiences are nonrepresentational.

43. Peikoff, 39-41, says something like this, though his point seems to be rather that the senses tell us only that *something* exists causing our experiences, rather than that they tell us nothing at all. I think my arguments following apply equally well to Peikoff's view.

44. See above, section II.3.

45. See Bonjour, 68-69; McDowell, 7-8, though McDowell confuses propositional content with conceptual content.

46. Evans, 229.

47. Wittgenstein, 194, contains a schematic version of the picture, derived from Jastrow, 295. Jastrow (from whom this version of the picture is copied) credits the magazine *Fliegende Blätter* as the original source but gives no bibliographic details.

48. McDowell, 56-57.

49. As a possible counterexample, consider a case in which a person has a very faint, fleeting visual impression, as might happen if he saw something move quickly and then disappear near the edge of his visual field, especially at night. In such a case, he might say, "I thought I saw something move there, but maybe I was just imagining it." I would not take this statement literally, at least not in the way I use "imagine"—I think the person means he might have suffered an illusion, not that he might have merely imagined there being something there, in the sense in which I am now imagining a white rabbit. Imagining that you see something in *that* sense is not at all like seeing it. You are probably now imagining a white rabbit, but that is not at all like seeing a white rabbit—not even seeing one very briefly or unclearly, etc.

50. Hume, *Treatise* I.III, p. 9. I have altered some spelling to conform to modern conventions.

51. Reid, 14, gives a similar account to mine, though I think he confuses seemings with beliefs (see section V.3 below). See also Reid's criticism of Hume, in Reid, 17.

52. Mortimer Adler draws this distinction very clearly, in addition to making the case that the confusion between these two things has had a great influence on modern philosophy. It is the first mistake discussed in his *Ten Philosophical Mistakes*. Cf. Kelley, 36, 67, where the point is made that one does not perceive one's means of awareness.

53. Kelley, 66-69, makes this point; Rand, 80-82, appears to be making a similar one.

54. Locke, *Essay*, I.i, section 8 (altering punctuation and capitalization to conform to modern style; italics Locke's).

55. Berkeley, *Principles*, section 1; italics Berkeley's.

56. Berkeley, *Dialogues*, 113.

57. Berkeley, *Dialogues*, 114.

58. Kant, *Critique*, B40-45.

59. See Barker; Strawson, 249-56.

60. Kant, *Critique*, B298. Cf. B303, where he says, "that which is not appearance cannot be an object of experience" and Bxvii, where there appears the phrase, "the objects [of our intuition], or what is the same thing, . . . the *experience* in which alone, as given objects, they can be known" (emphasis Kant's).

61. Kant, *Prolegomena*, Remark II, 36.

62. Kant, *Critique*, B45.

V. A Version of Foundationalism

1. What Is Perceptual Knowledge?

Perception is direct awareness of the external world. *Perceptual knowledge*, however, is not the same thing as perception. Perception is awareness in the form of perceptual experiences (that is, awareness wherein the type of apprehension involved is a perceptual experience). Knowledge is awareness in the form of beliefs (awareness wherein the type of apprehension is a belief). A perceptual experience is not a belief, so perception itself is not a kind of knowledge.

To see this, consider a hypothetical case. Jack comes home one evening, and as he walks in the door, he sees a large pink rat on the dining room table. He firmly believes that there are no pink rats in reality, that it is highly unlikely that a rat of any kind should be on his table in any case, and that people periodically have hallucinations. Jack concludes that there is not really a pink rat on the table, and that he is merely hallucinating it. It does not matter for the example whether Jack is reasonable in drawing this conclusion; it matters only that he may in fact draw it. In fact, let us suppose, Jack is mistaken; there is nothing wrong with his visual system. There really is a pink rat on his table (never mind how it got there), and it is causing his visual experience in the way middle-sized physical objects normally do, by reflecting light to his eyes and so on. In other words, Jack is perceiving (is perceptually aware of) the pink rat. But does he *know* that there is a pink rat on his table? No, for he does not believe it; in fact, he believes the opposite. This shows that perception is not a kind of knowledge, nor does perceptual experience imply belief, for it is possible to have perception in the absence of knowledge and belief.

Knowledge is traditionally defined, approximately, as justified, true belief. In other words, in order to know that something is the case, one must believe that it is the case, one's belief must be true, and one must be justified (in the internalist sense) in that belief. I say knowledge is defined "approximately" this way, because it is widely recognized that at least some fourth condition beyond the three just mentioned is needed, although there is no general agreement on what that condition is.[1] Here is a well-known example: suppose I look at a clock to find out what time it is. The clock reads 3:00 and I both correctly and justifiably accept that the time is approximately 3:00. But suppose that, although I have no reason to suspect this, the clock is actually stopped (even a stopped clock is right twice a day). In this case, I do not genuinely *know* that the time is 3:00, even though I have a justified, true belief that it is.[2] There is a voluminous (a bit too voluminous, in my opinion) literature on the definition of knowledge, mostly concerned with how one should deal with cases like this (so-called "Gettier cases"). My aim is not to resolve the disputes that have arisen in that literature, so I will only briefly mention how I think the definition of knowledge may be amended to deal with such cases: one may add the condition that there be no *defeaters* for the justification of one's belief. A defeater for your justification for *P* (where *P* is something you justifiably believe) is defined to be a true proposition that, if it were added to your beliefs, would render you no longer justified in believing that *P*. Thus, in the clock example, the proposition "the clock is stopped" is a defeater, and this explains why I do not have knowledge.[3]

Notice how this traditional definition of knowledge mirrors my account of awareness. In awareness, one must have an apprehension, its content must be at least roughly satisfied, and it must be nonaccidental that its content is satisfied. Knowledge is simply one form of awareness: the form in which the apprehension is a belief, the content of the belief is satisfied (since the belief is true), and it is nonaccidental that the belief is true (since the believer has an adequate and undefeated justification for it). Seen in this way, my proposed definition of knowledge as *awareness in the form of beliefs* is not incompatible with the traditional *justified true belief* definition; the latter is merely a more precise version of the former, in which it is specified more precisely what it takes for a belief to be *nonaccidentally* true.

Perceptual knowledge is a particular kind of knowledge, namely, the kind that involves perceptual beliefs. What is a perceptual belief? It is a belief that is directly based on a perceptual experience. I say "directly" because there are cases in which perceptual experiences lead to certain beliefs only through a chain of inferences—as in the case of scientific theories—and I would not call the beliefs at the end of the chain "perceptual beliefs." In general, an apprehension, B, is directly based on another apprehension, A, when B is based on A, and there is no intermediary apprehension, C, such that A causes B through causing C. Inference is a particular species of the basing relation; it is the process by which one belief comes to be based on another belief. When I say that I inferred Q from P, I am saying that I believed P, I came to believe Q, and my belief that Q was based on my belief that P.

From what I have said here and in chapter IV (section 2), it follows that perceptual knowledge, if it exists, would be a form of indirect awareness, but noninferential knowledge. (All inferential knowledge is indirect awareness, but not all indirect awareness is inferential knowledge.)

2. Do We Have Perceptual Knowledge?

There are perceptual beliefs—even an external world skeptic can agree with that. When we have perceptual experiences, we normally are prompted, without any intermediary thoughts or other apprehensions, to accept propositions about the external world. For instance, when I look at a tomato on the counter, the visual experience I have will typically cause me to believe, at the least, that there is a red, round thing there. (It is due to various background beliefs of mine that I accept the further proposition that the thing in question is a tomato. The latter belief, then, is not purely perceptual because it is based on my perceptual experience *together with* background knowledge.[4]) Furthermore, these beliefs are logically related to the experiences that cause them in the way appropriate for the "based on" relation: the content of my perceptual experience entails the content of my belief. As we indicated earlier (section IV.4.2), the content of a perceptual experience will normally not be the same as that of the perceptual belief it causes; rather, it will be far more specific and detailed. But we can be assured that it will entail the belief because there is a determinable-determinate relation between the two.[5]

It is easiest to explain the determinable-determinate relation with examples. Consider the relation between *shape* and *squareness*. Shape is a determinable property; squareness is a more determinate property, relative to shape. Similarly, *red* is a determinate, relative to the determinable *color*. A particular shade of red, say crimson, would be a determinate relative to *red* (and also relative to *color*). In these examples, we see that one property is more specific than, and falls under, the other. Crimson is a specific kind of red, so for a thing to be crimson implies that it is red, but not vice versa. Squareness is a particular kind of shape, so for a thing to be square implies that it is shaped, but not vice versa. Since our perceptual experiences are more fine-grained in their content than our concepts, and since the beliefs we form are constructed from our concepts, the properties represented in perceptual experience will typically be determinates, relative to those represented in beliefs. Thus, my perceptual experience might represent that there is a thing with a certain very specific color (one of the two million colors the visual system can distinguish), while my belief might represent simply that there is a red thing. The color represented by my visual experience will be a specific *kind* of red. This is why the contents of my perceptual experiences will entail the contents of my perceptual beliefs, but not vice versa.

The question of whether we have perceptual knowledge comes down to the question of whether our perceptual beliefs are true and justified, in the absence of defeaters. Although the truth condition is theoretically distinct from the justification condition (one can have true but unjustified beliefs or justified but false beliefs), we cannot really address them separately. An account of why our perceptual beliefs are justified just is, ipso facto, an account of why we should take them to be true (this is a tautology). If I could successfully argue that our perceptual beliefs are *true*, then, upon reflecting on that argument, we would also see that we are *justified* (by that very argument, if nothing else) in holding those beliefs. Conversely, if I could show that we are justified in our perceptual beliefs, then we would thereupon see that we should accept those beliefs (or rather, we should reaffirm them, since we have already accepted them prior to philosophical reflection), which is equivalent to accepting them as true. Although in general the proposition, "*S* is justified in believing *P*" does not imply "*P*," if *I* believe "I am now justified in believing *P*," I must believe "*P*" as well (unless I am irrational).

The skeptical challenges to our perceptual knowledge with which we are concerned are all arguments against the *justification* of our perceptual beliefs, not against their truth. The skeptic does not say that our perceptual beliefs are all false; he only says they may or may not be true. But the skeptic does not say they may or may not be *justified*; he says they *are not* justified (recall chapter II). Nor, by the way, does the skeptic say there are defeaters for our perceptual beliefs (again, there may or may not be defeaters). Thus, in answering the question of how we can have perceptual knowledge, the main issue to address is how our perceptual beliefs can be justified.

Some philosophers would seek to avoid skepticism by denying that justification is part of the meaning of "knowledge" in ordinary English.[6] They would maintain that we can have "knowledge" even if our beliefs are unjustified. I think these philosophers are mistaken, but that isn't really important. Notwithstanding the tradition of analytic philosophy, the important question here is not semantic. The important question is how we might justify our own beliefs about the external world, to ourselves; this question remains of interest even if I am mistaken about what "know" means in ordinary English. If you think I am thus mistaken, then you may regard this chapter as an inquiry after a special, philosophers' sense of "knowledge."

My position, then, is that our perceptual beliefs are justified *by* the perceptual experiences on which they are based. A perceptual experience can justify a belief in much the same way that a belief can justify another belief. If I believe P, and P entails Q, and I come to believe Q by correctly inferring Q from P, then my belief that Q is justified by my belief that P. The essential features of this situation are mirrored in the case of perceptual experiences and perceptual beliefs; namely, that there is an entailment relation between the two apprehensions and that the one causes the other by virtue of the logical relation between them.

But, it will be objected, one belief can only justify another belief if the first belief is, itself, justified. Similarly, therefore, shouldn't we say that a perceptual experience can only justify a perceptual belief if the experience, itself, is justified?

But the latter condition makes no sense. It does not make sense—it is a category error—to say that an experience is justified or unjustified. (A category error is the mistake of attempting to apply a predicate to a kind of thing to which it logically cannot apply. For instance, to say "The number 7 is red" would be a category error, since numbers cannot be colored; only physical objects and light can be colored.) You may be justified or unjustified in accepting a belief, but you cannot be justified or unjustified in having experiences; you simply have them. If I go near a fire, I just *will* feel a sensation of warmth; what would it mean to say I was "justified" in feeling warm?

To say that a person is unjustified in doing x is to say that, in some sense or for some reason, he shouldn't do x. Thus, you may say, "The American invasion of Vietnam was unjustified"; this would be to say that the Americans should not have invaded Vietnam. Interestingly, the predicate can also be applied to emotions. Suppose I say, "Your resentment toward Fred is unjustified; he hasn't done anything wrong." This would be the same as to say, "You shouldn't resent Fred; he hasn't done anything wrong." Likewise, if I say, "Belief in God is unjustified," this means, "One shouldn't believe in God." So the reason why an *experience* cannot be justified or unjustified is that it cannot be the case that you *should* or *shouldn't* have an experience.

There is a deeper explanation, for why it does not make sense to say a person should or shouldn't have a perceptual experience, and that is that perceptual experiences are automatic responses to external stimuli. Although I can choose to open or close my eyes, I cannot control what I will see if my eyes are open. My evaluations of my experiences will have no effect on those experiences. For instance, if I judge my present visual experience to be a mirage, and thus a misrepresentation of reality, this judgement will have no effect on the experience itself; I cannot stop "seeing" the mirage. Matters are otherwise when it comes to actions, beliefs, and emotions. If I come to judge that action A is morally obligatory, this will normally (except in cases of weakness of will) result in my doing A. If I come to judge that P is justified, this will normally result in my believing that *P*. If I come to judge that Fred did nothing wrong, this will normally result in my ceasing to feel resentment toward Fred, if I felt such resentment initially. Of course, it is possible that these results not occur—it is possible for a person to act, think, or feel irrationally. That is the point of the "should" statements, after all; they would have no point if our actions, thoughts, and feelings were automatic.

There will be some who will say that their feelings *are* automatic, in just the way I have said perceptual experiences are. I think this is false, because I think that an emotion is a kind of evaluation, or comes about through one's evaluation, of the events towards which one has the emotion. Rational-emotive therapy has demonstrated the possibility of controlling one's emotions through these evaluations.[7] Those who say they cannot control their emotions, I believe, are those who simply choose not to. But let us not argue this tangential point further; the point to make is that *if* emotions were purely automatic responses, then it would make no sense to speak of an emotion as justified or unjustified. And similarly, if (as is in fact the case) perceptual experiences are automatic responses, then it makes no sense to speak of them as justified or unjustified.[8]

But it is unclear where this leaves us, vis-à-vis the justification of perceptual beliefs. We have agreed that when a belief, B, is based on and logically supported by another belief, A, if A is justified B will be justified, and if A is unjustified B will be unjustified. Given that perceptual experiences are neither justified nor unjustified, it is difficult to know how to extend the analogy. We might say that, since perceptual experiences cannot be unjustified, perceptual beliefs based on them cannot be unjustified. But it would make just as much sense to argue that since perceptual experiences cannot be justified, perceptual beliefs cannot be justified.

Clearly, to explain why perceptual beliefs are justified, it is not enough to say that they are based on perceptual experiences that are neither justified nor unjustified. Consider another kind of state that is neither justified nor unjustified: imagination. Suppose I *imagine* that *P*, and this induces me to believe that *Q*, where *Q* is something that logically follows from *P*. I am neither justified nor unjustified in imagining that *P*. But obviously I am *unjustified* in believing that *Q* on the basis of it. Perceptual experiences likewise have no justificatory status, but I claim that a belief based on one is *justified*. Why?

3. A Principle of Foundational Justification

My theory is a version of foundationalism. Foundationalism says that there are certain beliefs, the so-called "foundational beliefs," which we are justified in holding and which do not depend on any other beliefs for their justification.

Perceptual beliefs, in my view, are foundational. Notice that the definition of foundational beliefs does not say that they do not depend on *anything else* for their justification; it says they do not depend on *other beliefs* for their justification. In my view, perceptual beliefs certainly do depend on something else for their justification: namely, perceptual experiences.

As we mentioned earlier (section II.1), foundationalists must explain what differentiates foundational beliefs from merely arbitrary beliefs. They must state a condition or set of conditions under which a person has foundational (noninferential) justification for believing a proposition. A "principle of foundational justification" is a principle identifying such a condition. A foundationalist might put forward any number of principles of foundational justification, to account for different kinds of foundational beliefs. I believe, however, that a single principle of foundational justification can account for all foundational beliefs.[9] The principle is what I call the rule of Phenomenal Conservatism (PC) (this is using "phenomenal" in the sense of "pertaining to appearances," not in the sense of "fantastic"):

(PC)   If it seems to *S* as if *P*, then *S* thereby has at least prima facie justification for believing that *P*.

In the remainder of this section, I explain what that means.

First, note that its seeming to *S* as if *P* is a distinct state from *S*'s believing that *P*.[10] This is important, since otherwise PC would be granting foundational justification, automatically, to all beliefs, and this is not what we want; we want to identify a special class of foundational beliefs, to be distinguished from merely arbitrary beliefs.

One kind of seeming-as-if state is perceptual, and the argument showing this state to be different from belief was that it is possible for it to seem to you as if *P*, even when you do not believe that *P*; in fact, even when you know that ~*P*.[11] There are also other, nonperceptual seemings, that is, cases in which its seeming to you as if *P* is not an aspect of your perceptual experience. There are memory-related seemings:[12] for example, I seem to remember that Saturn is the fifth planet from the sun. The argument showing this to be different from belief parallels the argument in the perceptual case: we can easily imagine a case in which it seems to me as if *P* in just this way but in which I do not trust my memory and so do not believe that *P*. (The argument would be at least as strong for experiential memory as it is for factual memory.) Likewise, there are intellectual seemings: when I think abstractly about the proposition, "The shortest path between any two points is a straight line," it seems to me to be true. Philosophers commonly call these intellectual seemings "intuitions." Intuitions can be distinguished from beliefs by means of the same kind of argument we have used above: it is possible for a person to have the intuitive sense that P but not to trust his own intuitions, and so to not believe that P. As a case in point, consider the intuitively obvious proposition, "In a plane containing a line and a point not on the line, there exists exactly one line parallel to the given line passing through the given point." There are some physicists who say that this proposition, as obvious as it seems, is false. Nor do these scientists lack the intuitions the rest of us (and the rest of the mathematicians and scientists in history) have. They admit that the proposition *seems* obviously true, but they say that our intuitions on this matter are not to be trusted and that there is powerful empirical evidence against it. (I refer, of course, to the non-Euclidean geometry used in Einstein's general theory of relativity.) The point here, as in the earlier examples, is not whether the scientists are reasonable to make this judgement, but simply that it is possible to make such a judgement. This suffices to show that its seeming to one, intellectually, that P is different from one's believing that P.

Next, we consider the notion of prima facie justification.[13] When a belief is said to be prima facie justified, two things are meant: first, that the belief does not depend on other beliefs for its justification, and second, that the belief's justification can be defeated by countervailing evidence. In other words, prima facie justification is both *foundational* and *defeasible*. Now, many people feel this combination of properties to be paradoxical, but it really is not. Compare the legal concept of the presumption of innocence: the defendant is presumed innocent, until proven guilty. This means that the defense need not present evidence proving the defendant's innocence (though they *may* do so, of course). If no proof is brought forward during the trial, neither of the defendant's innocence nor of his guilt, then the defendant is acquitted. But of course, this does not mean that a defendant can never be convicted. If the prosecution brings forward enough positive evidence that the defendant is guilty, then the presumption of innocence is overcome and the defendant is convicted.

Prima facie justification in epistemology works similarly. According to phenomenal conservatism, the epistemological default position is to accept things as they appear. The appearances are presumed true, until proven false. That means that when it seems as if P and no evidence emerges contravening P, it is reasonable to accept P. (Since, as I claim, phenomenal conservatism is the sole principle of foundational justification, "evidence against P" would consist of other things that seem to be the case and that, directly or indirectly, either contradict or render it improbable that P.) But that does not mean that P can never be refuted, of course; it is possible that sufficient evidence will emerge against P to overcome its presumption. Prima facie justification only provides us with an initial starting point; it does not guarantee that we have to end up where we started.

For a concrete example, take the Müller-Lyer illusion (figure 5.1).

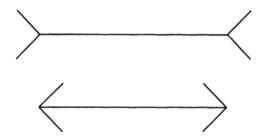

Figure 5.1. The Müller-Lyer illusion.

The top line appears to be longer than the bottom line, so other things being equal, you would be reasonable in thinking that the top line is longer. However, you can get out a ruler and measure these lines. If you do this, you will find them to be of the same length. At that point, it would be reasonable for you to revise the initial belief and conclude that the lines are really of the same length. This is because you know that measurement is generally a more reliable way of determining lengths than just eyeballing things. Of course, your new belief, that the lines are of equal length, is also based on how things seem, including what you seemed to see when you were measuring the lines; there is no (rational) way around that. It is just that you rightly take the latter seemings to be more reliable. As to why we take measurement to be more reliable than unaided visual length-estimates, I think this is partly a matter of past experience (beliefs based on measurements tend to exhibit fewer and less serious conflicts with each other and with other beliefs than unaided visual estimates) and partly due to the fact that measurement relies on situations in which what seems to be the case is particularly clear and unambiguous—which, of course, is the point of measurement procedures. This example shows that we normally treat perceptual beliefs as having just the sort of presumption of truth that phenomenal conservatism attributes to them.

Now why do I say, in my statement of PC, that S has "at least" prima facie justification? Well, I don't want to rule out the possibility of cases in which S would have incorrigible justification for believing that P. That is, I want to allow that there may be (as in fact I think there are) cases in which S has justification for believing P not dependent on other beliefs, and in which this justification *cannot* be defeated by further evidence. An example would be my present belief that for every number x, $(x + 1)$ is greater than x. I think I am not only justified in believing that, but furthermore, no future evidence could disconfirm it. Similarly, suppose I have a splitting headache. At this time, it seems to me that I am in pain, and I believe I am in pain. Again, I think my belief that I am in pain is not only justified, but justified in a way that is immune from countervailing considerations.

Those examples were not examples of *perceptual* beliefs, of course. I do not believe there are any examples of perceptual beliefs that have incorrigible justification. But I intend phenomenal conservatism to be a general principle of foundational justification. It explains not only why perceptual beliefs are noninferentially justified, but also why any other belief that is noninferentially justified is such. And this is important, for it means that my account of perceptual knowledge does not depend upon ad hoc principles of justification contrived specially to let in knowledge of the external world; I propose to account for perceptual knowledge by the same general principle I apply to all other kinds of knowledge. This should make my account more persuasive for those who are skeptical about perceptual knowledge but who allow knowledge of other kinds (that is, external world skeptics).

Notice that phenomenal conservatism does not hold that from the proposition, "It seems to me as if P" one may infer P. That would be a principle of inferential justification. What makes you justified in believing P, under PC, is not that you believe or know that it seems to you as if P, and you thereupon get to conclude that P; rather, it is the mere fact that it does seem to you as if P that makes you prima facie justified in believing P. Thus, to satisfy the antecedent of PC one does not need to have any beliefs—one does not even need to have the concept of an appearance, nor the concept of justification. In the case of perceptual beliefs, it is our perceptual experiences themselves—and not our assessments of, or beliefs about them—that justify our initial beliefs about the external world.

Even so, however, note that I am not saying a perceptual belief, or any other kind of foundational belief, *cannot* be supported by other beliefs. I am saying it *need not* be supported by other beliefs. These are two quite different things. Foundational beliefs are defined to be beliefs that do not depend upon other beliefs for their justification; they are not defined as beliefs that are not supported by other beliefs.[14] To return to the legal analogy: the presumption of innocence in a criminal trial means that the defense is *not required* to give positive evidence of the defendant's innocence. It does not mean the defense is *prohibited* from giving positive evidence of the defendant's innocence. If they have such evidence to give, all the better for them. So there could arise a case in which the defendant's acquittal was overdetermined: suppose the prosecution failed to prove the defendant's guilt, and, in addition, the defense was able to prove his innocence. There is certainly no contradiction in that, and in that case, there would simply be two conditions, each sufficient for acquitting the defendant. Likewise, there can be cases in which a belief has two kinds of justification, both a foundational one and an inferential one.

Incidentally, this is more than a merely theoretical possibility. There are many cases in which a belief has both kinds of justification. Suppose, for instance, that I see a red ball on the table. I am foundationally justified in believing that there is a red sphere there, due to the character of my perceptual experience. You happen to be in the same room with me, and I ask you, "Do you see a red sphere there?" whereupon you answer, "Yes." This gives me a second, inferential justification for thinking there is a red sphere there.[15] Obviously, the existence of this second justification does not remove or change the character of the original, noninferential one.

Lastly, notice that phenomenal conservatism does not assert, as a general rule, "If it seems to someone as if P, then P." If it did, phenomenal conservatism would be false, for there are many cases in which it seems as if P but P is not the case. Nor does phenomenal conservatism assert or imply, "Most of the time, when it seems as if P, P is true." The latter is true, but it just is not what PC is about. Phenomenal conservatism is epistemological, not metaphysical. It says that when it seems as if P and there is no evidence to the contrary, it is *reasonable to believe P*. Compare the legal presumption of innocence again: the principle is not that defendants in general are innocent; it is not even that most defendants are innocent (in fact, quite the reverse is the case). Rather, it is the normative principle that if the prosecution fails to prove the defendant's guilt, he should be acquitted.

A corollary is that phenomenal conservatism is a necessary truth, not a contingent one. There is no possible world in which phenomenal conservatism is false, although there are possible worlds in which most of the things that appear to be so are not so. Recall the brain-in-a-vat scenario. If you were a brain in a vat, then most of the things that seemed to you to be the case would in fact not be the case. Nevertheless, it would still be reasonable for you to believe those things, given your situation, and given that you would have no evidence of your being a brain in a vat. The diabolical scientists stimulating your brain make it so you have a bunch of false beliefs, but they do not make it so you have *unjustified* beliefs; in fact, their method of getting you to adopt the false beliefs is precisely to give you justification for them.

4. In Defense of Phenomenal Conservatism

Why should we accept my proposed principle of foundational justification? I claim that PC is self-evident, once it is seen in its proper light. To see it in its proper light, we have to remind ourselves of two things. The first is that the notion of "justification" we are talking about is internalist, rather than external-ist. That is, we are talking about what propositions are justified from the subject's own point of view. Thus, if P were false, but there were no way that S could reasonably be expected to guess that, then its falsity would have no bearing on S's justification for believing P in the internalist sense. What is "unjustified" in the internalist sense is what one could be blamed for believing.[16]

The second thing we must remember is that the notion of justification we are concerned with is epistemic (rather than, e.g., prudential or moral). Epistemic justification is the kind of justification that is assessed from the standpoint of the pursuit of the truth and the aversion to error. The relation between justification and truth is like the relation between expected utility and utility; that is, the acceptance of (only) justified propositions is what constitutes the rational pursuit of the truth.

Now consider an account of rationality offered by Richard Foley: "A decision is rational as long as it apparently does an acceptably good job of satisfying your goals."[17] This is plausible. Notice the need for the qualifier, "apparently." In order for a decision to be rational, it is not necessary that it *in fact* will satisfy your goals. A rational person can be mistaken about what will satisfy his goals, in which case he will do the thing that it appears to him will satisfy his goals rather than the thing that actually will. To return to my example from chapter II: it would have been irrational for the fisherman to just throw the pearl back into the ocean—even though that action would in fact have satisfied his goals better than keeping the pearl.

Now, if my goal is to have true beliefs and avoid having false ones, and if P seems to me to be true, while I have no evidence against P, then from my own point of view, it would make sense to accept P. Obviously, believing P in this situation will appear to satisfy my epistemic goals of believing truths and avoiding error better than either denying P or suspending judgement.

Another thing that will help to bring the self-evidence of PC into focus is reflection on the way you actually do form beliefs (omitting the cases of self-deception and leaps of faith, which are cases of epistemically irrational belief). When you are conscientiously seeking to know, you weigh a proposition in your mind. What determines whether you accept it or not? Well, in some cases you consider an argument for it. But this will help only if you accept the premises of said argument. How do you decide whether to accept a premise of an argument? You do not, in real life, demand an infinite series of arguments. Rather, you consider the premise on its own: if it is sufficiently obvious (to you) you accept it; otherwise, not. Moreover, it is difficult to imagine what possible alternative a person critical of this procedure could have in mind.

Should you, perhaps, accept the propositions that seem *false* instead? Surely this cannot be rational. Accept all and only the propositions that *are in fact* true? But acting on this advice is the same thing as accepting the propositions that seem true to you. Imagine I have a child who is having difficulty with fruit names. I tell him to put all the fruits that he takes to be apples into a basket. When he's done, I empty the basket, start over, and tell him this time, put all the fruits that *are* apples into the basket. From *my* point of view, I might seem to have said something different, but (leaving aside the implication the child may pick up that he did it wrong the first time, which is not part of the literal meaning of what I said) from the child's perspective I have essentially just repeated the same instruction, and he will obviously just do the same thing.

Or perhaps you should accept nothing at all? But half of your epistemic aim is to gain true beliefs. When *P* seems to you to be true and there are no grounds for doubting it (no defeaters), what more are you looking for? This is as good as it gets. Why should you withhold belief in *P*, keeping in mind the internalist sense of "should" (recall section II.6 above)—because it is still *possible* that *P* is false? But this seems to be just an extreme and unreasonable bias toward the "avoiding error" part of your epistemic goal, as against the "believing truths" part. You would not let the mere possibility that *P* is *true* suffice for you to *accept* it, so why let the mere possibility that *P* is false suffice for you not to accept it?

Consider, in fact, the argument you have just read. No doubt some philosophers will accept it, while others will not. Which ones will accept it? The ones to whom it seems correct, of course. Even if you do not accept it, you still will be thinking in accordance with the rule of phenomenal conservatism. The difference will merely be that to you, it does not seem correct. There is no (rational) escape from the reliance on how things strike *you*. (Even if you decide to rely on the opinions of a reliable expert, you will still be relying on how things seem to you: what the expert seems to you to be saying, and who seems to you to be an honest and reliable source.)

Because of this fact, any attempt to deny the principle of phenomenal conservatism will be self-defeating, for all thought and reasoning presupposes the principle in a certain sense. Even the reasoning put forward by philosophical skeptics, even as they try to present grounds for doubting all appearances, depends for its force on the way things appear to the skeptic and his audience. To illustrate, reconsider the following argument in favor of philosophical skepticism, the infinite regress argument:

Argument A:
1. In order to know anything, I must have an adequate reason for believing it.

2. In order for a reason to be adequate, I must know it to be true.
3. I cannot have an infinite series of reasons.
4. A series of adequate reasons cannot be circular.
5. Therefore, I cannot know anything.[18]

This argument, on the face of it, carries some force. Some work will need to be done to respond to it, to show, in the face of the argument, how we can have knowledge. But now compare the following "argument" for the same conclusion:

Argument B:
1. $3 = 5$.
2. Therefore, I cannot know anything.

This "argument" carries no force at all, so that it is not even clear whether it deserves to be considered an argument. *This* form of skepticism does not call for a response; there is no philosophical work to be done in explaining how knowledge is possible in the face of it. Similarly, consider the following anti-skeptical "argument":

Argument C:
1. There are seventeen inhabited planets in the Andromeda galaxy.
2. If there are seventeen inhabited planets in the Andromeda galaxy, then skepticism is false.
3. Therefore, skepticism is false.

Just as argument B does not call for a response, argument C does not count as a response. Just as we do not need to take argument B seriously, the skeptic does not need to take argument C seriously.

Why? What is the difference between (A) and (B)? The difference is not that (B) has a false premise, for (A) has a false premise too (which one, we will see later). Most of the arguments that have been presented throughout the history of philosophy have contained one or more false premises (for philosophical arguments are almost always logically sound, but their conclusions are usually false). Still, they have not been bad in the way that (B) and (C) are. What we are trying to account for is not why arguments (B) and (C) are *unsound*, but why (B) and (C) are not serious arguments at all; why do they not have a place in the discussion of philosophical skepticism?

Notice that in a way, this issue is prior to the question of whether philosophical skepticism is true, for unless we (at least implicitly) have a way of distinguishing what counts as a serious argument from what doesn't, we cannot even approach the issue, philosophically. This does not mean the skeptic would win dialectically; it means the practice of dialectic could never get started. We would have no conception of what it would be to motivate skepticism, or anything else.

What is wrong with argument (B) is that, not only does it have a *false* premise (like most philosophical arguments), but its premise *doesn't even appear* true; indeed, it seems obviously false. Hence, it doesn't even give us a prima facie reason for doubting that I can have knowledge. Similarly, the premises of (C), while not obviously false, do not particularly seem true either. Hence, we do not take them even prima facie as grounds for thinking I can have knowledge. This is why neither (B) nor (C) requires philosophical discussion or response.

The above illustrates the way in which the rule of phenomenal conservatism is presupposed in the practice of dialectic: what we count prima facie as motivating a position is a matter of what at first seems true. Clearly the intuitively *plausible* (true-seeming) premises of (A) are taken as prima facie justified; else the argument would give no motivation at all to skepticism. (Also clearly, but less importantly for our present purposes, they are taken as *only* prima facie justified, or else discussion of the issue would terminate once the validity of the argument was agreed upon.) If phenomenal conservatism is false, then dialectic as we practice it is fundamentally and intrinsically irrational. In calling it "intrinsically" irrational, I mean to imply that the problem would be irremediable; there is nothing that could be recognized as a form of dialectic or reasoning that would not be irrational. As a result, it is impossible coherently to argue against phenomenal conservatism. In engaging in argumentation, one is presupposing that there is a distinction between serious arguments and mere strings of arbitrary statements such as (B) and (C). If phenomenal conservatism is false, we cannot draw this distinction in practice. Thus, the skeptic who would argue against phenomenal conservatism labors at pulling the rug out from under his own feet. And if the skeptic eschews argument altogether, we shall hardly be concerned by our failure to "answer" him.

I think, in fact, that the lesson is even more general than I have just indicated—that is, the rule of phenomenal conservatism underlies not only our practice of argumentation (the attempt to convince others through giving expression to one's reasoning), nor, even, just the practice of reasoning. I think the principle of phenomenal conservatism underlies *judgement* in general. I think reflection will reveal that all judgement, whether inferential or not, is a process in which one accepts a proposition on the basis of how things seem to oneself. If phenomenal conservatism is false, so that the way things seem to oneself is irrelevant to epistemic justification, then all judgement must be irrational. And this is something which no philosopher, not even a skeptic, can accept.

5. Questions and Objections

(1)
Phenomenal conservatism seems to be overly liberal in doling out justification: whenever it seems to us as if P, that affords us prima facie justification for P. But doesn't it seem to us as if P whenever we believe that P? Didn't you, in fact, just assure us that beliefs are always formed on the basis of how things seem to the believer? Therefore, how can a belief ever be irrational according to your theory of epistemic rationality?

Reply:
There are three general ways that a belief can be irrational. The first is when the subject has grounds for doubting the proposition believed that ought to, but don't, cause him to revise the belief. Remember that phenomenal conservatism is only a principle of prima facie justification.

Here is an illustration of this case: To a casual observer, it looks as if the sun moves around the earth. Therefore, other things being equal, it would be reasonable to assume that the sun does in fact move; the heliocentrists have the burden of proof. Nevertheless, if I, right now, were to believe that the sun orbits the earth, my belief would be irrational. This is because I know that the opposite belief has been established scientifically, and I also know a bit about the sort of experiments that establish it. That is to say, I have evidence against the belief that the sun orbits the earth which, epistemically, should overrule that belief. However, I might be dogmatic and refuse to reconsider the belief in the light of that evidence, in which case my belief is unjustified.

Phenomenal conservatism, then, does not imply that all beliefs are justified, full stop. Nevertheless, the question may arise whether it implies that all beliefs are prima facie justified, which in itself would seem at least odd, though not as obviously unacceptable as the claim that all beliefs are justified. The answer to this question, however, is no, which brings us to the second way that a belief may be unjustified.

A belief can fail to be even prima facie justified, if the believer adopts it for reasons other than that the proposition believed seems to be the case. I said above that all *judgement* involves accepting a proposition on the basis of how things seem to oneself. However, not all *beliefs* are formed on the basis of how things seem to oneself. (The fact that "judgement" and "belief" appear to most philosophers to be synonymous is perhaps a testament to their rationality.) Judgement is a particular process by which a belief can be formed, but there are other ways of forming beliefs too, which do not depend on how things seem to the subject.

What ways? Well, there are two that I know of: self-deception and faith. (On reflection, the latter may turn out to be a species of the former.) In self-deception, a person adopts (or retains) a belief, not because it seems to be true, but because they *prefer* to believe it. A special case of this is wishful thinking—adopting a belief because one wishes it were true. For instance, say a man's son has been accused of a serious crime. Despite powerful, and almost conclusive, evidence against the son, the father continues to believe his son is innocent. What sort of factors are causing the father's belief? Not attention to how things honestly seem. It is not as if the father has something wrong with his reasoning capacity, such that he can't perceive the link between evidence and conclusion. For we may suppose—also perfectly realistically—that this same father, if any other boy were accused of a similar crime and similar evidence were brought forward, would conclude that the boy was guilty. The evidential situation could be the same; the only difference would be the emotional situation. If the father is "unable" to see how the evidence points to his son's guilt, it is because he does not *wish* to see that; rather, he chooses not to *accept* it. The general point: it often happens that what appears to be the case is something that it would be emotionally painful for a person to believe. People generally try to avoid pain. As a result, people often refuse to accept those propositions. On the other side, it often happens that what does not appear to be the case is something that it would be emotionally pleasant to believe. People generally seek pleasure. Hence, they often choose to accept, to talk themselves into, such beliefs. And those beliefs are epistemically irrational.

Compare the case of religious faith. Suppose a person has been presented with a certain wafer, which for all the world appears to be an ordinary piece of bread. Nevertheless, he believes it is a part of the body of Christ. Why? Because he has been told very solemnly, by an authority he respects, that this belief is essential to his religion. But why does he accept that religion, when it contradicts the evidence of the senses? I am not speaking here of those Catholics who have sophisticated philosophical arguments to defend their religion, but of the average Catholic, who takes his beliefs on faith.

To take a "leap of faith" is precisely to choose to believe something that does not appear to be the case, or even appears false. If I believe that there is a cup on my desk because I am seeing it, that is not called "faith." If I choose to believe that there is a cup on my desk, even though I can't see anything here, *that* is a leap of faith. Faith is typically associated with authority—for example, someone else tells me that there is a cup here even though I don't see anything, and I decide to take their word for it. (No one would just decide on their own that the communion wafer turns into the body of Christ.) This decision could be prompted by a feeling of respect for the authority figure, a desire to remain part of the community he represents, and even moral beliefs about the virtue of holding certain beliefs and/or the vice of questioning them.

There is a parallel here (as in so many other places) between epistemology and ethics. Unjustified belief is belief which is epistemically blameworthy, just as immoral action is action that is morally blameworthy. True immorality results when a person is aware of what ought to be done, and chooses to act otherwise. It happens because people have other, nonmoral sorts of motivations, including self-interest and various emotional motivations. If a person is entirely unaware that his action will result in some harmful consequences to others, and there is no reasonable way he could be expected to be aware of that, then the occurrence of such harmful consequences does not make his action blameworthy. Blameworthy actions occur only when other motivations override a person's sense of morality. Nor is a person who lacks a sense of morality immoral; he is amoral, just as animals are amoral. Likewise, irrational beliefs occur when other motivations override a person's epistemic goals, the goals of having true beliefs and avoiding false ones.

But there are really two kinds of blameworthy action—those that result from evil intent[19] and those that result from negligence. If a person is unaware of the harmful consequences of his action because he simply chooses not to investigate the issue, when any reasonable degree of caution would have resulted in awareness of them, then he can be blamed for negligence. And this suggests our third and final way that a belief can be unjustified: a belief might be unjustified, despite its seeming to be true, if the believer fails to exercise due caution in accepting it (fails to investigate the issue, to gather evidence). Exactly what is "due" caution is, of course, a matter for debate, and I will not attempt to answer that in detail. My purpose here is only to explain how unjustified beliefs can come about, in the light of my claim that mere appearances are sufficient to generate prima facie justification. Consider an example.

Suppose that Smith has decided to investigate the issue of creationism versus evolution, which he has heard a little about. He goes to a lecture by a creationist and listens to all the arguments the creationist presents. At the end of this lecture, it appears to Smith that the theory of evolution is unreasonable and counterintuitive. Smith accepts creationism, and that is the end of his investigation. Notice that this case need not involve any self-deception or leaps of faith in Smith's weighing of the arguments; the creationist lecturer might have presented arguments that honestly seemed correct when Smith heard them. Nevertheless, I would consider Smith's belief to be unjustified, or *insufficiently* justified, due to Smith's failure to investigate the other side of the issue. This is epistemic negligence. In order for Smith to be justified in accepting creationism, he would have to also attend a lecture (or read a book, or some such) by an advocate of the theory of evolution, to see whether they could make evolution seem reasonable.

This is a fairly uncontroversial point—that rational belief requires a reasonable attempt at investigating the issue. But is it consistent with phenomenal conservatism? Phenomenal conservatism would seem to imply that creationism is justified for Smith, since it seems true to him, and—due to failure to listen to what the evolutionists have to say—Smith has no evidence against it.

I think, however, that Smith really does have grounds for doubting creationism. In general, there are at least two different kinds of "grounds for doubt" that can defeat a prima facie justified belief. One is evidence against the proposition believed—that is, if P is what is prima facie justified, evidence that supported $\sim P$ would obviously be grounds for doubting P. But another kind of defeater would be evidence that the means by which one formed the belief is unreliable.[20] (Notice that this isn't the same thing—even if the means by which I came to believe P are unreliable, that doesn't tend to justify $\sim P$.) Smith knows that there is a controversy between evolutionists and creationists, and he knows that he has not investigated the other side of the controversy. These facts are not evidence for the theory of evolution, but they are sufficient evidence that Smith formed his belief in creationism in an unreliable manner. Note that the situation would be different if Smith were unaware that there was any controversy about the issue, and if he thought the creationist was presenting the received view.

To sum up: a belief may be unjustified if (a) one forms it for reasons other than how things seem (e.g., self-deception), (b) one has evidence against it that one chooses to ignore, or (c) one has reasons for thinking one's belief-forming method was unreliable (including that one was negligent in the investigation of the issue).

(2)
Richard Foley has presented a compelling argument against a thesis called "epistemic conservatism," which is very similar to phenomenal conservatism.[21] Epistemic conservatism holds that, if a person believes that P, *the mere fact that they believe it produces at least some degree of prima facie justification for* P.

Foley imagines a case in which S *has almost, but not quite, enough evidence for* P *to make it rational for him to believe it. Suppose* S, *irrationally, accepts* P *anyway. As soon as he formed this irrational belief, if epistemic conservatism is true, it would immediately become rational—for now, in addition to the evidence* S *originally had for* P, *there is also the fact that he believes it, and this pushes* P *over the threshold for rational belief. This result is counterintuitive, and so we should reject epistemic conservatism.*

How does phenomenal conservatism relate to epistemic conservatism? Does Foley's argument apply to phenomenal conservatism as well?

Reply:

Foley's argument succeeds in refuting epistemic conservatism as he defines it, but it does not apply to phenomenal conservatism.

Matters will be somewhat clearer if we redefine "epistemic conservatism." Let's say that an epistemic conservative is a person who believes there is some sort of representational mental state such that its mere occurrence makes one at least to some degree prima facie justified in believing its content. Then we can distinguish two different forms of epistemic conservatism: A *doxastic* conservative holds that the mere occurrence of a *belief* provides some form of justification for that belief, so all beliefs have at least some prima facie justification automatically.[22] ("Doxastic" means pertaining to beliefs.) A phenomenal conservative, on the other hand, holds that the *appearance* that *P* provides some kind of justification for believing that *P*. Foley's argument, I think, only refutes doxastic conservatism.

Suppose we tried to modify Foley's case to make it applicable to phenomenal conservatism. The only way to do this, while keeping the structure of the case the same, is to imagine that at first, *S* has almost enough evidence to make it rational to believe *P*, and then on top of that, there occurs a state of its seeming to him as if *P*—for instance, *S* might have a perceptual experience or an intuition representing that *P*. This appearance state substitutes for the belief in the original version of the story. (But the appearance is neither rational nor irrational, unlike the belief.) Is *S* now justified in believing that *P*?

It seems to me that he is. When the example is changed in this way, I no longer have the intuition that it would be irrational to believe *P*. If you still do, consider the example I discuss under objection (3), which is a similar case.

(3)
Phenomenal conservatism would seem to imply not only, as any foundationalist holds, that it is possible for a belief to be justified when one has no argument for it, but also that a belief can be justified even when one believes it on the basis of a bad argument. For it might happen that a person gives a fallacious argument for P, that they do not notice the fallacy, and that as a result, it seems to them that P. In this case, according to PC, a foundational justification will arise in lieu of the failed inferential justification.

Reply:
Phenomenal conservatism does indeed imply that a belief based on a

fallacious inference can be justified. This result, however, is not a problem for the theory, because the result is correct and not counterintuitive.

Consider the case of the Unfortunate Mathematician. A certain mathematician, let's say, has just constructed a proof of *P*. His argument is valid and sound, the premises are self-evident, and he exercised all due care in constructing it (he checked it over carefully, etc.), so he both believes and is justified in believing that *P*. Now he goes on to construct an argument for another mathematical proposition, *Q*. This second argument appears to him just as sound as the first. Furthermore, he has no reasons to doubt *Q* and no reasons to suspect his method of forming the belief that *Q* to be unreliable. He has exercised the same due caution in checking over this second argument as the first, and he found no errors in it. Each step appeared perfectly correct as he checked it, just as in the first argument. Unfortunately, however, the argument contains a subtle error in step sixteen, rendering it invalid. Since he doesn't know about this error, he continues to accept *Q*. Is his belief rational?

I think yes. Remember that we are talking about internalist justification, and keep in mind the alternatives open to the mathematician. In this situation, he must either accept *Q*, deny *Q* (which amounts to accepting ~*Q*), or suspend judgement. But surely it would not be rational for him to deny *Q*. He may have a fallacious argument for *Q*, but he has no argument at all against *Q*. Should he suspend judgement? Well, he already accepted *P*, and we agreed that that was rational. As far as he can tell, the case for *Q* is exactly as strong as the case for *P*; therefore, how could he be expected to refrain from believing *Q*? If he accepts *P* but declines to accept *Q*, it would surely be appropriate for someone to ask him why. And what reason would he be in a position to give? Given his epistemic position, it is as rational to believe *Q* as it is to believe *P*, and since *P* is justified, we must conclude that *Q* is justified as well.

Obviously, if he becomes aware of the error in the "proof," or even comes to have reason to suspect there is an error, then his belief is no longer justified. But this is also true in the case of the valid proof of *P*—if he comes to have reason to suspect there is an error in it, he will also cease to be justified in believing *P*.

(4)
What if it seems to one person as if P, but it seems to another person as if ~P? What should we believe then?

Reply:
Each person should believe what seems to himself to be correct after a careful examination of the issue. If it seems to John that *P* and it seems to Sally that ~*P*, then John will believe *P*, and Sally will believe ~*P*. If you are a third

party observer, then you should believe whatever seems to *you* to be the case.

This brings out the point, obvious in any case, that internalist justification is relative to an individual. One person may be justified in believing that *P*, while another person is not. Since different people have different experiences, interests, cognitive abilities, and so on, it is not realistic to think that what propositions are justified should be the same for everyone.

(5)
But is there any way for John and Sally to resolve their disagreement?

Reply:
There are two ways: either John makes it seem to Sally that *P* is true, or Sally makes it seem to John that *P* is false. No one has ever resolved a disagreement, except by one of those methods. (By "resolving" a disagreement, I mean convincing the other person. Hitting them over the head or shooting them doesn't count.) When you give someone an argument, what you're trying to do is simply to change the way things appear to them. You do this by drawing their attention to some other things that seem true to them, which support your conclusion. That is all you can possibly do. Of course, if they don't find your premises plausible, then your argument won't work; it won't persuade them. Disagreement is often unfortunate, but it is also a fact of human life. It is not the responsibility of a theory of knowledge to produce a technology for inducing universal agreement.

(6)
Does phenomenal conservatism imply that "truth is relative"?

Reply:
No. It implies that *justification* is relative to an individual. Justification is not the same as truth. You can be justified in believing something that, in reality, is false, and you can be unjustified in believing something that is true. This is where it is important to see, again, that phenomenal conservatism is not a metaphysical principle but an epistemological norm. It does not hold that things must be as they appear (which would indeed imply that reality is subjective, with multiple different "truths"), but rather that it is reasonable, other things being equal, to believe things are as they appear.

(7)
If justification is separate from and does not imply truth, then why should we care about justification? Why not just focus on truth?

Reply:

Although believing only what is justified does not guarantee you of getting only true beliefs (nothing within your power will), believing only what is justified for you is *doing the best you can* to get to the truth.

Here is an analogy. Suppose you want to shoot some baskets. The best thing to do is to carefully aim the ball at the basket, and then throw it. Will this guarantee you of making a basket? No, but it's the best you can do. It'll do a lot better (in all probability) than throwing the ball without aiming, or not throwing the ball at all.

When trying this technique, some people will have much better results than others. Some people will make a lot of baskets; others will make relatively few. The latter group of people are still doing the best they can: all they can do is aim the ball and throw it, and they cannot use someone else's aim to do it.[23]

Similarly, when you believe the things that are for you justified, this won't guarantee that you'll never be wrong. But you'll be doing the best you can. You'll do a lot better (in all probability) than if you tried believing the things that seem false.

This is what epistemic justification is about: does one believe "responsibly," so to speak, when one accepts *P*? The task for an epistemologist, in my view, is to address this question with respect to the main kinds of beliefs that we hold. If accepting *P* is part of doing the best one can to pursue truth and eschew error, then accepting *P* is justified in the relevant sense; no more could be asked.

Notes

1. This is not to say that all epistemologists accept that the first three conditions I have stated are necessary for knowledge, but all epistemologists agree that they are *not sufficient*. See Gettier.

2. Russell's example, *Human Knowledge*, 154.

3. There are further refinements required to the definition, having to do with distinguishing "misleading defeaters" from "genuine defeaters," but these details do not concern us here. See Klein, "A Proposed Definition of Propositional Knowledge," and Lehrer and Paxson.

4. Admittedly, even this description is oversimplified. It would be hard to identify the background beliefs of mine that lead me to categorize this object as a tomato. "All red, round things are tomatoes" won't do, nor do I have concepts adequate for describing the exact sort of shape and color that tomatoes have (unless you trivially count "shaped like a tomato" and "the color of a tomato"). What I seem to have is a much more diffuse mental state than a belief or collection of beliefs; roughly, I have a *conception* of tomatoes, which makes possible the classification of objects as tomatoes

(or nontomatoes as the case may be) on the basis of observed features, although the conception also involves features tomatoes are supposed to have that I am not now observing (for example, the tomato should have seeds inside it). So my belief in a tomato will be based on this conception of tomatoes, plus my present visual experience.

5. Evan Fales, ch. 5-6, defends this view of the relation between perceptual experiences and beliefs. Fales also discusses and answers traditional objections to the notion of noninferential, perceptual knowledge. See my review of his book for a summary.

6. See Nozick, 172ff.; Dretske, "The Pragmatic Dimension of Knowledge"; Goldman; and Lewis.

7. Ellis, *Reason and Emotion in Psychotherapy*. See also papers 2 and 3 in Ellis and Grieger for a review of the empirical evidence supporting rational emotive therapy.

8. There is one sort of exception, which occurs in the viewing of ambiguous drawings such as the Necker Cube and several of the illustrations in Jastrow, 283-95. In these cases, an observer can often choose to see the picture in one way or another; for instance, in viewing the Necker cube, one can choose to view a particular square alternately as the front face or the back face of the cube depicted, so that the content of one's visual experience is, in that sense, dependent on the will. This calls into question my proposed explanation in the text for why experiences are neither justified nor unjustified, because in such a case I still do not think it would make sense to characterize one's experience as justified or unjustified. It would not make sense, for instance, to speak of one's being justified in seeing the Necker cube in a certain way.

9. That is, I think the principle accounts, for every foundational belief, for why that belief is justified. Additional principles, or a stronger principle, would be needed to account for the *degree* of justification each such belief has.

10. Chisholm has observed that "appear" words are sometimes used to express tentative judgements, though I do not think that this refutes my contention here. See chapter IV, note 39.

11. See section IV.4.2-3.

12. The concept of a memory appearance is related to, but distinct from, Shoemaker and Parfit's concept of a "quasi-memory." Quasi-memories are states similar to experiential memories (as distinct from factual memory), except that it is conceptually possible to quasi-remember someone else's experiences (but it is not conceptually possible to quasi-remember things that never happened at all) (Shoemaker, "Persons and their Pasts," 271; Parfit, 14-15). "Memory appearances," on the other hand, are states like memories (experiential or factual), except that it is possible to have a memory appearance of something that is not true or that never happened.

13. A number of foundationalists, probably most foundationalists these days, rely on the notion of prima facie justification. See for example Audi, *The Structure of Justification*, 307-10; Pollock, *Contemporary Theories of Knowledge*, 177-78. For the argument that there is nothing inconsistent about this, see Alston, "Has Foundationalism Been Refuted?"

14. Alston makes this point, along with several other important clarificatory ones, in "Has Foundationalism Been Refuted?"

15. There are at least two inferential steps here: first, from the fact that you spoke certain words to the fact that you see, or at least think you see, a red sphere there, and second, from the fact that you see or think you see a red sphere there to the conclusion that there probably is a red sphere there. According to Burge (though I think he is wrong), I would actually have foundational justification for believing that you see the red sphere; however, the second inferential step would still be necessary, even on his theory. Moreover, there is no difficulty in generating any number of examples in which I would have a further, inferential justification for thinking there is a red sphere there.

16. See section II.6.

17. Foley, *Working without a Net*, 8. I do not know, however, whether Foley would agree with the use to which I have put his theory.

18. This is an abbreviated version of the argument from section II.1.

19. To be more precise, the distinction should be made between doing evil knowingly, and doing it unknowingly as a result of negligence. Doing something *knowingly* is not exactly the same as doing it *intentionally*. If *x* is neither my end nor a means to my end, but I know that it will occur if I do *y*, and I proceed to do *y*, then I bring about *x* knowingly but not intentionally. The law of double effect notwithstanding, a person may be blamed for bringing about evils knowingly, whether intentionally or not.

20. Compare Pollock's distinction between undercutting and rebutting defeaters in *Contemporary Theories of Knowledge*, 38-39. The distinction, with different terminology, originates in Pollock, "The Structure of Epistemic Justification."

21. Foley, "Epistemic Conservatism."

22. Chisholm takes this position in *The Foundations of Knowing*, 14.

23. I owe this analogy to Ben Kovitz (in email).

VI. Objections to Direct Realism

I have just defended two traditional "direct realist" theses: first, that in perception, the things of which we are directly aware are the real, physical objects, and second, that as a result of perception, we know noninferentially that there are external objects having certain observable properties. I think this is the view of common sense, on both counts. But it is also a view that has been subjected to a bewildering variety of objections and been often rejected by philosophers with disdain. I call it "direct realism," but it is also often called "naive realism," a name which reflects both its appeal to common sense and the assessment of many philosophers that it is open to clear and decisive objections. That assessment is given rather forthrightly in the passage from David Hume that I quote below, under our first objection.

Let us, then, see what these objections are, and how a direct realist might respond to them.

1. The Argument from Perspective

Referring to direct realism, David Hume wrote:

> But this universal and primary opinion of all men is soon destroyed by the slightest philosophy, which teaches us that nothing can ever be present to the mind but an image or perception. . . . The table which we see seems to diminish as we remove farther from it; but the real table, which exists independent of us, suffers no alteration; it was, therefore, nothing but its image which was present to the mind. These are the obvious dictates of reason; and no man who reflects ever doubted that the existences which we consider when we say *this house* and *that tree* are nothing but perceptions in the mind, and fleeting copies or representations of other existences which remain uniform and independent.[1]

The second sentence above is the entirety of the argument for indirect realism that Hume considered so obvious and so conclusive that no person who reflects could possibly doubt its conclusion. It is sometimes called "the argument from illusion," but I beg leave to change its name, since the example to which Hume here appeals is an example of the phenomenon of *perspective*, not an example of an *illusion*. (There are things more properly called "illusions," discussed in the subsequent section, which I think the direct realist should deal with in a different way.) The phenomenon we're talking about is, in the most general terms, that the character of your experiences regularly varies depending on the condition of you, the observer, and/or your relation to the external objects, even when there is no change in the characteristics of the physical objects that you are ostensibly perceiving. When you move farther away from an object, it "looks smaller," even though there is no change in the actual size (or any other property) of the object itself. Similarly, when you view an object from different angles, it may appear different shapes, even though the object itself does not change its shape. Allegedly, this proves that what you are really aware of is not the physical object but something else, something dependent on you, the subject.

But how *exactly* is this conclusion supposed to follow? Perhaps the implicit premise is that awareness (or at least a certain kind of awareness, such as *perceptual* awareness or *direct* awareness) requires a tracking relation between the character of one's mental state and the character of the object of awareness. In other words, it requires that the properties of the experience should vary alongside variations in (some of) the properties of the objects of awareness. For example, if the object changes its shape, the character of the experience should change in some suitable way to reflect that; conversely, if the object does *not* change, then the experience should not change.[2] I think this is a plausible condition for awareness, and I think something like it follows from the content-satisfaction condition that I laid down in chapter IV. Now, says the indirect realist, since the character (specifically, the content) of our experiences depends on factors that have nothing to do with the character of the physical objects we're supposedly (that is, according to direct realists) perceiving, we have to conclude that our experiences do not really count as awareness of those objects after all.

To avoid this conclusion, direct realists need not challenge the general premise about the nature of awareness. We can instead find properties of the external object that do vary alongside the variations in our experience to which the indirect realist is calling attention. In order to see this, we need to draw a distinction between two properties that a physical object can have, which I shall call *linear size* and *angular size*. Linear size is what we ordinarily think of as "size," that is, the sort of thing that you can measure in feet or meters. On the other hand, angular size is the sort of thing you can measure in degrees or radians. The angular size of an object, relative to a given point, is defined as the angle the object subtends at that point. In other words, suppose you have a point A. Imagine lines connecting A to the extremities of a table, as in figure 6.1. Those lines form an angle at point A. The size of that angle is what I call the "angular size of the table, relative to point A."

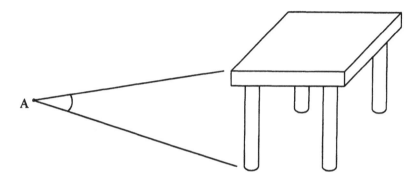

Figure 6.1. The angular size of a table, relative to a given point in space.

What the sense of sight makes one aware of, directly and in the primary sense, is the angular sizes of objects, relative to the point at which the observer is located. Obviously, the angular size of an object will vary (assuming the object keeps the same linear size) depending on how far away from it one is. Given this, that the table will look smaller as you move away from it is precisely what we should expect if we are seeing the real table. This change marks no illusion; in fact, as Thomas Reid pointed out in his response to Hume, it is evidence *in favor* of our seeing the real object. The character of our experience tracks the angular size of the object in just the way it should, so this phenomenon poses no problem for direct realism.[3]

If this response works, we could also introduce a property to be called "angular shape," in order to account for variations in the apparent shapes of objects depending on their orientation relative to us. The ordinary shape of an object is a function of the *ratios* of its sizes along different dimensions, or, in other words, the ratios of the distance relations among its parts. Object A is "the same shape" as object B when for each pair of parts of A, there is a corresponding pair of parts of B, such that the distances between any two parts of A are in a fixed proportion to the distances between the corresponding parts of B. That statement sounds a bit convoluted, but if you reflect on it, I think you will see it is correct (the reason for the talk about proportions or ratios is to allow for objects with the same shape but different sizes). The "angular shape" of an object, then, will be understood analogously to ordinary shape, except that angular sizes take the place of linear distances. And we can maintain that angular shapes of objects are directly perceived by the sense of sight.

Here is perhaps a simpler way to think about the kind of "shape" I am saying we perceive directly by sight. Consider the shape of the shadow that an object would cast onto a certain plane, if light were shined on the object perpendicular to the plane—for instance, you can think about the shape of the shadow that a table casts on the ground, when light is shined from directly overhead. That shape is called the *projection* of the table onto the two-dimensional surface that is the ground. (The shape of the actual table is three-dimensional; the shape of the projection is two-dimensional.) We can regard visual experience as responding directly to the *projected* shapes of objects, relative to a plane perpendicular to the line of sight. If you rotate the object, its projected shape will typically change (example: if you rotate the table about a horizontal axis, then the shape of its shadow will change). Our visual experiences vary in the right way to track the projected shapes of objects, which makes that what we are aware of. Of course, with experience, everyone learns to associate appropriate three-dimensional shapes with the two-dimensional projected shapes of which we are immediately aware, so we normally only form beliefs about the actual three-dimensional shapes of the objects we see.

If you are tempted to wonder whether this account of the objects of visual awareness is really compatible with direct realism, it is essential to keep clearly in mind what is the issue between direct and indirect realists. The issue is whether the immediate objects of awareness in perception are subjective or objective—whether they are mental phenomena or physical phenomena. What I have done is to concede the relational character of these objects, but not their subjective character. The angular size of an object is a relational property, varying depending on your location. But it is not subjective—it is a perfectly objective, physical fact that an object has a certain angular size relative to a given point in space. That angular size does not depend in any way on your consciousness. This is why my response to the argument from perspective leaves me well within the territory of direct realism.

In my view, then, the argument from perspective rests on a confounding of two distinctions: the *objective versus subjective* distinction and the *intrinsic versus relational* distinction. Perspectival variation shows that what we are directly, visually aware of is not an *intrinsic* property of the external object, since it depends on our position. Indirect realists then make the mistake of concluding that it must therefore be something *subjective*, that is, something in the mind. I propose a third alternative: that it is an *objective, relational* property.

A relational property is a property that depends on the relationship between two or more things. An intrinsic property is a property of an object that does not depend on the object's relation to anything else—that is, a property that is nonrelational. An objective, relational property, then, would be a property that depends upon a relationship but does not depend upon the mind. I have observed that angular size is objective and relational. It should be clear that the same is true of angular shape. I will give one more illustration, because it is important to see what my general strategy is and to understand that it can be deployed against any version of the argument from perspective, not just the example Hume cites and not just arguments concerning vision.

Suppose you keep one hand in a bowl of ice-cold water for a minute, while at the same time the other hand is immersed in hot water. Then you simultaneously plunge both hands into a third container full of lukewarm water. What you would find is that the same water feels warm to the first hand and cool to the second hand. Traditionally, opponents of direct realism try to use this phenomenon to show that we do not really perceive the actual temperature of the water, for one and the same tub of water cannot simultaneously be both warm and cool. That is, our sensations of hot and cold cannot constitute awareness of an intrinsic feature of the water, since our sensations vary depending on the condition of us, the perceivers, even when the water is intrinsically the same. Therefore, argue the opponents, what we are aware of is just our own sensations.

How should a direct realist explain what goes on in this experiment with the three tubs of water? One might try saying that you are aware of the temperature *difference* between the water and your hand. But there is a better answer: your sensations make you aware of the heat *transfer* between your hand and the water. The water "feels cool" to the one hand because heat is flowing from the hand to the water. For the other hand, heat is flowing from the water to the hand, so it feels warm. This also explains why a hot piece of metal feels hotter to the touch than a piece of wood or plastic at the same temperature: the metal transfers heat to your hand faster, since it is a better conductor.

Notice the strategy of this response: I concede that the property we are aware of in the example, the property we *detect*, is not an intrinsic property of the water (temperature). But nor is it something subjective (a sensation). Instead, I propose that it is objective but relational (heat transfer). This enables it to vary depending on the physical condition of the observer. Notice that the fact that the heat transfer between your hand and another substance depends upon the condition of your hand, as well as the conductivity of the substance, does not make it at all subjective. It is a perfectly objective, physical fact that heat is being transferred at a certain rate to your hand, or out of your hand.

I am not saying, here, that all the properties we detect through perception are relational; some of them, at least, are intrinsic. For instance, by the sense of touch, one can be aware of the ordinary, three-dimensional shapes of objects. What I am saying is that in the typical cases in which the character of our experience normally varies without an accompanying variation in the intrinsic properties of the external objects we're ostensibly perceiving, this is because we are detecting relational properties.

2. The Argument from Illusion

For the next argument, we make one more use of the optical illusion involving the stick half-submerged in water. The stick looks bent but is in fact straight. Can this phenomenon be used to show that we are not directly aware of the stick?

What if I try to explain this case analogously to the way I explained the perspectival variations discussed in the last section; how would that go? I would have to find a property (most likely a relational, but nevertheless objective property) of the stick that genuinely changes when it is put into water, so that my experience could be tracking that property. I might try citing the way the stick is disposed to reflect light. But in fact, nothing about the *stick's* disposition to reflect light is altered when it is partially submerged in water. The submerged part of the stick is still reflecting light in all directions, just like the above-water part is. It's just that the direction of the light is changed when it moves from the water to the air. Therefore, if I wanted to pursue this strategy, it would seem that I would have to claim to be perceiving a property of the stick-plus-the-medium (the "medium" including the water and air between the stick and my eye)—something like the pattern in which it is disposed to transmit light to my eye. This is starting to sound implausible (to me, anyway), and it also sounds incompatible with the content-satisfaction condition that we imposed on awareness earlier (sections IV.1 and IV.3.2), for my experience seems to be representing *the stick* as being *bent*, rather than representing the stick-cum-medium as having some disposition to transmit light. In any case, this is not the strategy I want to pursue. I think it best to grant that this case is a genuine illusion—meaning a case in which our experience misrepresents reality (unlike the cases discussed in the previous section).

The argument from illusion needs two stages. First, the indirect realist wants to argue that in this case, what one is immediately aware of cannot be the actual stick, and that it must be, instead, a sense datum. Second, the indirect realist wants to argue that if we are aware of a sense datum in this case, then we are also aware of sense data in *normal* cases, even when there is no illusion.

The second step seems right to me—it would be most implausible to hold that when you look at the half-submerged stick you are aware of something of a radically different kind from what you are aware of when the stick is all the way out of the water, and it would be even less plausible to hold that when you look at a stick you are aware of a sense datum, but not when you look at other objects. But I reject the first stage of the argument: I don't think that, because the stick appears bent when it really is not, it follows that you are not directly aware of the stick. Let's try to see how the indirect realist might argue that it does.

Here is a logically sound argument:

1. When you look at the stick, you are directly aware of something that is bent.
2. No (relevant) physical object is bent at this time.
3. Therefore, the thing you are directly aware of is something nonphysical.

If (3) is true, then it would seem that we must posit a sense datum as being the thing that is bent. This argument, however, is factually unsound; specifically, its first premise is false. When you look at the stick, you are directly aware of something (namely, the stick) that *looks* bent, but it is not in fact bent. At any rate, this would be the natural description of the case, and we have seen no reason so far why one should accept that the thing one is aware of is *really* bent.

Now, suppose we modified the argument, to take account of this response, as follows:

1. When you look at the stick, you are directly aware of something that appears bent.
2. No (relevant) physical object appears bent at this time.
3. Therefore, the thing you are directly aware of is something nonphysical.

Now, of course, the problem is that premise (2) is false; there is a relevant physical object, namely the stick you're looking at, that appears bent.

Third pass: what if we make both premises clearly true, like so:

1. When you look at the stick, you are directly aware of something that *appears* bent.
2. No (relevant) physical object *is* bent at this time.
3. Therefore, the thing you are directly aware of is something nonphysical.

But now (3) does not follow from (1) and (2).

Final try: we can add another premise to make the desired conclusion follow, like so:

1. When you look at the stick, you are directly aware of something that appears bent.
2. No (relevant) physical object is bent at this time.
3. If you are directly aware of a thing, then the thing is the way it appears.
4. Therefore, the thing you are directly aware of is something nonphysical.

Premise (3) is plausible, particularly in view of my content-satisfaction condition for awareness. It would seem that genuine awareness of something—and especially direct awareness—should give one access to the way the object actually is. If we accept this premise, then, along with premise (1), we can infer that the thing you are directly aware of is bent. That plus (2) will give us the desired conclusion that the thing you are directly aware of is not a physical object.

However, (3) is not true absolutely and without qualification. Rather, I think, if you are directly aware of a thing, that thing must be at least *roughly* the way it appears, in some important respects. I think one can, perfectly plausibly, allow that the object might fail to be *exactly* as it appears. So one can allow that in this case, one is directly aware of the stick, the stick appears bent, but the stick is not actually bent. This becomes clearer if one notices (a) that one is aware of the top half of the stick (the part out of the water), and there is no problem with that (at least as far as the content-satisfaction requirement goes), and (b) that one is also aware of the bottom half of the stick, and there is no problem with that either.[4] One's experience merely misrepresents their spatial relation to each other.

One final observation about this argument. I think this last version of the argument is the most plausible one—in fact, the only plausible one. Unless the indirect realist includes premise (3), I think he really has no argument, for we could always say that we are aware of something that appears bent but isn't. But at the same time, the indirect realist *cannot* consistently endorse (3) without qualification. For if (3) is true, we can also construct a conclusive argument against indirect realism:

3. If you are directly aware of a thing, then the thing is the way it appears.
5. During perception, the things I am directly aware of appear to be real, physical objects.
6. Therefore, the things I am directly aware of are real, physical objects.

The indirect realist cannot accept this argument. But the argument is certainly logically sound, and (5) is pretty clearly true. I might add that the objects of my awareness appear to be located in space, outside my body, that some of them appear to be solid, heavy, and to have all the other characteristics of physical objects. Therefore, what could an indirect realist find wrong with the above argument? He would have to say that (3) is false. But that means that he cannot use (3) to argue against direct realism, and so the argument from illusion collapses.

3. The Argument from Hallucination, Part 1

An illusion is merely an experience in which the object one is perceiving is not exactly the way it appears. A hallucination is an experience, introspectively similar to perception, in which there is no object one is perceiving. For instance, one might, due to some abnormal brain condition, hallucinate a tomato, even when there was nothing at all tomato-like in the offing, that is, nothing tomato-like that was causally related to one's experience. What is it that one is aware of in such a case?

I cannot, with any plausibility, treat this case either in the way I treat perspectival phenomena or in the way I treat illusions; I cannot say there is really some objective, relational property of some external object (what external object?) that one is aware of, and I cannot say that one is aware of an object that simply appears a bit different from the way it is. No, if there is to be an object of awareness in this case, it will have to be a mental item—a mental image, or "sense datum"—since no physical object will do.

If we accept that, the indirect realist will then try (as in the argument from illusion) to push us towards accepting that this same thing is also the object of awareness in normal perception. Why? Well, it is possible to have a hallucination induced by the same sort of brain state as that which occurs during normal perception. If in the hallucination case, that brain state causes one to have a mental image, then the mental image must also occur during normal perception. And then, why wouldn't one be aware of the image during normal perception, if one is aware of it during the hallucination?[5]

Fortunately, we do not need to accept the first stage of the argument. We do not need to accept that hallucinating is being aware of a mental image, nor do we have to find some physical phenomenon that one is aware of. For hallucination is not awareness at all. It is, so to speak, pseudo-awareness—that is, a mental state that seems like awareness of something (and, in terms of its *intrinsic* properties, *is* just like perceptual awareness) but is not in fact the awareness of anything, for awareness is a relation between the subject and the world, and the hallucination fails to have the right *relational* properties. This is clear in terms of my account of awareness in chapter IV.[6]

Now, an advocate of sense data might concede that I have given a consistent and even plausible account of the phenomena of perspective, illusion, and hallucination. But, he might argue, the sense data theory is simpler, and so in that respect better, than the direct realist theory. For the sense data theory explains all three phenomena in the same way—they are all explained by the hypothesis that one is aware of sense data—whereas the direct realist has to give three very different accounts of what is going on in these three kinds of cases. That seems to be an advantage, even if only a small one, for the sense data theory.

I think, however, that there is a deeper and more important sense in which my theory is equally as simple as the sense data theory, and in which it does make possible a unified understanding of perspective, illusion, and hallucination. Fundamentally, what separates me from the sense data theorists is this: the sense data theory tries to account for perception and related phenomena by positing a special kind of nonphysical object of awareness, to be the bearer of the properties that appear to us to be exemplified in our immediate environment. I account for perception and related phenomena by appeal to a special kind of mental state, perceptual experience, that *represents there to be* objects having certain properties, and then I characterize perceptual awareness as a matter of that state's being related to the world in a certain way. Thus, the sense data theorist gets to account for perspectival variations, illusions, and hallucinations by simply attributing appropriate properties to the involved sense data. I, in parallel fashion, account for these phenomena by attributing appropriate *representational contents* to our perceptual experiences. The differences in what I say about what we are aware of in those cases then arise from my account of what awareness is: a perceptual experience counts as awareness of the phenomenon that causes it and at least approximately satisfies its content. My claims (a) that we are aware of objective, relational properties of physical objects in perception, (b) that in the case of illusions, we are also aware of physical objects, though they are not quite the way they appear, and (c) that hallucination is not awareness of anything, all flow from that account; they are the natural things to say given my account of awareness. This is what makes my treatment of these cases more than just a series of ad hoc assumptions to escape from objections.

4. The Argument from Hallucination, Part 2

Richard Fumerton objects specifically to the epistemological thesis of direct realism, which he takes to be that we are justified in believing in external objects because we are directly acquainted with them. He asks us to compare a case in which a person sees a table with a case in which a person has a perfectly vivid and realistic hallucination of a table. Assume that the hallucination is qualitatively just like a perception, and that the subject has no reason for suspecting that he is hallucinating, so he is justified in believing that there is a table there. Fumerton offers the following argument:

1. The person with the hallucination has the same justification for believing there is a table as does the person who is seeing the table.
2. In the case of the hallucination, the person's justification for believing there is a table does not consist in his being directly acquainted with a table.
3. Therefore, in the case of normal perception, the person's justification for believing there is a table does not consist in his being directly acquainted with a table.[7]

"Same justification" in premise (1) must be understood to mean "justification of the same kind." In other words, the premise is that whatever makes it reasonable for the person with the hallucination to believe in the table is the same as what makes it reasonable for the person with the perception to believe in the table. This seems right to me.

Premise (2) is also true, because the person with the hallucination is not acquainted with a table (we can suppose there isn't any table around for him to be acquainted with).

And step (3) follows from (1) and (2).

I agree with Fumerton's argument—except that I don't think it refutes direct realism. It is an argument against *a* form of direct realism, but it is not an argument against my version of direct realism, because I do not say that our justification for believing in external objects consists in our being directly acquainted with them. I say that our justification for believing in external objects consists in the fact that, when we have perceptual experiences, external objects seem to us to be present, and there is no evidence in general against this. The person with the perfectly vivid hallucination also has an experience such that a table seems to him to be present and also (we assume) has no evidence against this; therefore, on my account, he has the same kind and degree of justification for believing in the table as we normally do when we see tables.

My view is certainly a form of what Fumerton calls "epistemological naive realism," since I say that beliefs about external objects are noninferentially justified, but it is not damaged by this argument.

5. The Argument from Double Vision

I promised to come back to this argument, after my earlier presentation of it (chapter I). If you look at your finger while it is out of focus, you will seem to see two fingers; alternately, you can induce double vision by pushing on one eyeball. Recall that the argument went, essentially, like this:

1. In the case of double vision, you see two of something.
2. There are not two (relevant) physical objects that you're seeing.
3. Therefore, what you see is something nonphysical.

I accept premise (2). Premise (1), however, is false. Since there are not two objects there to be seen, it cannot be correct to describe the case as one of seeing two of something. How, then, should one describe it?

One possibility is to treat double vision as a kind of hallucination. We could then say: "You are not *seeing* two of something; you merely *seem* to be seeing two things. In fact, what you are doing is *hallucinating* two of something." However, this does not appear to be the most plausible description of the case. While looking at your finger out of focus, close the left eye. When you close the eye, you will find that suddenly there only appears to be one finger. Now you are genuinely perceiving the finger that is in front of your face, since your visual experience correctly represents, and is appropriately caused by, the finger. If you then close the right eye and open the left, you will again genuinely perceive the finger in front of your face (but it will seem to shift position). However, according to the view under consideration here, when you open both eyes, now you are hallucinating, even though your experience is caused in the same way by the physical finger. So the apparent-finger on the left, say, is real when only the right eye is open, but the addition of the apparent-finger on the right when you open the other eye makes it turn into a hallucinatory finger.

Alternately, one might try saying that you are seeing the real finger, and, in addition, you are also hallucinating a second finger. That would raise the question, "Which of the apparent fingers that I seem to be seeing is the real one; the one on the left, or the one on the right?"

But it is fairly clear that on my account of perception, the kind of double-vision we're talking about is an instance of perception and therefore is not hallucination. For the experience one is having is caused in the normal way by the physical finger (light rays bounce off the surface of the finger, form images on your retinas, etc.), and the characteristics of the physical finger match the way the finger is represented in the experience—except, of course, for the fact that there's only one of them. To put that another way, if we want to speak in terms of two finger-images, *each* image counts as a perception of the one finger, since each is caused by and correctly represents the finger.

Thus, the correct description of the case is this: There is a single, physical object that you are seeing; however, that object seems to be in two places. That is, your visual experience incorrectly represents the finger in two different places.[8] This is a case of a visual illusion. In accordance with what we said in section 2, this does not require us to say that there actually is any thing that is in two different places, nor that there are two things in two different places. An illusion is precisely a situation in which things are not as they appear. If we accept, in the case of the bent-stick illusion, that the thing one is aware of appears to be, but in fact is not bent, we should be equally prepared to accept that in the double-vision case, the thing one is aware of appears to be, but in fact is not, in each of two different locations.

6. The Time-Gap Argument

Suppose you are looking at a star, up in the sky. Suppose the star is (or was) one thousand light-years away. That means that it takes 1000 years for light to travel from the star to where you are. Now, suppose that the star was actually destroyed 300 years ago. You would still be "seeing" it, because light it emitted before it was destroyed is still traveling towards Earth. People on Earth will continue to "see" this star for another 700 years. But wait—how can you be seeing something that doesn't (now) exist?

So what is it that you're really seeing? Indirect realists have a ready answer, of course: a sense datum of a star. And just as in the arguments from illusion and hallucination, there will now follow a second stage of argument where the indirect realist tries to show that, if we accept his account of this case, we should also accept his account of all cases of normal perception. For suppose that there is a second star, also 1000 light-years away, next to the first one, but that this second star has not been destroyed and continues to exist now. Could we, with any plausibility, claim that what we are seeing in these two cases is a radically different kind of thing? If the first case is one of seeing a sense datum of a star, isn't the second case also one of seeing a sense datum? After all, one's experience has exactly the same kind of etiology and the same introspectible character in the two cases. The only difference is that in the one case, the star was destroyed 700 years after it emitted the light that's now causing your experience—but that has no effect whatever on you or your experience. So if a sense datum exists in the one case, why wouldn't it exist in the other?

If you buy this argument, you will also have to accept sense data for all the objects around you. For in the case of *any* perception, there is always at least some time gap. When you look at your own hand there is a (very small) delay between when the light bounces off its surface and when you have an experience of seeming to see a hand. So if the time gap argument shows you are not really seeing a star, it also shows you are not really seeing your hand.

But perhaps one might give a different answer to the question that started this. Perhaps what you are really seeing is simply the *light* emitted by the star, rather than either the star itself or a sense datum. The light from the star continues to exist at the time you have the visual experience, so there's no problem, right?

Well, almost. There is still a delay (very short) between the time light rays strike your retina and the time you have a visual experience, required for the signals to reach your visual cortex and your brain to process the information. In fact, the particular photons causing your visual experience do not exist at the time your experience occurs, having been absorbed by your retina. Therefore, if the time gap argument shows that you're not really seeing the star, it must equally well prove that you are not really seeing the light either. Nor, for the same reason, could you be seeing retinal images. I assume no one will be tempted to say you're seeing your brain. So the only thing left for you to be seeing appears to be a sense datum.

After this elaborate argument, my response may seem disappointingly simple. What are you aware of when looking at the star 1000 light-years away? You are aware of the star, as it was 1000 years ago. I see no reason why one should not be able to perceive something in the past. Obviously, the time at which your perceiving occurs cannot be before your experience occurs. But why must the time of the *perceived state of affairs* be identical with the time of the *perceiving*?

Here is another example. You're in a large baseball stadium. You watch the batter hit the ball. A second after you see this, you hear the crack of the bat striking the ball, due to the fact that sound travels slower than light. Should we say that you are not really hearing the bat striking the ball, since that event no longer exists? Wouldn't it be more natural to say simply that you hear the event a second after it happened? And similarly, if you can hear an event after the time at which it happened, why shouldn't you be able to see an object after the time at which it existed?

It might be said that the events and states of affairs that we perceive always seem to be happening *now*, that is, at the time at which we are perceiving them. I am not sure this is right—I am not sure that the time of an event is represented in a perceptual experience of the event, rather than merely the character of the event. But even if we grant that perceptual experiences of events always represent them as happening in the present, we can still maintain that we are perceptually aware of events in the external world—we can just recognize that there is an illusory element to our perception in the case of distant events. Our experience represents them as occurring now, even though they actually happened earlier. Provided my earlier response to the argument from illusion succeeds, this will not present a problem.

Does that mean that *all* perceptual experiences have an aspect of illusion, with respect to the times at which things are perceived as happening? Not necessarily. If the time gap is very small, it might not make the experience illusory. The reason is that our experiences might not be infinitely precise in their representational content—our experience need not represent an event as taking place at a single, exact time. Consider the following example.

Try flipping the light switch for the room you are now in to off, and then flip it on. You observe light appearing when you flip the switch on. Judging purely by your experience, how long did it take for the light to appear after you flipped the switch? For most lights (excepting some fluorescent lights) the answer is that there was no noticeable delay. As far as you could tell from your experience, the light went on *immediately*, that is, at the instant you flipped the switch. What this shows is that your experience does not clearly represent the time at which the switch-flipping occurs to be different from the time at which the appearance of light occurs. But, on an intellectual level, we know that there had to be a delay, however slight, between those two events and, furthermore, between the time of the brain event corresponding to feeling yourself flip the switch and the brain event corresponding to seeing the light. Presumably, then, there was a time gap between your two experiences, although you don't *experience a time gap* between the events.

What can that mean about the representational content of your experience? One way to interpret it is to say that one or both of your experiences is illusory; either the one experience represents the switch-flipping as happening later than it actually did, or the other represents the light-appearance as happening earlier than it actually did, or both. And we seem to be forced to say, incidentally, that at least one experience represents the event it is of as happening at a time different from the time the experience itself happens.

I do not find this the most plausible interpretation, however. For one thing, it would seem hard to understand why our experience should contain exactly this sort of distorted time indexing. If there had been a comparably small delay between the two events but in the reverse direction (that is, if the light had flooded the room just a tiny moment *before* you flipped the switch), I think things would have seemed the same—that is, the events also would have seemed simultaneous as far as you could tell. Therefore, we would have to say that your perception makes distortions in opposite directions in these two cases. We would have to lay down a rule something like this: if *A* happens just slightly before B, the experience will represent A as happening later than it actually did, but if A happens just slightly after B, the experience will represent A as happening earlier than it actually did.[9] This would strike me as odd.

For another thing, I expect that we could have a sequence of perceived events, say $(A_1, A_2, \ldots, A_n)$, such that each event in the series appears, as far as the observer can tell, simultaneous with the next one in the sequence, but such that A_1 definitely seems to precede A_n. In other words, a series of imperceptible time delays might add up to a delay that is very clearly noticeable. And this would be incompatible with the view according to which our experience assigns a determinate (if incorrect) time to each event in the series.

The alternative, then, is that our experiences have *indeterminate* contents. In other words, an experience will represent an event as happening more or less at such-and-such time, rather than at exactly such-and-such time (this is assuming, for the sake of simplicity, that we are talking about instantaneous events). There are philosophical puzzles about indeterminate representations. Note that the distinction between determinate and indeterminate representations is not merely the distinction between assigning a single instant of time to an event and assigning a finite time interval during which it happened. For the same sort of considerations that show that we cannot, on the basis of experience, assign perfectly precise time-instants to events we observe will equally well show that we cannot assign perfectly precise intervals either—the boundaries of the interval must themselves be indeterminate. This is one of the strange things about the phenomenon of indeterminacy, or vagueness, of representations.

Note, however, that this situation is far from unique to perceived time. The perceived colors of things are also indeterminate, since it is possible to have a series of colors, $(C_1, C_2, \ldots, C_n)$, such that C_1 is observably distinguishable from C_n, but C_1 is indistinguishable from C_2, which is indistinguishable from C_3, and so on. The contents of our beliefs are also frequently indeterminate, owing to the indeterminacy in our concepts. To take a well-worn example: a man with only one hair on his head is bald, and a man with 10,000 hairs is not, but there is no precise number of hairs you have to have (or mass of hair, or anything else) in order not to be bald. The boundary between bald and hairy is indeterminate. And therefore, the content of the belief that John is bald is indeterminate. Thus, we might say that perceptual experiences are in good company.

Now, how does this help with the time gap argument? I say that it enables us to avoid the displeasing conclusion that (due to the delay between external events and our perceptions thereof) our experience always misrepresents the times at which things happen. For if our experiences are indeterminate with respect to the times at which things seem to happen, that means there is a range of times that could count as satisfying the content of the experiences. So if my experience represents that E happens more or less at t, it's okay if E happens at $t - 1$ millisecond. 1 millisecond is not a perceptible time interval, so a delay of that length between the event I perceive and my experience is not enough to make the event fail to correspond to the content of my experience (in other words, it is not enough to say that the event seemed to happen at a time different from the time it did happen).

7. The Causal Argument

It is well known that an object does not directly cause a perceptual experience in an observer—that there are intermediary processes that must take place in order for one to perceive a thing. In order for me to see the cup on the table, for instance, light rays have to travel the distance between the cup and my eye. Then electrical signals have to travel down my optic nerve. Then my brain has to process the information. All these events intervene between the object I take myself to be seeing and my experience of seeming to see it. Therefore, must we not conclude that I am not "directly aware" of the object?

This sort of worry rests upon a misunderstanding of the term "direct awareness." If being directly aware of a thing meant being aware of it with no causal intermediaries between it and your state of awareness, then direct realism would be swiftly dispensed with on empirical grounds. But if being directly aware of a thing means having awareness of it not based upon one's awareness of anything else, then these considerations are irrelevant, for the aforementioned processes intervening between the cup and my experience of a cup do not include any states of awareness. They are simply blind physical processes, with a mental state at their end. This mental state, this experience, is not based upon any other mental states, and its object is the cup out there, rather than any of the intermediary processes. Brain processes cause my visual experience, but I am not seeing brain processes; I am seeing the cup.[10]

8. The Illusoriness of Secondary Qualities

According to this next objection, the physical objects around you are really colorless. The colors you think you are seeing on the surfaces of physical objects either do not exist, or exist only in the mind, as properties of sense data. A number of considerations support this startling conclusion.

First, there is the way that the apparent colors of things vary depending on the lighting conditions. An object will appear to be a slightly different color under indoor, fluorescent lighting than in daylight and a very different color under, say, a red light. It would seem contradictory to say the object has two or more of these colors simultaneously; therefore, if colors are really out there, in the object, we must ask: what are the *correct* lighting conditions, that is, the lighting conditions under which the object manifests its true color? But there seems to be no nonarbitrary answer to that. You might want to say that the object must be under white light, of course (so the color the object manifests under the red light is an illusion), but one would still have to choose between sunlight; indoor, incandescent lighting; fluorescent lighting; and so on. Well, perhaps the true color is seen when the ambient light contains all the wavelengths in the visible spectrum, in equal amounts (measured by energy). But since sunlight does not satisfy this condition, this would mean that objects are generally not the colors we perceive them to be. Furthermore, the apparent colors of things will also depend upon the *brightness* of the ambient light. When the light is dim, things take on a more bluish look than they do in bright light. And how is one to pick a privileged level of brightness?

It seems that any answer one gives to the question *Which of the colors we seem to see under various lighting conditions is the true color of the object?* will have to be merely stipulative. One can make a stipulative answer if one likes, of course—for example, for some purposes it might be convenient to call the color that manifests under bright, direct sunlight the "true color." But the point is that there is nothing in the nature of the object itself that forces such a decision. There seems to be no reason why it would not be equally legitimate for someone else to stipulate that the 'true color' of an object be the color it manifests under 50-watt fluorescent lights. And that only means that the object does not have any true color in and of itself. And yet we seem to see colors actually on the surfaces of the external objects. So that appearance is an illusion.[11]

Put this another way: assume that color is really an objective property of the surfaces of physical objects. Then a physical object can have one and only one color (in a given place at a given time). But there is no way for us to determine what the real color of an object is, since it appears different under different lighting conditions, and we have no reason to believe one of these lighting conditions to be better than the others. Nor do hypotheses about what is the true color of an object entail any testable predictions about anything else observable. But if we can never know the true color of anything, then why believe things have any true colors at all? Ockham's razor would seem to dictate the elimination of such unknowable and explanatorily useless properties.

Second, if you bought that argument, consider the variations in color perception among normal humans. Without even considering colorblind people, it is common to have two people disagree about the color of an object—for example, *A* says the shirt is red, *B* says it is orange. The simplest explanation for this is that *A* and *B* have slightly different visual experiences, such that the shirt appears to *A* more similar to the paradigmatic red objects (e.g., ripe apples, fire engines) than to the paradigmatic orange objects, while for *B* the reverse is the case.

A related experiment asks people to identify "unique green" on the color spectrum. Unique green is defined as a color that looks completely green, not at all yellowish and not at all bluish. Different people will pick out different samples as unique green, with wavelengths of reflected light varying by up to 30 nanometers (this is a very definitely noticeable difference).[12]

If colors are really out there in the objects, this raises the question *Whose color perceptions are right?* It seems that different people perceive the same object as having (slightly) different colors and that the object cannot really have both (e.g., an object cannot simultaneously be orange and red). But again, there is no nonarbitrary way of picking out a privileged individual or class of individuals to be the bearers of the veridical color perceptions. If we wanted to, we could maintain that objects have real colors, but we just do not *know* whose color perceptions (if anyone's) are accurate. But again this would go against Ockham's razor, the simpler theory being that there are no such properties, and that different people simply experience different qualia in response to the same physical stimulus.

Third, we can make almost the same argument again by appealing to the more radical differences in color perception among species. Some animals can only perceive differences of light and dark, and not differences of hue.[13] The way objects look to them cannot be the way they look to us. Moreover, it would seem that those animals must perceive objects to have colors *incompatible* with the colors we perceive the same objects to have. If I look at an apple and see it as being red, and the animal sees that same object as being grey, then one of us must be wrong, misled about the real color. Again, it would seem arbitrary to declare ourselves the ones with the correct perceptions. One might want to appeal to the fact that we have greater discriminatory capacities than those animals. But then, there are other species that can see more colors than we can;[14] so if that consideration determines whose perceptions are "right," we will have to admit that our perceptions are wrong.

We take a different tack in our fourth argument for the illusoriness of color:

1. If an object is composed entirely of parts that are colorless, then that object is colorless.
2. All middle-sized physical objects are composed entirely of subatomic particles (protons, electrons, neutrons, and so on).
3. Subatomic particles are colorless.

4.   Therefore, all middle-sized physical objects are colorless.

Premise (1) appears to be a necessary truth. In other words, if A and B are each colorless, then the aggregate (A + B) is not going to be, say, purple; rather, it must also be colorless. Premise (2) is something we know from modern physics. Likewise, it seems, for (3)—at least to the extent that modern physical theory does not attribute colors to subatomic particles. (The physicists do have a theoretical property called "color" that they attribute to quarks, along with "charm" and "strangeness," but it has nothing to do with color in the sense that we're talking about.) You might say that, since no one can see an individual subatomic particle, we do not really know that they are not colored. But there is no reason to believe they are; the hypothesis, say, that protons are brown would have no explanatory value in physics or chemistry; it would make no difference to anything that we observe. Furthermore, the supposed brownness of the protons would have nothing to do with the brown that we often see, for example, in tree branches or dirt, since it would not have anything to do with wavelengths of light reflected to our eyes, as does the latter. Given that, it is of questionable intelligibility that the protons could even be brown in the same sense as tree branches and dirt are.

   Finally, notice that the hypothesis that middle-sized physical objects are really colored, like the hypothesis that elementary particles are colored, has no explanatory value in understanding color perception. In the scientific account of what causes our visual experiences, including our apparent seeing of color, one need not mention the actual colors of anything. This is quite different from our perception of, for example, the shape of an object. If you want to explain why the table causes me to have an experience representing a rectangular, brown object, you have to cite the rectangular shape of the table, but you do *not* have to cite the brown color of the table. Rather, you cite the pattern of wavelengths of electromagnetic radiation that reflect off the surface of the table. And although a scientist might be able to identify properties of the surface of the table that explain why it reflects light in just that way, these properties would not include the intrinsic "brownness" of the surface. Well, and what does that mean? That seems to mean that even if there is brownness in the surface of the table, we're not perceiving it, since it is causally irrelevant to our experience. Only the "scientific" properties of the surface, such as the kind and arrangement of molecules in it, are causally relevant.

   Such are the arguments for the illusoriness of color. These arguments leave two alternatives open—if one accepts that physical objects aren't colored, one might thence conclude that nothing has color, or one might conclude that colors are properties of sense data, rather than being properties of physical objects. On the former view, our seeming perceptions of color are just hallucinations or illusions. On the latter view, physical objects reflect certain kinds of light to our eyes; our brains process the signals arriving and construct mental images with colors in them. The colors are *correlated* with the wavelengths of light, but the colors are properties of the images, not the physical objects. The widespread impression that physical objects have colors is due to the widespread tendency we have to confuse our sense data with the real (physical) objects.

I believe that similar arguments can be given for tastes, smells, and sounds, to the effect that they are not in the objective, physical world either. Be that as it may, for the sake of brevity we focus only on colors.

Now, the only things we ever see are colored things. The visual field is filled with nothing but colors—one could make the argument that the only primary objects of visual awareness are patches of color (that is, whenever one sees anything that isn't itself a color, one sees it only *by* seeing some colors). One makes out the shape of an object by discriminating its color from that of its background. But we just argued above that physical objects are colorless. Therefore, it can't be the physical objects that we're seeing. It must be only sense data (or nothing at all). In sum:

1. If a thing has no color, it cannot be seen.
2. Physical objects have no color.
3. Therefore, physical objects cannot be seen.

Or, if you prefer: all physical objects are invisible.

Well, at this point, it would seem that something has gone wrong, for this conclusion is hardly to be believed. I think the argument can be attacked in both its premises.

To begin with, (1) is quite disputable. Take a case in which we would, even from a common sense standpoint, admit that one is not seeing the (real) colors of physical objects: let's say that Bob has a pair of severely green-tinted glasses. When he puts on the glasses, everything looks green or black, regardless of what is (as we would ordinarily say) its true color. So now Bob has a red tomato in front of him. He puts on the glasses, and the tomato looks a very dark green or black. In this case, Bob is not seeing the color of the tomato, nor is he seeing the color of anything else in the environment (assume that nothing else nearby is anywhere close to the color it appears). Notice that this is the intuitive conclusion—I don't mean this in the sense that the tomato doesn't have a color; I mean that, even according to the common sense view in which the tomato has a color, Bob is not seeing its color. Even so, it would be quite farfetched to claim that Bob is not even seeing the tomato at all. (If this were so, then night-vision goggles, which make everything look green, would be a sham, since their whole purpose is to enable the wearer to see things at night.) How might this be explained, according to my account of perception? A natural explanation is to say that Bob sees the tomato by virtue of seeing the shape of the tomato. Bob can do this, since there is no distortion in the tomato's apparent shape (notwithstanding that the shape is discriminated by means of the visual experience's representation of the distribution of colors in the field of view).

Thus, it seems that, if physical objects can have colors, it is possible to see a physical object even though its actual color is radically different from its apparent color. If you accept that, then you should also accept the possibility of a case where one sees a physical object even though it has no actual color. Suppose that Bob's glasses also have the effect of making perfectly transparent objects appear green (of a different shade from the background). In this case, besides distorting Bob's color perception, the glasses would give Bob a cognitive advantage—intuitively, they would enable him to see otherwise transparent objects. In fact, if you like, you can imagine that the glasses were designed for this very purpose, and it certainly seems logically possible to suppose that they could succeed in this aim, though of course they could not succeed in making Bob see the color of the transparent objects. And this seems to be true for exactly the same reasons that it is true to say Bob sees the tomato.

Perhaps physical objects, on the indirect realist/skeptical view we're combating, are not equivalent to *transparent* objects, despite the fact that both sorts of things are colorless. Still, it is hard to see why, if being able to make out the shape of the transparent object suffices for perceiving it, being able to make out the shape of any physical object would not suffice for perceiving it—in which case physical objects could be perceived in the same way that Bob perceives the tomato and the transparent object in my thought experiments, even if we granted that physical objects have no color.

So much for premise (1). Premise (2) is also highly doubtful. There have been a number of philosophical theories about the nature of color, including:

a. There is no such thing as color.
b. Colors are properties of sense data.
c. Colors are dispositions that physical objects have to cause experiences of certain sorts in us.
d. Colors are dispositions that physical objects have to reflect light in certain ways.
e. Colors are complex properties of the surfaces of objects, including perhaps their textures and the electron structures of the molecules they contain, that explain the dispositions spoken of in (c) and (d).
f. Colors are undefinable and irreducible properties of the surfaces of physical objects. By calling them "irreducible" I mean they are not

identical with any of the things spoken of in (c), (d), or (e), nor with anything else along those general lines.

The arguments we just discussed are all arguments against position (f), assuming that if one rejects that view, one must then accept either (a) or (b), which of course creates problems for direct realism. To preserve direct realism against this assault, I don't need to determine what is the correct theory of color. This is fortunate, since in fact I do not know. All I need to do is show that (a) and (b) are not the most plausible alternatives. Alternatives (c), (d), and (e) all allow that physical objects are colored and so present no problem for direct realism as far as the present argument is concerned. It will suffice, then, to show that something along the lines of (c), (d), or (e) is more plausible than (a) or (b).

I think that (b) is implausible primarily because I don't believe in sense data. The reasons for that, however, will have to wait until chapter VII. I think (a) is implausible because it just seems obvious that I'm seeing a brown thing now. And I think (a) and (b) are both implausible *if* they imply that physical objects are invisible.

I propose to elaborate position (d), as perhaps the most natural and widely held sort of view. According to this view, colors are kinds of spectral reflectance distributions, which is to say, roughly, complex dispositions that surfaces have to reflect various wavelengths of light in various amounts.[15] The main philosophical objection to such a view derives from the problem of metamers. Metamers are different spectral reflectance patterns that nevertheless look the same to the human eye (in fixed lighting conditions; see figure 6.2). In other words, it is possible to have two surfaces that have very different spectral reflectance distributions, but that nevertheless look the same to us, so that we would classify them as the same color. If the surfaces have different spectral reflectance distributions but the same color, this would seem to show that colors are not just spectral reflectance distributions.[16]

The response to this objection is that what counts as "the same" or "different" is relative to a classification scheme, and the system of categories used by the scientists studying spectral reflectance distributions need not be the same as the one used by ordinary language.

To explain what I mean about relativity to a classification scheme, look at the following two inscriptions:

The cat is on the mat.
The cat is on the mat.

Are those inscriptions the same or different? Well, in one way, or in one system of classification, they are the same inscription. They both contain the same sequence of words, and if that is what you care about, then that makes them "the same." Suppose, for instance, that you are quoting what another author has written. If the author used a different typeface from the one you use in making the attribution, that does not count, in that context, as his having written something different. Likewise, if you are a judge examining a copyright infringement claim, the difference in typefaces does not count as a relevant difference; the above two inscriptions would count as "the same" for those purposes. On the other hand, if you are a typesetter, the above inscriptions will not count as the same; for typesetting purposes, the substitution of the second inscription for the first would be a material alteration, as it would not in the previous two contexts. The set of categories used by the typesetter makes finer discriminations than that used by the judge and the author, but neither of them is more *intrinsically* right than the other; each of them simply is appropriate to its own context. If you use the typesetter classification in deciding the copyright claim, then you are using the wrong system of classification for that context.

I once saw a comedienne on television have an exchange with a man in the

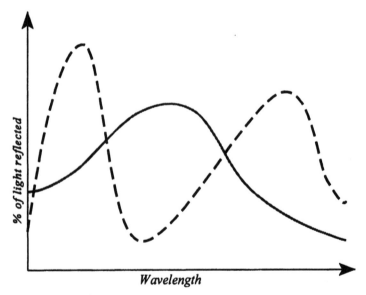

Figure 6.2. Metamers. Surfaces with the two spectral reflectance distributions shown would look the same. The diagram is qualitatively but not quantitatively accurate. Cf. Hilbert, 86; Hardin, *Color for Philosophers*, 47, 75.

audience that went something like this:

Comedienne: What kind of car do you have?
Man: A Pontiac Firebird.
Comedienne: Ask me what kind of car I have.
Man: What kind of car do you have?
Comedienne: A white car.

The idea of the joke is that the man from the audience and the comedienne have different systems of classification for cars. For him, the make and model are important, so different color Pontiac Firebirds would count as "the same kind" of car. For her, two white cars count as "the same kind," but a white Firebird and a green one would count as different kinds of car. Again, what is the same or different is relative to a system of classification.

Taking this point, then, we can say that there are two different systems for classifying colors. The scientific classification of spectral reflectance distributions (which are, in fact, colors) makes finer discriminations than the ordinary, everyday classification, but this does not make the latter wrong in an intrinsic sense; it simply answers to different interests. In the everyday sense, two surfaces will count as "the same color" when we can't tell them apart visually. But for scientific purposes, we can slice colors more finely. In other words, a word like "red" covers a set of different (from the scientific standpoint) spectral reflectance distributions that all cause a similar quale in us, and for a thing to be red is just for it to have one of the spectral reflectance distributions in that set.[17]

I am not asserting that this theory is true, because I don't have strong grounds for rejecting alternatives (c) and (e). What I am asserting, however, is that this theory is at least better than theories (a) and (b).

We turn, now, to the first argument for the illusoriness of color: the apparent colors of things vary depending on the lighting conditions, so what are the conditions under which we perceive the true colors of objects?

The obvious answer is: *normal* lighting conditions. That means reasonably (but not blindingly) bright, white light. So the pink look of objects under red light is just an illusion, as is the bluish look of objects in dim light. This corresponds with our ordinary way of thinking—people will often, if having trouble discerning the color of an object, try taking it into more favorable lighting conditions—specifically, bright, white light—in order to determine its true color. We don't think that at night, the grass has actually turned gray, and we don't think that when we shut off the lights, everything is black.

But what of the differences in apparent colors of objects under different kinds of bright, white lights such as sunlight, incandescent light bulbs, and fluorescent light bulbs? Which of those lighting conditions is most "favorable"? Here, I think the answer has to be that all species of bright, white light are equally good. That is, each kind of bright, white light is a possible, legitimate interpretation of "normal lighting conditions." Since a given visual experience represents a given object as having the spectral reflectance distribution that causes experiences of that kind (that is, experiences with that particular sort of sensory quale) *under normal conditions*, this means that there are multiple, equally legitimate interpretations of what spectral reflectance distribution a given visual experience represents an object to have. That is, the experience has a content that is to some degree indeterminate. Notice that I am not saying there is any indeterminacy in the objective world; rather, there is an indeterminacy in the mapping from mental states onto the states of the world that they represent.

The vagueness of words in ordinary language provides an example of the same sort of indeterminacy; for example, there is no objective fact of the matter as to exactly how many seconds a person must have been alive in order for him to count as "old," so the content of "old" is indeterminate. It can equally legitimately be interpreted as picking out any of a range of distinct properties.

This means that there is no fact of the matter as to whether a surface really possesses a certain very specific shade of red, when that shade is one that people "see" under some normal lighting conditions but not under others—because there is no fact of the matter as to exactly what that shade *is*, that is, what class of spectral reflectance distributions it is. Nevertheless, there is a definite fact that a given, paradigmatically red object—say, a ripe tomato—is *red*, as opposed to orange, green, etc. This is because under *any* of the legitimate ways of interpreting what "normal conditions" are, objects with the spectral reflectance distribution that the tomato in fact has will cause the relevant sort of quale (a red* quale) under normal conditions. Under no conditions that could reasonably be considered normal will an object with that spectral reflectance distribution cause an orange* quale, or a green* quale, etc.

The second argument for the illusoriness of color appealed to the variations in color experiences among normal humans, while the third appealed to the variations among species. My response to these two arguments is the same. I say that these differences are differences in the qualia of the visual experiences, not in their contents. As a result, it need not be the case that one person, or one species, is "wrong." There is no uniquely right way for qualia to get matched up with spectral reflectance distributions.

To put that in other terms: color qualia are our means of detecting certain objective properties of the surfaces of objects (spectral reflectances). However, the same quale might detect different properties for different creatures. For one creature, Q might detect spectral reflectance distribution S_1, whereas in another creature, Q detects S_2. The property that the experience in question *represents* is determined by what, in the world, normally causes experiences with that quale. So a visual experience with quale Q represents there to be an object having that surface property that under normal conditions causes one to have experiences with Q. For the one creature, that surface property might be S_1, while for the other creature, it is S_2.

The fourth argument for the illusoriness of color went like this:

1. If an object is composed entirely of parts that are colorless, then that object is colorless.
2. All middle-sized physical objects are composed entirely of subatomic particles (protons, electrons, neutrons, and so on).
3. Subatomic particles are colorless.
4. Therefore, all middle-sized physical objects are colorless.

Given that colors are spectral reflectance distributions, we'll have to reject premise (1). A single electron may not have a spectral reflectance distribution, but the entire surface of which it is a part certainly does.

On the other hand, how do we account for the intuitive sense that (1) is true? Someone might well think that since (1) seems to be true about colors, although the analogous statement is not true about spectral reflectance distributions, that is reason for thinking colors are *not* spectral reflectance distributions.

To some extent we can explain away the intuition as being due to a limited experience: (1) is true of almost all of the things we can see. For instance, if you take a red piece of paper and cut it in half, you will find both halves to be red. If you take a clear piece of glass and join it to another clear piece of glass, the resultant glass will still be transparent. But, we may say, we don't have any direct experience with subatomic particles (we can't see them), and it just turns out that what applies to macroscopic objects does not apply to their microscopic parts. The sense that (1) is true derives from an induction based upon our experience with certain macroscopic objects, but this induction is fallible, and we have scientific evidence that shows it to be false by showing that subatomic particles lack color.

Another reply we can make is that (1) is not even true of all the objects we observe. For instance, a single drop of water, or even a glassful, is colorless. But a very large quantity of water, like a lake or ocean, is not colorless; it is blue. Similarly, a single pane of glass might be colorless, but twenty such panes put together might turn out to have a translucent, whitish color.

No air molecule is blue, nor is any moderately sized volume of air, but the sky is blue. The blueness of the sky, of course, is not a surface spectral reflectance distribution, since there is no surface there, and so one would have to give a different theory about what constitutes the sky's blueness from our theory about what constitutes the blueness of a blue surface (the sky is blue, incidentally, because air molecules scatter more short wavelength light than long wavelength light)—but that is not our concern here. Our concern is simply to undermine the specific argument against the reality of colors given above, by undermining the plausibility of its first premise. These examples indicate that a color can be, in a certain weak sense, an emergent property—a property that a whole has that is not possessed by any of its parts.

Notes

1. Hume, *Enquiry* XII.1, p. 152 (punctuation altered to conform to modern conventions).

2. The conditions here should probably rather be stated counterfactually, for example, "if the object's properties *were* different, the experience *would be* different in a parallel way." Compare Nozick's similar tracking conditions for knowledge (172-78).

3. Reid, 176-79. Reid's terminology is "apparent magnitude" (for angular size) and "real magnitude" (for linear size), but I consider that terminology misleading; it suggests that what we are aware of by the sense of sight is a mere appearance, which is not what the direct realist intends.

4. Austin, 29-30.

5. Compare the argument of section IV.3.1.

6. See chapter IV, sections 1, 3.2, and 3.3.

7. Fumerton, *Metaphysical and Epistemological Problems*, 78ff.

8. I do not mean that the visual experience has a self-contradictory content, like "There is a single finger which is simultaneously here and there." Rather, the visual experience represents that there is a finger here, and there is a finger there. Note the difference between "there seems to be a single finger both here and there," and "there is a single finger that seems to be both here and there."

9. There are other possibilities, of course—for example, that if A precedes B, A is represented as later than its actual time, but if A follows B, A is represented correctly, while B is represented as later than its actual time. My point is that the way A's time of occurrence is represented would have to change depending on what precedes or follows it. And what shall we say if A both slightly precedes B and slightly follows C?

10. Cf. Kelley, 75-79.

11. Russell, *The Problems of Philosophy*, 9-10, gives this argument, defending the view that colors are properties of sense data.

12. See Hardin, *Color for Philosophers*, 79-80; Byrne and Hilbert, "Colors and Reflectances," 272-74.

13. This includes some rodents and perhaps foxes and sheep. Contrary to commonly held belief, it does not include cats and dogs, which appear to have some color vision. See Jacobs, chapter 5.

14. Birds generally have better color vision than humans. Some are tetrachromats at least (having four primary colors), and possibly pentachromats, in contrast to our trichromacy. Hence, they can see colors (or perhaps I should say, experience color qualia) that we cannot. See Varela et al. for a summary of the relevant scientific evidence, which includes both physiological and behavioral evidence.

15. Here I follow Byrne and Hilbert, "Colors and Reflectances." This is only a theory of colors for physical surfaces, of course; it does not say what it is for a ray of light or transparent volume to be colored. The colors of physical surfaces are what we are mainly interested in for the purposes of defending the possibility of seeing physical objects.

16. Hardin, *Color for Philosophers*, 7, 46-8. My response to the objection roughly follows that of Byrne and Hilbert, "Colors and Reflectances," 265-67, 274-79.

17. Readers familiar with the philosophy of mind literature will appreciate the parallel between this view of colors and Davidson's anomalous monism (see his "Mental Events"). Ordinary, everyday-type colors supervene on spectral reflectance distributions—so there cannot be a difference in ordinary-color without a difference in spectral reflectance—but there is no type identity between any given kind of spectral reflectance distribution and any given ordinary-color. This is analogous to the relationship between mental and physical predicates in Davidson's (though not my) view.

VII. An Objection to Indirect Realism: The Problem of Spatial Properties

I have two major objections to indirect realism. One is epistemological: indirect realists make much easier targets for skeptics than direct realists do, as I think will become clearer in chapter VIII. To the extent that one regards the avoidance of skepticism as a requisite for an acceptable theory of knowledge (and I do—see chapter III), this is a strong argument for favoring direct realism.[1]

The other major objection, which I will focus on in this chapter, is metaphysical. The indirect realist says that in perception, we are directly aware (only) of some sort of mental phenomena, which we're calling "sense data."[2] The problem I want to raise for the indirect realist centers around the question *Where are sense data located?* I can think of five (nonarbitrary) answers the representationalist might give to this:

a. Sense data have no location.
b. Sense data are *literally* in your head, that is, in the space where your brain is.
c. Sense data are in the same places as the physical objects that cause them. For instance, your sense datum of a table, caused by looking at a table, is located where that table is.
d. Sense data are located wherever they appear to be.
e. Sense data are located in an alternate space, separate from the space of physical objects.

I do not find any of these answers to be believable; I will explain why in this chapter. My argument against sense data, in brief, is this:

1. In perception, the things I am directly aware of (at least sometimes) have

      locations.
2.   Only physical things have locations.
3.   Therefore, the things I am directly aware of in perception (at least sometimes) are physical things.[3]

To defend this argument, I need to rebut each of the five theories the indirect realist might put forward in answer to the question of where sense data are located. (The first of the five theories would amount to a rejection of premise 1. The others would amount to a rejection of premise 2.)

1. "Sense Data Have No Location"

This answer would appeal to those indirect realists for whom the mental phenomena in question are mental states or properties (where these are distinct from physical states, including brain states)—states which perhaps represent things in space but which are not themselves in space.[4] However, I find this answer implausible, for the following reason:

1.   In perception, I am immediately aware of things with *spatial properties* (things with shapes, sizes, and spatial relations to each other).[5]
2.   Whatever has spatial properties has a location.
3.   Therefore, the things I am thus aware of have locations.

Premise (2) seems self-evident. If a thing has no location, that means it does not occupy space, and if it does not occupy space, then it has no size or shape. For example, an abstract object such as the number 2 has no spatial location. It is not in Taiwan or on the moon. It also has no size (in the sense of length, height, and/or depth) or shape.

      Could the indirect realist plausibly reject (1)? Well, I certainly *seem* to be aware of things with shapes, sizes, and so on. When I look at the book on my table, I am (as far as I can tell) aware of something green and (in profile) rectangular. I am also aware of other things around it (a cup, the surface of the table, and so on), but all of these things have shapes too. If there is some shapeless, nonspatial entity in the offing, I have no inkling of it. Nor can I recall ever having been visually aware of such a thing. Nor, as a matter of fact, can I even imagine what it would be like to enjoy visual awareness of such a thing. I am, admittedly, sometimes aware of nonspatial things. I am aware of the number 2, the fundamental theorem of calculus, and my own thoughts and feelings, and I don't think any of these things are in space. But I cannot imagine what it would be like to be *visually* or *perceptually* aware of those things. And if sense data (or "appearances") are nonspatial entities, then I'm pretty sure they are not among the things I am aware of now, merely insofar as I am seeing the book. Insofar as I see this book, the green rectangular thing seems to be the only relevant object of awareness (plus the book and the book's surface and properties, if these are not the same as the green rectangle).

Perhaps, in response, the indirect realist will say that the thing I am immediately aware of only *seems* to have spatial properties, whereas in actuality, it is a mental state that has no spatial properties. Perhaps it seems to have spatial properties in part because it *represents* spatial properties—though it isn't quite clear how this works. (My *belief* that the book is rectangular represents a spatial property too, but this does not tend to make my belief itself seem rectangular.)

This move would involve a shift from the traditional indirect realist position—traditionally, indirect realists introduced sense data in order to explain how it was possible for physical objects to appear different from the way they are. Now we find that sense data themselves can appear different from how they are (with a vengeance—they can appear to have shapes and colors when in fact they have none), and so according to the traditional motivation for introducing sense data, it would seem that we should now introduce sense data of sense data. To avoid this unencouraging step, our indirect realist will need to eschew the traditional motivation for sense data as I have just described it. There are several different arguments for sense data, so this may not prove to be a problem.

The more serious problem, in my view, is that the position now under discussion is incompatible with the conception of awareness sketched in section IV.1. There, I defined awareness of x as a kind of relation to x in which (among other things), x at least roughly satisfies the content of a representational mental state. That is to say, a person counts as aware of a thing only if he has an at least roughly adequate representation of it. It follows from this conception of awareness[6] that it is conceptually impossible for a thing to appear utterly different from the way it is. Some cases of illusion are allowed—a thing can have a somewhat different shape and color from the shape and color it appears to have, and there is no sharp dividing line indicating how much "distortion" is too much. However, if an object has no size, shape, location, or color (since a color requires a size and shape) at all, then I think it is clear that it cannot appear as, say, a green book—that would be a too radical divergence between appearance and reality, if anything would. If I have a mental state representing there to be something green and rectangular, the object of this mental state cannot be a colorless, shapeless entity. For this reason, I do not think the indirect realist can sustain the position that the objects of awareness in perception are things that merely appear to have locations but actually do not.

Given the assumption that sense data lack spatial properties and given that our perceptions are (at least apparently) of things with spatial properties, the external, physical objects would certainly be better candidates for the objects of awareness than sense data. Which would mean that, since being the immediate objects of awareness in perception is a defining characteristic of sense data, sense data do not exist.

I need to be careful here about stating the point of distinction between my own view and that of the sort of indirect realist we're discussing here (the sort who says, "Sense data have no location"). I, of course, believe in the existence of mental states called "perceptual experiences" which, in my view, have no location.[7] Nor do I deny that we can be aware of such states, even directly aware of them (by introspection). What I deny is that I am aware of a perceptual experience *insofar as* I perceive, for example, this book. More specifically, I deny that my awareness of the book is *based on* an awareness of a perceptual experience or other mental state. This is shown by the fact that I can see the book without at the same time enjoying awareness of any (relevant) nonphysical thing.

2. "Sense Data Are in Your Head"

At first glance, this answer seems naive—as if, when I see a green book, there must be a green, book-shaped thing in my head. Scientific investigation (brain surgery, brain scans) will not bear out such a hypothesis.

Of course, the sense datum theorist could plead that sense data are invisible to all but the person whose sense data they are. And even that person could not "see" them with his eyes—if you had your skull opened up while still conscious and you had mirrors set up so you could look at your brain, no one thinks that in addition to seeing your brain and the surrounding scenery, you would also see a miniature image of the whole scene embedded somewhere in your brain. Sense data, if they exist, are not perceived by directing your sense organs at them. Rather, you are *automatically* aware (without the use of any sense organ) of a sense datum when you have it, and you get sense data by directing your sense organs at other (external) things. This explains why, even if sense data are in your head, no one ever sees them there.

Still, why might someone be tempted to locate sense data in the head? Suppose you wanted to be an indirect realist but without being committed to the existence of nonphysical things. You might, then, think that mental phenomena (including sense data) *are* just states, processes, and/or properties of the brain. Since brain states are located in the brain, that must be where the sense data are.[8]

Understood this way, the view seems less naive than it seemed at first glance. Yet, while this reasoning permits us to attribute locations and other spatial properties to sense data, it does not give us *the right* spatial properties. The thing I am apprehending is green and shaped like a book. Although my current brain state *might* have a shape (I am not sure whether states can have shapes), it is not green or book-shaped. So this theory fares little better than the last one. We still run afoul of the content-satisfaction condition on awareness: I seem to be seeing a green book. The actual green book satisfies the content of this visual experience. My brain, or some part, state, or property of it, does not, not even remotely. Therefore, while my visual experience might be of the book, it cannot be of my brain, or some part, state, or property of my brain. That is why I am not seeing my brain.

The indirect realist might avoid this objection by holding that the sense data in my head really do have the shapes and colors that I seem to perceive objects to have—that is, there is a green rectangle in my head now. This position is odd enough that I do not know whether anyone actually holds it,[9] so I won't spend too much time on it.

First, note that the position now under consideration rules out identifying sense data with brain states, since the two have different spatial and other properties (including color, smell, and so forth). No brain state of mine typically has the color, shape, smell, and so on of the sense data I am allegedly aware of (except in the rare case where I am looking at, smelling, or otherwise observing a brain), so my sense data are not brain states. With that understood, it seems that there is now no reason why sense data should be thought to be in the head.

Second: If visual sense data have the properties that I appear to see (e.g., "green," "rectangular"), what about tactile properties? Shouldn't we also say that when I touch something I have tactile sense data and that these tactile sense data have the properties that I appear to be feeling? I think the sense data theorist will agree. Now, when I touch the book, I seem to feel something solid ("solid" here being used in the sense of "hard," rather than "filled all the way through")—in sense data language, we would say I am having a sense datum of solidity. Thus, my sense datum is actually solid. So there is a solid, rectangular object in my head. It appears when I touch the book and disappears when I stop touching it. Why doesn't it get in the way of the brain material that's already in there? The old maxim that two things cannot occupy the same space at the same time would seem to apply here. It is true that my brain is a bit mushy, so a solid object, if it wasn't too big, could push the brain material aside—but I doubt anyone believes that is what is happening.

There is one further argument that could be deployed here, which is the argument from indeterminacy, but I will defer it to section VII.6.

3. "Sense Data Are in the Same Place as the Distal Object"

The "distal object" is the object that you normally think you're perceiving—for example, the book when you think you're perceiving a book. Of course, it is questionable whether you can be said to perceive a book if the sense data theory is true; in this case, the distal object is merely the distant object "out there" that causes your sense data.

So, according to this view, my sense datum of a book is in the same place as the actual, physical book that is causing me to have the sense datum, though perhaps the sense datum is only at the book's surface and not its interior.

Like the position discussed in section 2, this view runs into the objection that two objects cannot be in the same place at the same time. Why doesn't the sense datum get in the way of the physical object that's already there? The indirect realist would have to plead that sense data are special in this respect, as in so many others—unlike the case with two physical objects, a sense datum can be colocated with a physical object or another sense datum, as in the case where two people see something in the same place at the same time. There could even be thousands of sense data in the same place at the same time, for instance, at the outer surface of the pitcher's body during a baseball game. I do not claim that this view is logically contradictory, only that it is bizarre and counterintuitive.

Consider a further consequence. I go outside at night with my eyes closed. I turn my head skyward and then open my eyes. At the instant my eyes open or very shortly thereafter, I have an experience of seeming to see thousands of stars. If this involves my having sense data, and the sense data are located at the surfaces of the distal objects causing them, then what happens in that instant is that thousands of my sense data are "transmitted," so to speak, to various places across the galaxy, some of them thousands of light-years from Earth. All that is proximately caused, since my experience is proximately caused, by the electrochemical reactions in my brain.

One problem is that this seems to conflict with the theory of relativity. The reason is that, according to relativity, there is no objective time ordering to spacelike separated events, and that apparently implies that such events cannot be causally related. To explain that in simple terms:

Figure 7.1 is a spacetime diagram, representing different locations in spacetime. In reality, of course, spacetime is four-dimensional, but I cannot draw a four-dimensional object on a piece of paper, so I have suppressed two spatial dimensions, representing space as just the horizontal dimension on the page. Also, relativity does not permit an *objective* separation between spatial and temporal dimensions, so this is really a picture of spacetime *as represented in some particular frame of reference.*

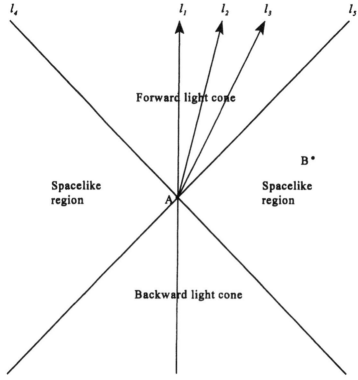

Figure 7.1. Spacetime. The vertical direction is the temporal dimension, the future being up on the page. The horizontal direction is spatial.

If an object is stationary (in the reference frame used by the diagram), its path through spacetime will be a vertical line, since it has the same spatial coordinates at each different time. For example, if an object at point A were to remain stationary, it would trace out line l_1. If the object moved to the right at a constant velocity, its path (that is, the set of spacetime points it occupied) would look like l_2. The faster it was moving, the more *slanted* the line would be. Thus, l_3 represents a faster motion to the right than l_2 does. I use lines l_4 and l_5 to represent the speed of light; if someone sends out light rays to the left and right from point A, they trace out the lines marked l_4 and l_5. (The portion of the lines *below* A represent the paths of light rays, traveling toward each other, that would meet at point A.) The region of spacetime above point A but between lines l_4 and l_5 (all the places that it would be possible to get to from A by traveling at or below the speed of light) is A's forward light cone. It is also called A's "absolute future," because the points in that region are in A's future according to any reference frame. The backward light cone (A's absolute past) can be defined analogously.

Now, the important point is this. According to the theory of relativity, if an event is in the forward or backward light cone of A, then it has an absolute temporal relation to an event located at A; it is either definitely after the event at A or definitely before it, respectively. *Otherwise*, however, its temporal relation to A is relative to a reference frame. Which is to say: if an event is outside A's light cone, then there is no objective fact as to whether it is before A, after A, or simultaneous with A. Take point B, for instance. According to some inertial reference frames, an event occurring at B is earlier than an event located at A; according to other inertial frames, it is later; and according to still other inertial frames, they are simultaneous—all of these reference frames being equally good. (The reference frame of the diagram has B occurring later than A, since B is drawn higher up on the page.)

Events in one another's light cones are called "timelike separated," while events outside one another's light cones are "spacelike separated." So we can sum up the important principle as, "Spacelike separated events have no absolute time ordering." This is an important principle of relativity theory.

Now to return to the sense data. We have "established" that, an instant after I open my eyes, the events going on in my brain cause a sense datum to appear at the location of a star thousands of light-years away. These two events are certainly outside one another's light cones (nothing traveling at or below the speed of light could get from my brain to the star in the instant it takes for me to have the experience). Thus, according to relativity theory, there is no objective time ordering to the events. But this is inadmissible for the sense datum theorist. He needs the sense datum's appearance to happen at the same time as, or very shortly after, the brain events, since the sense datum is supposed to exist during precisely the time I have the experience of seeming to see a star. Thus, the present version of the sense data theory is incompatible with the theory of relativity.

This should refute this version of indirect realism to the satisfaction of those who accept the theory of relativity. I will not press the objection too hard, however, because there are other phenomena (having to do with Bell's Theorem) that seem to contravene the theory of relativity in the same way,[10] which the indirect realist could use to argue that the operative part of relativity theory is false. So I would rather place the emphasis on some more common-sense-based arguments.

Consider dreams and hallucinations. In these cases, there are no distal objects, so no places for the sense data to be located, according to the present theory. Yet the indirect realist would be hard pressed to deny that sense data exist in these cases. After all, hallucinations are one of the central kinds of phenomena that sense data are supposed to explain.

We might try locating the sense data involved in hallucinations somewhere different from those involved in normal perceptions. Perhaps hallucination sense data are located at the apparent location of the hallucinated object—but then why not just locate all sense data wherever they appear to be, as in the theory of section VII.4? Now the argument from hallucination (see section VI.3) comes back to haunt the indirect realist: since a hallucination sense datum could be proximately caused by the same brain state as a normal perception sense datum, shouldn't the effects be the same, including with respect to their locations?

In fact, this brings out the hitherto unnoticed arbitrariness in the answer of this section. The experience I have when I look at the star is *ultimately* caused by the star thousands of light-years away. But it can also be said to be caused by the state of the electric and magnetic fields (at an appropriate time) at any given point in between the star and my eye. If the electric and magnetic fields had been in the appropriate state at the appropriate time, whether or not any of the earlier events in the causal chain had happened, I would have had the same sense datum, or one indistinguishable (by me) from it. Would the sense datum have been in a different place if the earlier parts of the causal chain leading to its occurrence had been absent, but the later parts duplicated? Why would that be so?

The *immediate* cause of a sense datum, if there are such things as sense data, is a brain state. No information as to the actual location of the source that sent the photons to my eyes—whether it was a thousand light-years away or fifty miles away—is physically recorded in that brain state, so I do not see how it could be determining where the sense datum appears. More colloquially, the sense datum would have no way of "knowing" where it is supposed to appear.

4. "Sense Data Are Wherever They Appear to Be"[11]

This answer is the most natural one, if you're going to grant spatial properties to sense data at all. If sense data have the shapes, colors, and other properties that we seem to perceive, why not also the positions?

This may also get the indirect realist out of the problem with the theory of relativity. For, when I look at a star, although the star may be thousands of light-years away, it (or the sense datum I directly apprehend) certainly doesn't *look* thousands of light-years away. In fact, you probably cannot visually tell the difference between the distance of an airplane in the sky and the distance of a star, except for the fact that the airplane may move in front of the star—and even then, you can't tell just by looking that the star isn't just a few feet behind the airplane. Thus, we don't require a sense datum to appear thousands of light-years away. The sense datum of the star might appear only, say, a few thousand feet away. (How far away it appears depends on the acuity of your depth perception.)

Whether this actually gets the indirect realist off the hook is questionable, since it may well be physically possible for a being to have an experience of seeming to see something very far away, such that it would be outside the forward light cone of his brain state. At least, there is no reason to think this is physically impossible. Still, there are, in my opinion, stronger arguments against this version of sense data theory.

Let us begin by considering dreams. According to the present theory, assuming that dreams involve sense data, when you dream about, say, a purple unicorn, there is a purple, unicorn-shaped thing in the room with you. If you dream that it is right in front of you, then, apparently, the sense datum is hovering above your bed if you sleep on your back or next to the bed if your head is turned to the side.

This seems pretty strange, but a sense data theorist would probably be prepared to accept it. Now, what if I am dreaming of a fictional place—for instance, I am dreaming about events taking place in Tolkien's Middle Earth? The indirect realist cannot say that then I have a sense datum that is actually in Middle Earth, since there is no such place. Perhaps the sense data are just around me, wherever I happen to be, rather than being in the fictional place.

Conceivably one might deny that dreams involve sense data, on the ground that they are qualitatively different from perceptual experiences. But the above reasoning could be repeated for vivid hallucinations (you could hallucinate that you were in Middle Earth), and hallucinations are a paradigm for the kind of case that sense data are supposed to be involved in.

So, let's say that when you have a visual hallucination, a sense datum comes into existence in front of you (in front of your eyes, since that is where the hallucinated object appears to be). We can raise a problem for this theory by invoking the brain-in-a-vat scenario. The brain in the vat is having nothing but hallucinations. Its whole life, perhaps, the brain has seemed to be living in Middle Earth. When the brain has one of its experiences as of seeing a unicorn, the unicorn sense datum appears "in front of" the brain. But since the brain doesn't have any eyes, what counts as "in front of" the brain? Perhaps where the frontal lobes are. But why should *that* direction count as "where the unicorn appears to be"? The brain in the vat has no awareness of its brain-in-a-vat-hood and no awareness of its own frontal lobes. The brain might not even know what a brain is. In what sense, then, does the unicorn the brain thinks it is seeing appear to be in that place which is in fact in front of the brain's frontal lobes?

The essential problem here is that, in certain cases, there could be *no such thing* as the place where a sense datum appears to be, even when the alleged sense datum would have to be one with spatial properties. Of course, to the brain in the vat, it appears that the unicorn is somewhere. But there is no real place such that the unicorn appears to be in that place. And so the answer, "Sense data are in the places where they appear to be," does not work.

Now, if you thought, in spite of what I have just said, that it is okay to locate the sense datum "in front of" the brain, you can imagine an only slightly stranger scenario. The brain in the vat is actually not shaped like a normal human brain. Instead, scientists have figured out how to create a spherical brain, perhaps through genetic engineering, and they use these for their brain-in-a-vat experiments, because the spherical brains fit better into the special kind of vats the scientists use. I have no reason for thinking this either physically or logically impossible. In this case, the brain has no front or back, so there is no logical place for the brain's sense data to be.

Perhaps, fortuitously for the indirect realist, the laws of nature somehow do not permit the creation of spherical brains in vats. Still, in a world that did allow the creation of spherical brains in vats (I do know that this is at least logically possible), couldn't the spherical brains have experiences qualitatively like ours? Would these experiences require the existence of sense data? If no, then why think that *our* experiences require the existence of sense data? If yes, where could the sense data be located? If sense data are located wherever they appear to be, it seems that this should be a necessary truth, just as it is necessary that sense data have the colors and shapes they appear to have.

5. "Sense Data Are in Phenomenal Space"[12]

Our fifth and final form of indirect realism holds that sense data exist in an alternate space, separate from the space that physical objects occupy. The laws (if any) that apply to this alternate space may differ from the laws of physical space. For instance, there may be no problem with transmitting influences faster than the speed of light in the alternate space, the alternate space may be Euclidean and unaffected by gravitational fields, and so forth. We can call this alternate space "phenomenal space" to distinguish it from physical space.

There remain interesting questions about phenomenal space: is there only one phenomenal space, or does every observer have his own, separate phenomenal space (the latter answer could explain why we can only perceive our own sense data)? Do tactile and visual sense data occupy the same phenomenal space? What about sounds and smells, which often appear to have some sort of location? These are all questions we would want to pursue if we believed in phenomenal space. There is no need to pursue them now, however.

I will detail three objections to the theory of phenomenal space. The third seems to me the strongest, while the first two are inconclusive, but I discuss all three because it is possible that the reader will find one of the first two objections more persuasive than the last.

First, the theory of phenomenal space runs into a conflict with special relativity, just as does the theory discussed in section 3. In this case, the problem is with the separation between space and time that the indirect realist must rely on. In sum:

1. According to relativity, space and time are not two separate things; there is only the single, four-dimensional manifold, "spacetime."
2. So, according to relativity, no event can be temporally related to a physical event without being spatially related to it.
3. According to the theory of phenomenal space, sense data are not spatially related to physical objects/events.
4. But, according to this same theory, sense data are temporally related to physical objects/events.
5. So the theory of phenomenal space conflicts with the theory of relativity.

Let's discuss the steps of this argument more slowly.

Step 1: According to special relativity, there is a single, four-dimensional object, "spacetime," that all physical events occupy. Any two events have a single, objective distance from each other in spacetime (N.B. not distance in *space* but in *spacetime*)—this distance is the same for all reference frames. However, how much of that distance is accounted for by spatial distance and how much by temporal separation is relative to a reference frame.[13] I explain this with an analogy.

Consider the points A and B in figure 7.2. Their distance from one another is 2 inches. That is an objective fact, not dependent on the coordinate system I choose. However, suppose I ask: what is the *horizontal* distance between A and B, and what is their *vertical* distance? (Or: what is the difference in their positions along the x-axis and what is the difference along the y-axis?) Your answer to this question depends on your orientation, or on the coordinate system you use. If you use the coordinate system with the axes I have labeled "x" and "y," then you will find that the horizontal distance is about 1 ¾" and the vertical distance about 1". On the other hand, if you are using the alternative coordinate system with the x' and y' axes, which you get by rotating the page a bit, then you will find the horizontal distance to be 2" and the vertical distance 0". Thus, *what is the distance between A and B* is absolute, but *how much of that distance is horizontal and how much is vertical* is not; it is dependent on

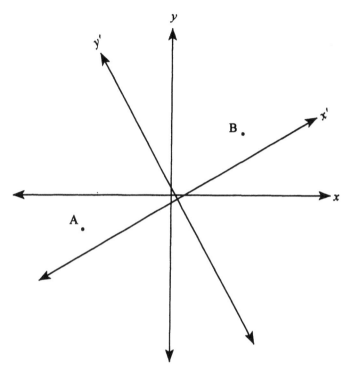

Figure 7.2. The relativity of horizontal and vertical distances to a coordinate system.

a choice of coordinate system. There is no one, privileged direction that has to be called "vertical"; you can rotate the page and, equally legitimately, call some other direction on the page "the vertical axis" (this point is perhaps clearer if you imagine the diagram drawn on a round piece of paper).

There is a similar phenomenon involving spacetime distance in the theory of relativity, with just the difference that we are talking about "distance" in a four-dimensional "space," where one of the axes of our coordinate system is labeled "time." Just as there was no privileged "vertical" direction on the page, there is also, according to relativity, no privileged "temporal" direction in spacetime. Different, legitimate coordinate systems are possible that label the t axis differently. Not just anything goes (and this is one point of disanalogy with the preceding illustration)—one cannot legitimately call just any straight line in spacetime the temporal axis (one cannot use a line whose points are at spacelike separation from each other—in the spacetime diagram in section VII.3, this means one cannot choose an axis slanted past l_4 or l_5 toward the horizontal). The important point, though, is just that different specifications are possible of what counts as the time dimension in spacetime. This is sufficient to explain why, in the theory of relativity, space and time do not exist as two separate things.

This point is connected with the point we made in section 3 about the relativity of the time order of events. This is, in a sense, the *reason why* the time ordering of events is relative to a reference frame, according to the special theory of relativity: different specifications of the temporal axis can yield different conclusions as to the time order of spacelike separated events. We don't need to go into details, but we should note that the two points—(i) that spacelike separated events have no objective time order, and (ii) that the "true" temporal dimension cannot be isolated in spacetime—are connected and stand or fall together. I do not wish to place too much emphasis on this argument, for the same reason I did not want to rest much weight on the related argument of section 3.[14] Nevertheless, I think it is worthwhile to understand this argument, and, while it would not convince me were I inclined to posit sense data to begin with, it may well convince some indirect realists.

Step 2: Since there is no objective specification of the time axis in spacetime, it seems to follow that nothing can be in (physical) time without being in (physical) space. Perhaps more accurately: An event either occupies spacetime, or it does not. If it occupies spacetime, then it has both spatial and temporal coordinates, in any given reference frame. If it does not occupy spacetime, then it has neither. In order for an event to have a temporal distance from a physical event, it must occupy the same spacetime as the physical event does, and it cannot occupy physical time but not physical space.

Step 3: According to the "phenomenal space" theory, since sense data occupy a separate space from physical space, they cannot be spatially related to physical objects—there cannot, for example, be a distance between a physical object or event and a sense datum. (As a related point, Putnam points out that it makes no sense to ask whether your mental image of a table is shorter or longer than the real table.[15])

Step 4: Any indirect realist must, however, hold sense data to exist in physical time, that is, to be temporally related to physical events. The reason is that a fundamental tenet of indirect realism is that sense data are *caused by* physical objects or events. The presence of a book on my desk is supposed to be now causing me to have a sense datum of a book. The sense datum is, therefore, supposed to occur after the time at which the relevant physical state of affairs occurs (or begins to occur). If I see a ball fall, then the sequence of corresponding falling-ball sense data occur at about the same time (with a slight time lag) as the ball is actually falling. In addition, of course, there are the brain processes that are going on in me at the same time that I am having the experience of the falling ball—this is scarcely deniable, without reverting to skepticism. Thus, step 5 seems unavoidable. If one accepts the theory of relativity, one should reject the idea of phenomenal space.

I turn now to the second problem for phenomenal space, a problem concerning the causal relations between events in physical space and events in phenomenal space. As noted, there must be such relations, because sense data are held to be produced by the interaction of physical objects with our sense organs and brains. At the same time, there are no spatial relations between physical objects and sense data, even though both have spatial properties—a sense datum cannot be next to a physical object, inside a physical object, four feet from a physical object, etc.

One objection to this involves a metaphysical principle of "local causality"; this is the principle that an object cannot act *directly* on another object unless the two come into contact. As earlier philosophers used to say, a thing cannot act where it is not.[16] For example, suppose there is a certain tree in New York that I would like cut down. I can't cut it down, myself, unless I can get to New York and to the place where the tree is. Furthermore, in order to have a *direct* impact on the tree, I must come into contact with it. Of course, I wouldn't normally try to cut down a tree with my bare hands (or teeth?). So suppose I use an axe. Then I am in contact with the axe, which contacts the tree. The thing I act directly on is the axe (I make it move in a certain way). This, in turn, affects the tree.

I might try to get the job done even less directly—say I call someone in New York and convince them to go cut down the tree. In this case, what I come into contact with is the telephone and the air in front of the receiver; I make sound waves that travel to the receiver, which then causes light signals to travel down the fiber optic cables all the way to New York.

The point illustrated here is that I can affect an object only by (a) coming into contact with it, (b) coming into contact with something else that is in contact with it, (c) sending something (an object, a signal, or in general, something that carries my influence through the intervening distance) that travels through the space between me and the object, or some combination of these (including sending something that comes into contact with another thing that then comes into contact with the object, etc.). Any way I do it, there has to be a spatiotemporally continuous sequence of causally connected states or events stretching from me to the object I am affecting.

This principle seems at least empirically true, given our common experience interacting with our environment. However, the indirect realist could just say that sense data are an exception to the rule. What we need in order to make out an objection to phenomenal space is for the principle to be *intuitively* correct. Many people have found it intuitive—it was the source of great puzzlement in the seventeenth century, when Newton's theory of gravity appeared to require action at a distance. For example, it appeared that the Earth exercises its gravitational influence on the moon without any intermediaries. (This was before the concept of fields was developed.) Newton himself said that the idea of action at a distance was so absurd that no person with a competent faculty of philosophical thinking could believe in it.[17] Assuming that one finds the principle of local causality intuitively appealing, then, one has reason to reject the theory of sense data located in phenomenal space—not because the theory requires action at a *distance*, of course, but because it requires action with no spatial relation at all between the cause and the effect. It would be conceptually impossible for a spatiotemporally continuous series of states or events to connect a physical event to an event outside physical space.

In the interests of fairness, however, I have to admit that this argument is inconclusive, because it rests on an intuition that (*pace* Newton) might reasonably be rejected on independent grounds. Two such grounds suggest themselves. First, even if one is not a representationalist, one might still hold that (at least some) mental states are caused by brain states but that (at least some of these) mental states do not have spatial locations (this, of course, presupposes that mental states are not simply identical with brain states). For instance, it does not seem to make sense to talk about the spatial location of an emotion, although emotions are caused by chemicals in the brain. We could reformulate our principle of local causality to allow this: we could say the principle is that an object at a given location cannot produce an effect at another location, unless there is a spatiotemporally continuous sequence of changes stretching from the time and place of the cause to the time and place of the effect. This is a reasonable interpretation of the slogan "a thing cannot act where it is not." A brain state causing a mental state would not violate this principle, even if the mental state was not spatially located, because this simply isn't a case of a thing at a given location causing an effect *at another location*. But a brain state causing a sense datum in phenomenal space would still violate the principle, since the sense datum is still located somewhere. However, the second ground for rejecting the principle of local causality is that Bell's Theorem apparently shows that quantum mechanics logically implies the possibility of instantaneous action at a distance[18]—and I don't have an answer to that.

We turn, then, to the third objection to phenomenal space, the objection that I think is the strongest. According to this third objection, if there were such a thing as phenomenal space, there would be no reasonable answer to the question of where in phenomenal space a particular sense datum would appear. In outline, my argument will be as follows:

1. Whenever a cause produces an effect, either the location of the effect is random, or it is determined in accordance with some law or laws of nature.
2. Laws of nature can always be formulated in terms of general characteristics and relationships.
3. Therefore, when a cause produces an effect, either the location of the effect is random, or there is some general relationship that the location of the effect uniquely bears to the cause. (from 1, 2)
4. If phenomenal space exists, there is no general relationship that a location in phenomenal space uniquely bears to any physical state or event.
5. If brain states produce sense data, the locations of the sense data are not random.
6. Therefore, brain states do not produce sense data in phenomenal space. (from 3, 4, 5)

Now let's examine each step of this argument in series.

Step 1: Note that this premise does not entail that all effects have a location; there could be a law according to which, when a certain sort of cause occurs, an effect with no spatial location ensues. I would count that as a case of the location of the effect being determined in accordance with a law of nature—the law determines the effect to have no location. Note also that (1) allows the possibility of irreducibly probabilistic laws concerning where an effect takes place—I would count that as the effect being "random." However, all effects that we're familiar with in everyday life are probably examples of effects whose locations are determined by some law or laws of nature. As an example, when you strike a match, this causes a flame to appear. The flame doesn't appear just anywhere, however—you wouldn't expect the flame resulting from the striking of the match to appear on your ear, or at the base of the match, etc.; it appears at the tip of the match. There are general laws of nature that explain why this is where the flame appears (there is a combustible material there, rubbing it against a rough surface generates friction, etc.). When I say that the location of the effect is "determined" in accordance with laws of nature, I mean that the laws of nature (together with a knowledge of the cause, including relevant environmental conditions) enable one to identify uniquely the place where the effect will occur—so that there would be only one place where the effect could occur. Thus, "determined" is a strong word in my usage; even so, (1) is a very weak premise, since it only says that *either* the effect's location is determined, *or* it is random, with the latter possibility including that there are probabilistic laws.

What other alternatives could there be to these two? Well, perhaps a third alternative to "determined" and "random" is "subject to free will"—thus, perhaps (1) would be false in a case in which an effect is produced by a cause, and a person with free will chooses the location where it will occur. However, we can simply say that this is not the sort of case we're interested in here. No one thinks that our sense data during normal perception are produced by our own free will, nor—more to the point—that we get to choose where in phenomenal space our sense data will appear. Thus, if someone wants to add a clause to (1) allowing for the possibility of locations determined by free will, we can simply add another premise that sense data are not in this case and get to the desired conclusion all the same.

Now, step 2: Laws of nature can always be formulated in terms of general characteristics and relationships. This is one of the defining characteristics of laws of nature. As an example, "Napoleon lost the Battle of Waterloo" is not the sort of thing we would call a "law of nature," because it is not general enough. It is a statement about one specific person and one specific battle. A law of nature would state a general relationship between certain kinds of causes and certain kinds of effects. So if you had a general statement saying that all people facing a battle in such-and-such general circumstances will lose that battle, that might be a law. (It is doubtful you could formulate any such true generalization, but that's beside the point.) To take the most famous law of nature, Newton's Second Law, $F = ma$: this law is formulated in general terms, in the sense that it says *whenever* you have a body with a (net) force acting on it, the body will undergo an acceleration proportional to the force and inversely proportional to the body's mass. It's a symptom of the generality of laws of nature that you don't need to use any proper names in order to state them. (E.g., "Whenever Mike Huemer drops an object, it will fall to the Earth" is not a law of nature; the operative law would give the acceleration due to gravity of any body toward any other body as a function of the bodies' masses and distance from each other.)

This brings us to step 3: From step 2, we can see that, if a law of nature determines the location at which a certain effect occurs, then the law must pick out that location by means of general characteristics/relationships. If the law is to *determine* the location uniquely, the location where the effect occurs must be the *only* location having a certain characteristic or standing in a certain relationship to the cause. But since spatial locations don't really have distinguishing characteristics, other than their relationships to each other (e.g., the distance between one location and another), this just means that the location of the effect has to be the only location bearing a certain relationship to the cause. As examples, there could be a law that says, "Whenever an event of kind A occurs, an event of kind B will occur *in the same place* as the type A event, x minutes later." Or a law could say, "Whenever a rigid body impacts a second rigid body, the second body will accelerate *in the direction perpendicular to the surface of the second body at the point of impact*." Examples of things that a law of nature could not say: "When a body strikes another body, the second body will move in the direction of *Mike Huemer's house*" or "When an event of type A happens, an event of kind B will occur *just outside of Constantinople*." (It is possible that my house could have some sort of attracting power that nothing else in the universe had, but even so, the law of nature would refer to the general *properties* that the house has that give it this attracting power, not just the fact that it's mine, and would say that any thing with those properties has this special attracting power.)

Step 4: I am assuming here that phenomenal space is intrinsically homogeneous—that is, other than the different sense data that may be at different places, one location in phenomenal space is just like any other location in phenomenal space. Furthermore, no location in phenomenal space is related, spatially, to any location in physical space (that is, it is not at any distance, nor in any direction, from a location in physical space); this is the whole point of calling it a separate space. Thus, it seems that, when a physical event occurs at a certain location in physical space, that physical event is related in exactly the same way (which is to say, apparently, in no interesting way) to any given location in phenomenal space as it is to any other location in phenomenal space. Notice how this problem is unique to the alleged causation between events in different spaces and does not arise for causation between events in the same space, for you can easily have a law of nature that says that when event A occurs, event B will occur at such-and-such distance from A. And now, I am not even ruling out action at a distance—but even in that case, there must be *some* general rule about where the distant effects occur. The problem only occurs if you say that when A occurs, B will occur somewhere that is completely spatially unrelated to the location of A. Then, as far as I can see, there is no way to state a general rule about where B occurs.

Step 5: The sense data theorist does not want to say that the sense data simply appear at random locations in phenomenal space. For in that case, the different sense data that I have, caused by different objects, should appear in unpredictable spatial relations to each other—for example, there would be no reason to expect that the book sense datum would appear on top of the desk sense datum whenever the physical book is on the physical desk. Nor, in fact, would there be any reason to expect the positions of sense data to remain constant over time—my book sense datum should be jumping all over unpredictably, if its spatial location is not determined by any cause.

Finally, step 6: If brains produced sense data in phenomenal space, then either the locations where the sense data appeared would be random (which is ruled out by step 5), or they would be determined in accordance with some general law or laws (which is ruled out by step 4). It follows that brains do not produce sense data in phenomenal space. Of course, our brain states *do* produce our sensory experiences, so we can conclude that sense data in phenomenal space are not part of the correct analysis of sensory experience.

6. The Argument from Indeterminacy

A final problem for sense data is what I call the argument from indeterminacy. The argument states that the location and other properties (e.g., color, shape, size) that an object of perception *appears to have* may be indeterminate, but the location and other properties that an object *actually has* cannot. Therefore, it cannot be maintained that objects of perception have exactly the location (or other properties) that they appear to have.

To explain the argument in more detail, I introduce some technical terminology. A "determinable" is a property that encompasses a range of more specific properties. For instance, "shape" is a determinable property, because it encompasses, as examples of it, various more specific shapes, such as "triangularity," "roundness," and the like. These more specific properties falling under a determinable are referred to as "determinates" for that determinable. So "triangularity" is a determinate of the determinable "shape." Similarly, "red," "yellow," "blue," and so on are determinates of "color." A determinate can also have its own, even more specific determinates falling under it. Thus, "scarlet" is a determinate of "red" as well as of "color."

Another useful concept is that of an exhaustive set of determinates. A set of determinate properties is exhaustive, relative to a given determinable, when the determinates, taken together, cover the whole range covered by the determinable. Another way to say this is to say that for anything to have the determinable requires that it also have at least one of the determinates in the set. For example, I think that {red, orange, yellow, green, blue, indigo, violet, purple, brown, grey, black, white} is exhaustive for color (unless I've forgotten some colors). On the other hand, {red, yellow, blue} is definitely not, because a thing can be colored but be neither red nor yellow nor blue.

I will say that an object has an "indeterminate" property (or: is indeterminate with respect to some property) if there is some determinable that the object possesses, and there is also an exhaustive set of determinates falling under that determinable, such that the object does *not* possess any of those determinates. Thus, for example, an object would be indeterminate with respect to color if the object had color, but was not red, not orange, not yellow . . . and so on, for each of the colors. It would also have indeterminate color if, say, it was red but did not have any particular shade of red.

The reader will see from these definitions that it is logically impossible for an object to have indeterminate properties. But an objection to this point might be brought, based on cases of vague predicates, the famous example of a vague predicate being "bald": in order to be considered bald, a person needn't be completely without hair on his head—if you have only a few hairs, you're still bald. However, there is no definite number of hairs that a person has to have in order not to be bald; we cannot say, for instance, "If you have 976 hairs, you are bald, but if you have 977, you are not." This is what is meant by calling "bald" *vague*. Because it is vague, there can be borderline cases, cases of people who are neither definitely bald nor definitely nonbald. Is this an example of how a thing might have indeterminate properties?

I would say not. In order for this to be a counterexample to my general thesis that no object has indeterminate properties, it would have to be the case that a person on the borderline between baldness and nonbaldness possesses some determinable but lacks every member of an exhaustive set of determinates falling under it. What would be the determinates that the person lacks in this case? Perhaps "bald" and "nonbald." Then what is the determinable? Perhaps "bald or nonbald," if you want to call that a property. But then, I do not know how it could be said that the person possesses this third property. *If* we accept that the person is neither bald nor nonbald, then I think it follows that he is not "bald or nonbald." If we accept that he *is* bald or nonbald, then I think it would be absurd to go on to deny that he is bald and also deny that he is nonbald. In short, vagueness notwithstanding, the assertion that there are indeterminate properties is simply a contradiction.[19]

Now, let's say that an object has an indeterminate *appearance*, if there is a determinable property and an exhaustive set of determinates of that determinable, such that the object appears to possess the determinable but there is no determinate in that set such that the object appears to possess that determinate. Thus, if an object appeared to be colored, but did not appear red, did not appear orange, did not appear yellow, and so on, then the object would have an indeterminate color appearance.

Notice that having an indeterminate appearance, so defined, is *not* a species of having indeterminate properties, and it is not a logical contradiction for an object to have an indeterminate appearance. Compare this case: It is possible to believe an object to be colored, without believing it to be red, nor believing it to be orange, nor . . . etc. If someone tells me that Smith bought a new shirt today, I will be of the opinion that the shirt has some color or other, but I may not have any opinions as to *which* color it has; I may thus not believe it to be red, not believe it to be orange, and so on. On my view, perceptual experiences are representational mental states whose contents are (sometimes) reported in sentences of the form "it appears to *S* that *p*" (just as the content of a belief is reported in sentences of the form "*S* believes that *p*"). Thus, just as there is no *logical* problem in the claim that a certain person *believes* that *x* possesses a determinable without believing it to possess any given determinate falling under that determinable, nor is there any logical problem in the claim that to a certain person *x appears* to possess a certain determinable without appearing to possess any given determinate falling under that determinable.

Notice, however, that this (alleged) possibility *does* conflict with the sense data theory. The sense data analysis of appearances (leaving aside the views discussed in section 1 and at the beginning of section 2) is that there is a special object that actually possesses all and only the sensible properties (color, shape, smell, etc.) that appear to us to be present during a given episode of perception, that we are immediately aware of that object, and that that explains why things appear to us the way they do. Thus, if there appears to be a sphere in front of me, I am having a sense datum that is actually spherical. Conversely, and equally importantly, if there does not appear to be a sphere, then I am not having a sense datum that is spherical. Because of this, the existence of indeterminate appearances would, *on the sense data theory*, imply the existence of objects with indeterminate properties. And so the sense data theorist cannot accept the existence of indeterminate appearances.

To refute the sense data theory, I will try to convince you that there are indeterminate perceptual appearances. I defended this point with respect to perceived time and perceived colors in section VI.6, and I suspect that similar arguments to the one in that section could be made for any sensible quality. Here I will consider two more kinds of indeterminacy in perceptual appearances.

a.   The apparent distances of perceived objects from the observer are to some degree indeterminate. In discussing the visual experience of a star as compared with that of an airplane, I noted that the two objects do not appear to be at significantly different distances. Of course, this would be true if both objects appeared to be at the same, determinate distance. But I don't think that is the case. Try looking at a star (or the sun, if it's daytime). How far away does it look? If there is a determinate answer to this, you should be able to produce it, simply on the basis of attending to your visual experience (no scientific knowledge necessary). For my part, I find that I cannot. In our earlier discussion of this case, I allowed the indirect realist to claim that the star appears only a few thousand feet away. But in fact I think this is wrong. What is correct to say is that, on the basis of my visual experience, I simply *cannot tell* how far the star is, other than that it's at least "pretty far": I cannot tell whether it is 1000 feet away, or 1000 miles, or 1000 light-years. This is not simply a matter of the fact that I know my eyes cannot discriminate such distances. Rather, even if I pretend to completely trust my senses, to take my experiences "at face value," I still form no definite conclusion as to how far the star is.

As I have indicated, I think the indeterminacy in this case is extreme. However, it is worth observing that, in order to make my case, any degree of indeterminacy will do. Thus, as long as you agree that your visual experience does not represent distances down to the millimeter, so that there is no answer to "exactly how many millimeters away does the star appear?", you agree that the star's apparent distance is indeterminate.

b. The apparent shapes of objects are to some degree indeterminate. There is a famous example, sometimes used by skeptics to illustrate the unreliability of our senses, involving a square tower that, when viewed from a distance, appears round. Or perhaps it is a round tower that appears square; I can't remember how the example is supposed to go. And that is significant, for it does not matter which I say—either way, the example is a realistic one, seemingly true to how our experience is. The reason it doesn't matter is that from a distance, there is no distinction to be made between "looking square" and "looking round." That is, the more accurate thing to say is that, whether the tower is in fact round or square, you *cannot tell* from your experience, when viewing it from a distance, which it is. It's not that it definitely looks round or definitely looks square. It's that your experience is neutral about its cross-sectional shape. (Why would your experience represent the tower to be definitely round when it was actually square, or vice versa?)

A similar example involves the viewing of written words. Try looking at the middle of a page of printed matter (well, finish reading this paragraph before trying the experiment). Now, *without moving your eyes*, attend to the words just a few lines above where your eyes are focused. Try reading them. It may take a little practice to avoid directing your eyes toward the place you're trying to read, but it can be done.

If you do this, you will find that you cannot read the words. The physical reason for this is that there is a great concentration of cones at the center of the retina (the fovea), making your vision at the center of the visual field much more acute than your vision even a small distance from the center. The *phenomenological* description of the case, I claim, is that the apparent shapes of objects at the center of the visual field are much *more determinate* than the apparent shapes of objects away from the center. Nevertheless, it is quite possible that you have never noticed this, owing to the fact that you automatically, reflexively direct your eyes towards any object on which you are trying to make out details.

Now, I ask the reader to do a simple further experiment and make an introspective judgement. Focus on the center of a page of printed matter, again. Attend to the words a few lines above where you are focused. And then, this time, move your eyes up toward those words, bringing them into the center of your field of view. When you do this, *does it appear that the words change shape?*

I claim that the answer is no. You are now able to make the words out, so the way they appear is not the same as the way they appeared before. Still, it does not appear that they changed shape. But if the words had a determinate apparent shape in the first case, then that shape either was or was not the same as the shape they appeared to have in the second case, after you focused on them. If it was the same, then you should have been able to read the words just as easily in the first case as in the second. If it was not the same, then the words should have appeared to you to change shape, for, if an object appears to be one shape at one time and then, a moment later, appears to be a shape incompatible with the first shape, then it appears to have changed shape. For example, if an object looks triangular, and then a second later it looks rectangular, then ipso facto it will look as if it has changed shape.

The fact that it does not appear to you that the words changed shape, then, shows that there was no determinate shape they appeared to be in the first case; that is the only alternative to the dilemma posed in the preceding paragraph. The correct thing to say about the words that are out of the center of your visual field, is not that they appear to be some other shape than the shape they really are, but that you simply cannot tell, going on the basis of your visual experience, what shape they are. Thus, suppose that one of these words you cannot make out is actually the word "content." It is not that it definitely appears *not* to be the word "content"—that isn't why you can't read it. After all, your visual experience doesn't lead you to make *false* judgements about what those words are; it just doesn't lead you to make definite judgements. It is rather that the word doesn't definitely appear *to* be the word "content" (nor any other given word). It does, however, definitely appear that there is some thing there, which perforce has some shape. Thus, this case fits our definition of indeterminate appearance.

Now, as I say, this phenomenon is a problem for the theory of sense data. For while it is not a logical contradiction for an object to have indeterminate appearances (fortunately, since objects do in fact have indeterminate appearances), it would be a logical contradiction for there to be an object with indeterminate properties. This consideration provides an argument against *any* theory which holds that (a) sense data are involved in typical cases of perception and (b) sense data have precisely the shapes, or the distances, or the colors, etc. that they appear to have—this applies to the positions discussed in sections 2, 4, 5, and probably 3, of this chapter. If sense data actually exist, they cannot have indeterminate shapes, or indeterminate locations, etc.

Notes

1. This was probably Thomas Reid's main objection to indirect realism. Reid writes: "These facts . . . give reason to apprehend that Des Cartes' system of the human understanding, which I shall beg leave to call *the ideal system*, and which, with some improvements made by later writers, is now generally received, hath some original defect; that this scepticism is inlaid in it, and reared along with it; and, therefore, that we must lay it open to the foundation, and examine the materials, before we can expect to raise any solid and useful fabric of knowledge on this subject" (*Inquiry and Essays*, 10-11).

2. This is an extension from the usual use of "sense data," which usually refers to putative mental objects that have the properties (e.g., the colors and shapes) that we appear to perceive. In this chapter, I use "sense data" for whatever mental states, objects, events, properties, or other kind of mental phenomena we are directly aware of in perception, assuming indirect realism is true. If indirect realism is not true, then there are no such things as sense data.

3. As always, I use "things" broadly, to include events, properties, and so on. The reason for the "at least sometimes" qualifier is that it may be doubted whether sounds or tastes are spatially located, and I do not wish to dispute that issue.

4. This seems to be one of the views to accommodate which Chisholm introduced the terminology of "I am appeared to redly" and the like (*Theory of Knowledge*, 29-30).

5. In view of the distinction drawn in section VI.1, one may ask whether I mean angular sizes and shapes or linear sizes and shapes. The answer is both; anything that has angular size/shape must also have linear size/shape, and vice versa.

6. Together with the assumptions, which I take to be analytic, that x appears some way to you only if you are aware of x, and that the way x appears to you is determined by the content of the mental state by which you are aware of x.

7. I am a dualist; if physicalism is true, then I suppose perceptual experiences are located in the brain.

8. See Russell, *The Analysis of Matter*, 383: "I should say that what the physiologist sees when he looks at a brain is part of his own brain, not part of the brain he is examining."

9. Aristotle held a similar view, with "your sense organs" substituted for "your brain"—that is, that perception is to be explained by your sense organs' taking on the properties of the perceived objects (*De Anima* II.11-12). Kant apparently held that this sort of thing would be required in order to perceive real things. See the passage in the *Prolegomena*, section 9 (29) that includes "It is even then incomprehensible how the intuition of a present thing should make me know this thing as it is in itself, as its properties cannot migrate into my faculty of representation."

10. See J. S. Bell, "Bertlman's Socks and the Nature of Reality." See also the remarks about relativity in section VII.5.

11. This seems to be Frank Jackson's view (*Perception*, 89, 102-3).

12. Price defends this view (111-13, 246-52). So does Russell (*The Analysis of Matter*, 252-53), in addition to the one mentioned in note 8.

13. See Einstein, 56.

14. In addition to the problems with Bell's Theorem that I mentioned earlier (note 10), it will perhaps not be amiss to remark that the empirical evidence for this aspect of relativity theory was never particularly overwhelming to begin with. Essentially, it rests on an appeal to Ockham's razor, the weakest kind of empirical argument: no observable phenomenon appeared to require for its explanation the introduction of a privileged frame of reference, it is impossible to identify that frame of reference if it exists, and so the physicists thought it would be simpler to deny its existence.

15. Putnam, 59.

16. This was a commonly accepted principle in medieval and modern philosophy, regarded as intuitively obvious. See for example Descartes, letter to Hyperaspistes, *Philosophical Writings*, vol. 3, 193: "I am not subtle enough to grasp how something can be acted upon by something else that is not present."

17. Letter to Bentley, in Turnbull, 254.

18. See J. S. Bell again.

19. A second objection might arise based on the alleged indeterminacy in quantum mechanics. This is not the place for an extended discussion of the interpretation of quantum mechanics, so I will limit myself to two brief remarks. First, if the Copenhagen Interpretation of Quantum Mechanics asserts the existence of objects with indeterminate properties in the sense I have defined, then the Copenhagen Interpretation of Quantum Mechanics is indeed self-contradictory. Second, there are alternative interpretations that are not self-contradictory, any of which is to be preferred to an incoherent theory.

VIII. The Direct Realist's Answer to Skepticism

Hopefully, I have shown that my version of direct realist foundationalism offers a more plausible account of perceptual awareness than its competitors. It is time to return at last to the skeptical arguments of chapter II. We are now in a position to understand exactly what is wrong with each of them.

The four arguments in question were

1. The infinite regress argument,
2. The argument from the problem of the criterion,
3. The "How can you get outside your head?" argument (Hume's argument), and
4. The brain-in-a-vat argument.

Of these, my answer to #3 is obvious. Hume's argument explicitly includes an anti-direct realist premise ("We have no experience of external objects"), which I reject. It is not necessary, then, to discuss this argument further. We proceed to the remaining three arguments.

1. The Infinite Regress Argument

The regress argument went as follows.

1. In order to know something, I must have a good reason for believing it.
2. Any chain of reasoning must have one of three structures:
    a. it is an infinite series,
    b. it is circular, or

    c. it begins with a belief for which there are no further reasons.
3. I cannot have an infinite series of reasons.
4. Circular reasoning cannot produce knowledge.
5. I cannot gain knowledge by structure 2c, for
    a. I would not know my starting beliefs to be true. (from 1)
    b. I cannot gain knowledge by deriving it from assumptions I do not know to be true.
6. Therefore, I cannot know anything. (from 1-5)

There was a further argument supporting premise 1 as against foundationalism:

7. Assume that I have a foundational belief, x.
8. Either there is no feature distinguishing x from an arbitrary belief, or there is some feature, F, such that x is distinguished from an arbitrary belief by the fact that x has F.
9. If there is no feature distinguishing x from an arbitrary belief, then x is not foundational.
10. There is some feature, F, such that x is distinguished from an arbitrary belief by the fact that x has F. (from 7, 8, 9)
11. If I were not aware that x has F, then the fact that x has F would not distinguish x from an arbitrary belief.
12. I am aware that x has F. (from 10, 11)
13. I have a reason for accepting x, namely, that x has F. (from 10, 12)
14. x is not foundational. (from 13)
15. No belief is foundational. (from 7-14, by reductio ad absurdum)

    The latter argument is invalid as written, since (14) does not follow from (13). A foundational belief is defined to be a belief that one *does not need* a reason for; it is not defined as a belief that one *does not have* a reason for. Nonetheless, I am not going to rest my response on that, because I think the argument could be reformulated to eliminate the problem[1] and because I think there is a more important mistake to focus on.
    In my view, foundational beliefs about the external world are justified by virtue of the fact that they are based on perceptual experiences. Normal perceptual experiences, in turn, are a nonconceptual and nonbelief form of direct awareness of external things. If this theory is correct, then, obviously, we can know things about the external world. But which step in the skeptic's argument is wrong, according to this theory?
    There are at least two possible ways of interpreting the skeptic's use of "to have a reason for." First: It could mean "to have a belief that supports." In this case, premise (1) says that I can know something only if I have a belief that

supports it. This is false, because I can know *x* by having a nonbelief state of awareness that supports *x*—such as a perceptual experience.

Second: It could mean "to have some sort of mental state (whether a belief, an experience, or something else) that renders justified." In this case, premise (1) is acceptable; however, step (5) is now wrong. (5a) does not follow from (1), since, in structure (2c), I might know my starting beliefs to be true by virtue of their being based on perceptual experiences.

Essentially, the skeptic's problem is that he overlooks states of awareness other than beliefs, failing to consider them as possible sources for the justification of our beliefs. Since, as I think, all beliefs are ultimately rendered justified by nonbelief states (appearances), it is not surprising that this omission leads the skeptic to conclude that there are no justified beliefs.

Let us return to the first interpretation of "to have a reason for," under which, I have claimed, premise (1) would be false. In this interpretation, it is stipulated that a "reason" for believing something must itself be a belief. In this case, what is wrong with the argument of (7)-(15), in support of premise (1)?

Well, there are two problems now. The first is that (13) does not follow from (10) and (12), since a state of *awareness* need not involve a belief. If my awareness that *x* has F took a nondoxastic form, then (13) would be false. The second problem, more to the point for my theory of perceptual knowledge, is that premise (11):

11. If I were not aware that *x* has F, then the fact that *x* has F would not distinguish *x* from an arbitrary belief.

commits what is called a "level confusion."[2] A level confusion is a confusion between, for example, (knowing that *P*) and (knowing that one knows that *P*), or between (being justified in believing that *P*) and (being justified in believing that one is justified in believing that *P*), or the like. In this case, the confusion is between (the conditions that make one justified in *x*) and (awareness of the conditions that make one justified in *x*). By hypothesis, *F* is what makes *x* justified—not *the awareness of* F. Premise (11) just straightforwardly confounds the two.

In the case of my version of foundationalism, F would be the property of seeming to be the case. As noted in section V.3, the thesis is *not* that a belief is justified because one *believes*, or *knows*, or *is aware that* its content seems to be true, but just because its content *does* seem to be true. This may seem like a small distinction, but a confusion of this kind is quite enough to generate the absurd conclusion in (15). Small mistakes of this sort can lead to much larger mistakes. Recall that any contradiction in one's premises is sufficient to derive any conclusion whatsoever. The confusion of a state of affairs with the awareness of that same state of affairs is, in fact, a kind of contradiction (notwithstanding that the state of affairs may itself be mental).

Besides the temptation of confusing levels, (11) may also draw spurious plausibility from its confusion with another, plausible constraint on principles of justification. This constraint is that whether and to what degree a person's belief is to be counted justified should be a function of his total mental state. If two people have exactly the same mental states, then what one person is justified in believing the other one is, regardless of what else might be going on in the environments of the two people. For instance, according to this principle, you and a brain in a vat being programmed to have all the same experiences as you, would have exactly the same degree of *justification* for your respective beliefs, even though of course the brain in the vat, unlike you, would be radically deceived (and its beliefs would be causally unconnected to the sorts of things it thinks it is perceiving, and its belief-forming mechanisms would be unreliable). This is the principle of *internalism about justification*.[3] This principle, which I think is true, is similar to (11), but does not entail (11), as shown by the fact that my version of foundationalism accepts internalism while rejecting (11). In my theory, foundational beliefs are justified by virtue of their relation to appearances, which are understood as internal, mental states; in this sense, internalism about justification is respected. However, it is not the case, in my theory, that what renders a belief justified is always something that one is aware *of* (that is an *object* of awareness), though it (the appearance state, that is) may well be a state of awareness (a *vehicle* of awareness).

2. The Problem of the Criterion

The second skeptical argument went as follows:

1. All my beliefs are formed by some method.
2. I am justified in accepting a belief formed by method M only if I first know that M is reliable.
3. I do not have an infinite series of belief-forming methods.
4. Therefore, I cannot know that my belief-forming methods are reliable. (from 1, 2, 3)
5. Therefore, none of my beliefs are justified. (from 1, 2, 4)

Premise (1) may be true, depending on how broadly one uses the word "method"—it is true if it means merely that there is some way one comes to hold a belief. Premise (3) also seems acceptable, though not beyond question— once we accept such a broad use of "method," it isn't quite obvious that the available "methods" of forming beliefs need be finite. Still, a skeptic can probably articulate some sense of "method" weak enough that it is reasonably clear that all our beliefs come from a "method" but strong enough that it is reasonably clear that we do not have infinitely many of them, and it hardly seems worth pressing this.

Premise (2), however, would clearly be rejected by any foundationalist, since by itself it implies the negation of foundationalism—any premise that begins, "In order to be justified in accepting a belief, I must first know . . . ," where this is supposed to apply to all beliefs, is a straight-out denial of foundationalism.

The essential error behind premise (2), from my standpoint, is closely related to the basic mistake of representationalism. The representationalist makes the mistake of confusing a means of awareness with an object of awareness. In fact, we are aware of the external world in and through having perceptual experiences; our perceptual experiences under normal conditions *constitute* awareness of the external world. But the representationalist mistakes the situation for one in which we are aware of external objects by *apprehending* our perceptual experiences and thence taking them as *signs* of external objects. Thus arises the problem of establishing discursively the correlation between sensory images and real objects.

The reasoning behind the problem of the criterion is the same, except more general. The "criterion skeptic," as we might call the proponent of this argument, does to all human cognitive processes what the representationalist does to perceptual experiences—which is to say, he regards them as alleged *signs of* the things we believe to be true and thereupon raises the problem of establishing discursively the correlation between our cognitive processes in general and the facts that they supposedly enable us to know. The solution lies in recognizing, for all that this may be tautological, that the *objects* of our cognitive processes are what we know, by virtue of their being the objects of our cognitive processes. The occurrence of certain cognitions in us (coming to form a belief by method M, as the argument we have been discussing puts it) does not in general function as a sign from which we must draw conclusions about what is true; rather, it just *is*, in normal cases, the knowing of whatever it is that is the content of the cognitive state. So when I do a calculation to determine that 18 × 33 is 594, the sequence is *not* like this: first, I do the calculation, come up with the answer 594, then notice that I believe that the answer is 594, and then, since I think I am generally reliable, conclude that the answer is really 594. Rather, it was the process of doing the calculation, itself, that justified me in believing that the answer was 594.

H. A. Prichard made a similar point, on which he is worth quoting at length. He said that the discipline of epistemology was focused on a misguided search for a general criterion of knowledge:

> [Epistemologists] look for some general procedure by which we can ascertain
> that a given condition of mind is really one of knowledge. And this involves
> the search for a criterion of knowledge, i.e. for a principle by applying which
> we can settle that a given state of mind is really knowledge. The search for
> this criterion and the application of it, when found, is what is called the
> Theory of Knowledge. The search implies that instead of its being the fact that
> the knowledge that *A* is *B* is obtained directly by consideration of the nature
> of *A* and *B*, the knowledge that *A* is *B*, in the full or complete sense, can only
> be obtained by first knowing that *A* is *B*, and then knowing that we knew it by
> applying a criterion, such as Descartes's principle that what we clearly and
> distinctly conceive is true.
>
>   Now it is easy to show that the doubt whether *A* is *B*, based on this
> speculative or general ground, could, if genuine, never be set at rest. For if,
> in order really to know that *A* is *B*, we must first know that we knew it, then
> really, to know that we knew it, we must first know that we knew that we
> knew it.[4]

What, you may ask, of the argument that we gave to support premise (2)
in chapter II? We tried to motivate (2) with an argument by analogy: you
wouldn't be justified in believing that the answers delivered up by the Magic
Eight Ball were true, in the absence of some further (non-eight-ball-based)
evidence of a correlation between eight-ball answers and facts in reality. That
seemed right. And then it seemed as though we could draw an analogy to the
"answers" delivered up by the five senses, or the intellect, and so on. What is
wrong with this analogy?

Well, just this: perceptual beliefs are foundational. Eight ball beliefs are
not. When I see a tree outside, my perceptual experience constitutes immediate
awareness of the tree. When, on the other hand, the eight ball produces the
answer "It is decidedly so" after being queried, "Is there a tree outside?", the
floating up to the window of the "It is decidedly so" answer does not constitute
anyone's awareness of anything (for the sufficient reason that it is not a mental
state). What I am directly aware of when I use the eight ball is not the alleged
fact reported by the eight ball, even if the eight ball's answer is correct; what
I am directly aware of is simply the eight ball itself, and some of its observable
properties. What I have foundational knowledge of, then, is that there is a
certain pattern of symbols showing in the little window in the bottom of the
eight ball, since that is what I actually see. If I, then, decide that there is a tree
outside, not having seen the tree nor otherwise made any further confirmation
of the fact, I will be making an inference, from the fact about the eight ball's
observable characteristics, to a conclusion about a tree outside. This inference
is, as it stands, neither valid nor cogent. In order to make it cogent, one would

have to add a further premise that patterns of symbols appearing in the eight ball's window are correlated in a certain way with the correct answers to questions that have been spoken prior to shaking the eight ball and turning it over. Thus, the skeptic's premise (2), or something very close to it, is eminently true of eight-ball reasoning. It does not apply to perceptual beliefs, on a direct realist account, where these are not based on reasoning analogous to that which would be needed to form beliefs with the use of a Magic Eight Ball.

Certainly, if one is a foundationalist, one is not going to declare just any belief to be foundational—and among the beliefs that probably no foundationalist would consider to be foundational are the eight-ball-based beliefs. Thus, it should cause the foundationalist no alarm to see that an argument based on analogy to eight-ball beliefs would lead to the conclusion that no beliefs are foundational—which is essentially what premise (2) declares.

In sum, then: in a case where I infer that *P* is true on the grounds of some other fact *Q*, where the latter fact is not logically connected to the former, I require a further premise asserting some kind of connection between *P* and *Q*.[5] But in a case where I am foundationally justified in believing that *P*, no such requirement applies.

3. The Brain in a Vat

Lastly, we come to the brain-in-a-vat argument:

1. Your sensory experiences are the only evidence you have for propositions about the external world.
2. The BIV scenario predicts that you would be having the same sort of sensory experiences as you are actually having.
3. Therefore, the sensory experiences you are actually having are not evidence that the BIV scenario isn't true. (from 2)
4. Therefore, you have no evidence that the BIV scenario isn't true. (from 1, 3)
5. Therefore, you do not know that you're not a BIV. (from 4)
6. Therefore, you do not know anything about the external world. (from 5)

This argument, I contend, depends on an indirect realist theory of perceptual knowledge—more precisely, the argument assumes that the skeptic's opponent is an indirect realist; it simply does not consider the possibility of a direct realist account of our knowledge of the external world. What I have in mind here is specifically the *epistemological* thesis of direct realism that I defended in chapter V, namely, the view that perceptual beliefs are foundationally justified.[6]

The argument has two problems, from the viewpoint of the epistemological direct realist. Premise (1) is false, and (5) does not follow from (4). Premise (1) is false, since our sensory experiences do not function merely as *evidence for* claims about the external world, at least not in the usual sense of that term—they are not like the footprints that are "evidence that" a person has passed through the area, where you infer that a person passed through the area from the presence of the footprints.[7] Rather, they simply constitute our awareness of the external world.

Premise (1) might be interpreted, not as saying that sensory experiences are evidence for claims about the external world (which, after all, the skeptic does not accept), but just that nothing *other than* sensory experiences constitutes such evidence. In that case, my criticism might seem misplaced, for my denial that we *need* evidence for claims about the external world is not inconsistent with premise (1) so interpreted. But there remains another reason for a direct realist to reject (1): If direct realism is true, then the actual physical facts—the character and arrangement of the physical objects in one's immediate environment—may well be said to constitute the evidence that one has for certain claims about the external world. For instance, the fact that the milk bottle in the refrigerator is half-empty (N.B. not my *belief* or *sensory experience* of the milk bottle) is evidence that I have been drinking some milk. This fact is not a sensory experience, so this is a counterexample to (1). Of course, the fact would not constitute evidence *that you have*, unless you were aware of the fact. But the realist thinks you can very well be aware of this sort of fact, so he has no reason to accept (1)—it certainly can't simply be asserted as a starting point in an argument against a realist.

Against the *indirect* realist, a modified version of premise (1) can be formulated: your sensory experiences are the only *ultimate* evidence you have for propositions about the external world, meaning that all conclusions about the external world must ultimately be based, perhaps through a long chain of reasoning, on facts about the sensory experiences. But of course, this could not be asserted as a premise if we are taking *direct* realism seriously.

Once we see why we should reject (1), we can also see our way to rejecting (4), which is inferred from it: I have *lots* of evidence that I'm not a brain in a vat! The fact that I have two hands, for instance. A brain in a vat doesn't have two hands, so that is conclusive evidence that I'm not a brain in a vat. The BIV scenario is supposed to explain all our evidence, but it does so only on an indirect realist's interpretation of what the evidence is: the BIV scenario can account for my having *a perceptual experience of* two hands. But it cannot account for my having two hands.

Step (5) also does not follow from (4), even if (4) were true. For a foundationalist, no evidence is required for foundational propositions. Thus, "you have no evidence for so-and-so" does not imply "you do not know so-and-so." The skeptic would have to add a premise that the denial of the BIV scenario also is not foundational.

I don't think it's foundational that I'm not a brain in a vat. But I do think there are some foundational propositions that obviously and directly entail that I'm not a brain in a vat—such as the proposition that I have two hands (when I can see them), that I have a body, and so on. If we accept that those beliefs are prima facie justified, then we must also accept that they provide excellent reasons for concluding that I'm not a brain in a vat, provided there are no defeaters for them. Is such an argument circular, or question-begging? Not in a direct realist theory—there is nothing logically wrong with starting from a foundational proposition and inferring an obvious logical consequence from it. One is entitled to *presume* that things are the way they appear, until proven otherwise. In this case, I appear to be a normal human being, not a disembodied brain.

For the skeptic to make a case, then, he would have to exhibit some sort of defeater for our perceptual beliefs, that is, some fact that undermines the prima facie justification those beliefs start with. Does the brain-in-a-vat hypothesis, itself, constitute such a defeater? It would, if I had some reason for accepting it—that is, if I had significant evidence that I am a brain in a vat. But I have no such evidence, nor have the world's skeptics proven interested in trying to provide that sort of evidence; they have sought to rest their case on the mere logical possibility of being a brain in a vat.[8]

What about that, then: does the fact that *it is logically possible that I am a brain in a vat* constitute a defeater for my perceptual beliefs? I don't think so. To allow that would be to defeat the point of the concept of prima facie justification. Suppose our legal system said that the defendant in a criminal trial should be presumed innocent, but that the logical possibility that the defendant is guilty was to be accepted as defeating that presumption. In that case, one might as well just say that there is no presumption of innocence. For when would it apply? I suppose it would apply if the defendant was accused of something like squaring the circle (where a law had been made against this), or trisecting an angle. But then, in those kinds of cases, there would be a *conclusive proof* of the defendant's innocence, so there would be no point in declaring a "presumption" of innocence. The point of talking about a presumption that P is that, in cases where there is no strong evidence either for or against P, we will assume P. If the so-called presumption only operates when P is logically necessary, then it does nothing.

No one who accepts the notion of prima facie justification in general could regard the logical possibility that a prima facie justified belief is false as a defeater. But of course, whenever it is logically possible for a belief to be false, there exists some possible scenario or hypothesis in which it would be false. So simply describing such a scenario cannot be regarded as providing a defeater.

Now, let us return to my alleged evidence that I'm not a brain in a vat. I claim that my two hands are conclusive evidence that I'm not a BIV. I have found few people who are willing to accept this offhand, even though everyone agrees that it follows from the existence of the hands that I'm not a BIV. I can think of two possible reasons for this.

First: they may have some indirect realist sympathies, even if only implicitly. It is important to see how my "proof" would fail on an indirect realist theory. Suppose that my only evidence for claims about the external world consists in my sensory experiences, and that in order to know about the hands, I have to infer their existence from the character of my experiences. In this case, the BIV scenario is a challenge to the inference. It says: "Well, here is an alternative explanation for that same evidence. What reason do you have for rejecting this alternative hypothesis?" In *that* context, I can't say, "The fact that there are two hands here," since that is just a hypothesis that I haven't yet established. I can establish my "hypothesis" that I have two hands only if I can show that it is the best explanation for the evidence that I have. Which involves, among other things, showing why it is a better explanation than the brain-in-a-vat hypothesis. Thus, I cannot, without circularity, show that the two-hands hypothesis is better than the BIV hypothesis by just appealing to the presence of the two hands. If I am an indirect realist, I have to play the skeptic's game: I have to entertain the BIV hypothesis and try to find ways in which it is an unsuccessful or unacceptable explanation for my sensory experiences.[9] As a direct realist, I don't have to do this; the skeptic, rather, would have to give *me* reasons for thinking I *am* a brain in a vat.

Second: People may have in mind an epistemological principle something like the following:

7.   One cannot know that *P* by means of method M if, if *P* were false, method M would still say that it was true.

Here is an illustration of what I mean by this. Suppose a person looks at a stopped clock to determine what time it is (whether he knows that the clock is stopped or not is immaterial for purposes of the example). He concludes that it is 3 o'clock. And let us suppose that, as a pure coincidence, it is 3 o'clock at the time he looks at the clock. Does he *know* that it is 3 o'clock? Certainly not. Why not? Well, if the time *wasn't* 3 o'clock, then the clock *would still have said that it was*—it just always says it is 3 o'clock, no matter what the actual time is. Speaking more broadly, the method that the person used to come to the belief that *P* was such that, if *P* were false, the method would still have resulted in the conclusion that *P* was true. It seems that this is sufficient to render his method inadequate as a way of finding out whether *P*.

Apply this to the brain-in-a-vat scenario. I come to the conclusion that I am not a brain in a vat, because it seems to me that I have two hands, and I know that it follows from this that I am not a brain in a vat. But, if I *were* a brain in a vat, and I applied this method, I would still come to the conclusion that I wasn't one. By using this method, one just automatically comes to the conclusion that one isn't a BIV, no matter whether one is really a BIV or not. Thus, it does not seem that this is a way of finding out whether one is a BIV.

Now, a direct realist might try saying that this is not so, because if I were a brain in a vat, I would not be using "the same method" to determine whether I was one: I would be using the method of relying on my (false) *sensory experiences* to conclude that I'm not a brain in a vat, whereas in the actual case, I use the method of holding up my hands and perceiving them. As a variant on this idea: my actual method relies on perception; if I were a brain in a vat, my method would be relying instead on hallucinations.

This response won't wash, however, for the reason that if it were valid, it could be used also to defend the guy who uses a stopped clock to determine what time it is. For we might say: "His method of finding out what time it was was to look at the stopped clock *at the time when it was right*, that is, at 3:00. In the alternate possible situation where it wasn't 3:00 at the time he looked, he would be using a different method—say, the method of 'looking at the stopped clock at 2:00,' or more broadly, looking at it when it is wrong." This motivates the idea that we should not allow the *truth* of a belief to be built, implicitly or explicitly, into the description of the "method" by which the belief is adopted, for purposes of applying principle (7).[10]

I must say that I find this one of the more initially plausible arguments at the skeptic's disposal. Nevertheless, I am not persuaded. I think (7) is false. Moreover, I think that (7) is incompatible with the rest of the skeptic's argument. The skeptic's argument requires the following assumption:

8. If you know that *P*, and *P* is incompatible with *Q*, then you know (or are in a position to know) that *Q* is false.[11]

The argument depends on this, in the sense that (5) together with (8) entail (6), but (5) without (8) does not entail (6). Which is to say: if it is possible to know something, even though you are not in a position to know some of the alternatives to be false, then from the claim that I don't know the BIV scenario is false, one couldn't infer that I don't nevertheless know all sorts of things about the external world, including that I have two hands. My having two hands is incompatible with my being a brain in a vat, but I might still know the former without being able to refute the latter, if (8) is false. Of course, you may think it is obvious that (8) is true, and I don't dispute that. I only want it recognized as a premise of the skeptical argument.

The new version of the skeptical argument, then, goes something like this:

7. You cannot know that P by means of method M if, if P were false, method M would still say that it was true.
8. If you know that P, and P is incompatible with Q, then you know (or are in a position to know) that Q is false.
9. Therefore, if you know that you have two hands, you know (or are in a position to know) that you are not a BIV. (from 8) But:
10. Any method you might use for trying to know you aren't a BIV is such that, if you were a BIV, that method would still lead you to the conclusion that you weren't one.
11. Therefore, you do not know (and are not in a position to know) that you aren't a BIV. (from 7, 10)
12. Therefore, you do not know that you have two hands. (from 9, 11)

In this new version of the argument, there are three premises; (7), (8), and (10). I think (10) is beyond dispute. However, principles (7) and (8) are not both true.[12] I happen to think it is (7) that is false, but for now, I only want to convince you that at least one of them must be false. To see this, let P be any proposition that I know. Now let Q be the proposition that I am mistaken in believing P (this means that I believe it but it's false). Q, obviously, is incompatible with P. Let's assume that, because I realize this, I believe $\sim Q$, that is, I believe that I am not mistaken in believing P. Now, do I *know* that $\sim Q$? According to principle (8), the answer is yes. But according to (7), the answer is no, for: if I *were* mistaken in believing that P, then I would still think that I wasn't mistaken. People who are mistaken don't think they are mistaken; if they did, they wouldn't hold the mistaken belief. (Sometimes a person will say, "Well, it looks like I'm mistaken," but this means that something he previously said or thought was mistaken; he does not believe this thing at the same time that he is saying it is mistaken.) Which is to say: if Q were true, then I would still think Q was false. Which is to say: if $\sim Q$ were false, then I would still think $\sim Q$ was true. According to (7), this means that I don't know $\sim Q$.[13] Since (7) and (8) entail contradictory answers as to whether I know $\sim Q$, at least one of them must be false.

One reply for the skeptic would be as follows: "Actually, (7) and (8) are not logically incompatible with each other. Your demonstration started with, 'Let P be any proposition that I know.' So, *if there is* any proposition that you know, then as you have shown, (7) and (8) would give contradictory verdicts as to whether you know ~Q. However, I hold that there is no proposition P such as you have stipulated, because nobody knows anything. Thus, your demonstration cannot get started."

Well, the first part of that is right—my demonstration did assume that there is at least one proposition that someone knows. However, let's take note of the following facts. First, that the brain-in-a-vat argument was supposed to be an argument for skepticism about the external world, not an argument for *universal* skepticism, and most people who find some persuasive force in the BIV argument are not universal skeptics. We have also seen that there are special problems in the area of self-refutation for global skeptics, that do not apply if one is only a skeptic about the external world (III.1).

Second, once we have seen that the BIV argument relies on (7) and (8) and that (7) and (8) are incompatible given just the existence of at least one thing that someone knows, we are unlikely any longer to find the BIV argument persuasive. The skeptic's reply in defense of the joint compatibility of (7) and (8) depends on assuming that no one knows anything (which would suffice to make (7) and (8) both true, regardless of what "know" means)—but it is not because we thought *that* was true that we initially found the BIV argument persuasive. We found the BIV argument persuasive when we thought it was an argument to show that we don't know the propositions that would be false in the BIV scenario. Moreover, if we did accept (7) and (8), the BIV argument would be unnecessary; the skeptic would have a direct argument that no one knows anything, without the need of any talk about brains in vats. He could simply point out that (7) and (8) can only be jointly true if no one knows anything. Specifically, the skeptic could say: "The reason you don't know anything is because you never know that you're not mistaken. And the reason for that is that if you were mistaken, you would think you weren't mistaken." But few are likely to find *that* argument convincing. It is a bit like the following skeptical scenario: "Maybe you're an intelligent dog who thinks he's a human." Granted, if I *were* a dog who thinks he's a human, then I would still think that I wasn't such, but this hardly seems to show that I don't know I'm not a dog who thinks he's a human.[14] Yet according to (7) it would.

Well, if (7) and (8) are incompatible, modulo the assumption that someone knows something, why is it that they both seem plausible at first glance? Not that all initially plausible principles are true, but one would like to have some sort of diagnosis of the mistake, if indeed there is a mistake.

Perhaps the plausibility of (7) and (8) stems from two different conceptions of "knowledge," the "internalist" conception and the "externalist" conception. The internalist conception is, roughly, that to know something is to be correct in believing it and to have adequate justification for believing it. The externalist conception (or rather, *one* externalist conception) is, roughly, that to know something is to be correct in believing it, and to have formed the belief by a method that is *reliable*. This is called an "externalist" conception because the reliability of a method (unlike the justification for a belief) does not just depend upon what goes on inside the subject's mind but, rather, on the facts external to the mind. Principle (7) is closely related to the externalist conception of knowledge: for a belief-forming method to be reliable, it seems that it must be the case that if a given proposition were false, the method would (or at least probably would) not yield the result that it was true. Principle (8), on the other hand, is closely tied to the internalist conception: if I have a justification for believing something, then I must also have a justification for denying anything that is incompatible with it. (If nothing else, I have the deductive argument, "*P* is true; *Q* is incompatible with *P*; so *Q* is false," and deductive arguments are a paradigmatic way of justifying beliefs.[15]) I won't try to resolve the dispute between internalists and externalists here; I am not sure that it is more than semantic. However, it may be that the skeptic who adheres to both (7) and (8) is being drawn by both conceptions simultaneously: he is trying to be an internalist and an externalist about knowledge at the same time. Since this is not really possible, the only thing that can come of it is for one to conclude that there's no such thing as knowledge.

This diagnosis doesn't seem to fully explain our intuitions, however. For the following principle, closely related to (7), also seems plausible:

7'. If I know (or justifiably believe) that, if *P* were false, method M would still say that *P* was true, then I am not *justified in believing* that *P* is true on the basis of an application of method M.

For instance, in the stopped clock example, if one knows (or justifiably believes) that the clock is stopped and so would read "3:00" regardless of the actual time, then one is not justified in believing that it is 3:00 simply on the basis of reading the clock. The skeptic could make his argument using (7') instead of (7): "You know that, if you were a brain in a vat, your method of 'proving' that you aren't one could still be used, and would still yield the result that you weren't one. Therefore, knowing this, you are unjustified, that is, unreasonable, in believing on the basis of this method that you aren't a BIV."

I still say that (7') is incompatible with (8): Again, let *P* be any proposition that I know. I believe that I am not mistaken in believing *P*. But I also know that, if I were mistaken in believing *P*, I would still think (on the basis of the same method) that I was not mistaken. According to (7'), it follows that I am, *eo ipso*, unreasonable to think that I'm not mistaken—although according to (8), again, I know that I'm not mistaken.

Although the substitution of (7') does not save the skeptic's argument, it does serve to show that the spurious plausibility of the argument need not depend upon a shift between internalist and externalist conceptions of knowledge.

More likely, I think, is that the plausibility of (7) and (7') depends upon the same mistake as the argument from the problem of the criterion: a neglect of the phenomenon of direct awareness and an assimilation of what are actually cases of foundational knowledge to cases of inferential knowledge. It is certainly right that I cannot justifiably believe that it is 3:00 on the basis of reading a clock if I know that the clock would give that reading no matter what time it was. But this is also, just as clearly, a case of inferential belief—specifically, a case in which I infer what the time is from something I take to be a sign of it and in which I would need to first have a justified belief in some kind of connection between the clock readout and the actual time. We should be wary of drawing from this case conclusions about cases of (allegedly) foundational justification. If the problem in the clock case is either

a. that I am not justified in believing that the time on the clock is correlated with the actual time (as when I know or have reason to suspect that the clock is stopped), or
b. that although I justifiably believe this, my belief is false (as when the clock is in fact stopped but I have no reason to suspect that it is stopped),

then what we have is simply a case of an inferential belief in which one of the premises of the inference is false (as in (b)) or unjustified (as in (a)). According to this analysis, the same problem cannot apply to my alleged knowledge that I am not a brain in a vat, since I am neither mistaken nor unjustified in the belief from which I infer this (namely, the belief that I have two hands). The skeptic doesn't want to say that the reason I don't know I'm not a BIV is that in actual fact, I have no hands. He wants to say that I'm not *justified* in believing this, but I have given an account of why this belief is justified, and we have seen no reason so far to doubt it—the analogy to the clock case fails, because my belief that I have two hands is foundational, whereas the belief that the time is 3:00 is inferential.

To summarize: In both cases, I have a belief that is inferred from another belief. The skeptic thinks there is a parallel between the two cases, as follows:

	Premise	*Conclusion*	*Defeater*
Clock case	The clock reads 3:00.	It is 3:00.	If it were not 3:00, you would still have concluded by this method that it was.
BIV case	I have two hands.	I am not a BIV.	If you were a BIV, you would still have concluded by this method that you weren't.

I think, however, that the cases are more accurately portrayed as follows:

	Premises	*Conclusion*	*Defeater*
Clock case	a. The clock reads 3:00. b. The reading on the clock is correlated with the actual time.	It is 3:00.	Premise (b) is false.
BIV case	I have two hands.	I am not a BIV.	???

I have put "???" in the last box, because, if direct realism is true, there is nothing to put there that would be analogous to "premise (b) is false." That is why the stopped clock case is not a good analogy for showing that I don't know I'm not a BIV.

Now, to show that I am wrong, the skeptic will have to come up with another case, one that I cannot analyze in the way I have analyzed the stopped clock example. The skeptic will want to show that (7') also, intuitively, applies in cases where I infer something directly from a perceptual belief, that is, without the aid of something like premise (b). Thus, consider this example: while walking through the desert, I seem to see an oasis up ahead. Taking my experience at face value, I believe that there is an oasis. But then I remember that people in the desert are reputed sometimes to see mirages of oases, and it occurs to me that this could be a mirage. I conclude, however, that it isn't just a mirage, because there really is an oasis there. This does not seem very logical. The skeptic would say this is comparable to my conclusion that I'm not a BIV; thus:

	Premise	Conclusion	Defeater
Oasis case	There is an oasis there.	It is not a mirage.	It could be a mirage, and if it were a mirage, you would still have concluded by this method that it wasn't.
BIV case	I have two hands.	I am not a BIV.	You could be a BIV, and if you were a BIV, you would still have concluded by this method that you weren't.

Now, the problem with the parallel the skeptic wants to draw, in my view, is that mirages are an actual phenomenon. We know mirages exist, and in the example, I was in the sort of conditions in which I know or believe that mirages tend to occur. Thus, the "could" in "It could be a mirage" has considerably more force than the "could" in "You could be a BIV." Brains in vats are not an actual phenomenon. Moreover, we neither know nor have reason to believe that there are any brains in vats. That is why I think the defeater in the oasis case is legitimate, whereas the alleged defeater in the BIV case is not. As discussed above, the mere logical possibility of a scenario in which I would be mistaken in some belief does not constitute a defeater for that belief; the scenario must be supported by some evidence. This is why "If you were mistaken about P, you would still believe you weren't mistaken" does not work as an all-purpose defeater. Since there is no legitimate defeater for my belief that I have two hands, it stands as presumed true, and the BIV scenario, contradicting that belief, remains presumed false.

We need to be clear about what I am trying to accomplish at this point. Of course, one *could* delete the phrase "It could be a mirage" and claim that the defeater is simply, "If it were a mirage, you would still have concluded that it wasn't one." In that case, one could draw a parallel to the case where I believe I'm not a BIV, even though if I were a BIV I would still have concluded I wasn't one—this would be what principle (7') invites us to do. However, I have already argued that (7') is incompatible with (8), and what I am trying to do at this point is simply to offer a plausible diagnosis of the mistaken intuition that (7') is true: the cases in which (7') seems to apply are actually cases in which two conditions hold, the latter being overlooked by the skeptic: first, that if P were false, your method of coming to believe it would still have resulted in the conclusion that P; and second, that there is some reason for thinking that P might be false.

4. Conclusion

What have we learned from our encounter with skepticism? For one thing, we learned that skepticism is false—you really do know that you have hands and that this book you are reading exists, in case you were wondering. But more importantly, we saw the power of direct realism, and in particular of the version of direct realism presented in chapters IV-V, in accounting for this knowledge. We have seen that indirect realist theories are vulnerable to skeptical assault where my version of direct realism is not. That I take to be a strong argument in favor of my theory of perception.

Perceptual knowledge—knowledge of the characteristics of the things we ordinarily perceive—is often thought of (rightly, I think) as a central and paradigmatic kind of knowledge, and it forms a natural starting place for the theory of knowledge. Thus, Descartes began his great epistemological excursion by observing, "Whatever I have up till now accepted as most true I have acquired either from the senses or through the senses."[16] Of course, Descartes was later to go on, in true rationalist style, to argue that in fact the knowledge gained by the senses was derivative, and inferior to purely rational knowledge. Like me, Descartes saw the refutation of skepticism as an occasion to make a larger point about the structure of human knowledge. The point that I make, however, is quite different from, and almost diametrically opposite to Descartes's. I think our discussion of the refutation of skepticism has shown that perceptual knowledge is foundational, and that the knowledge gained by the senses is exactly on a par with the knowledge gained by pure reason—both are justified in the same way, under a single principle of foundational justification. I think that Descartes, Locke, and the other representationalists failed to refute skepticism, and that their failure is instructive. It reveals a fundamental mistake that they made: they mistook a cognitive process for a special, internal object of cognition.

Most philosophers who have made this mistake have not gone on to embrace skepticism—I think they had a little too much sense for that, and could not quite stomach a conclusion that was so directly at odds with their thought and practice in everyday life. Even so, I believe that such a mistake must have a profound effect on one's thinking, the more profound the more consistent one is. One such effect I have hinted at earlier: if one holds premises that in fact imply either global or external-world skepticism, even if one does not embrace those forms of skepticism, one may easily be moved towards less radical forms of skepticism, skepticism concerning more controversial claims. The reason is that here one's common sense (such as it is) would not serve as the check preventing one from drawing out and embracing the logical consequences of one's mistaken assumptions. This means that such a fundamental epistemological mistake as we have seen can produce very widespread errors about what sorts of things we are justified or unjustified in believing.

A second effect of the mistake, I suspect, is to produce a kind of discomfort, the more so the more philosophically minded one is, with the whole of one's beliefs about the external world, and perhaps the whole of one's beliefs about everything. I say this because the arguments indirect realists have been able to produce for the existence of external objects generally seem disappointingly weak at best, and it is open to question whether they have any cogency at all. The indirect realist who is honest with himself can never quite be sure that he is not being irrational in holding beliefs about the physical world, for all that he may find it unavoidable to do so. Hume, indeed, happily embraced this conclusion, being both a skeptic and an indirect realist. Which is to say: he believed in external objects, but he also believed there was no logical reason to do so. He thought that this illustrated the general conclusions, (a) that reason is impotent to produce knowledge and (b) that human beings are irrational. He thought this was a valuable lesson for people to learn, too, for purposes of putting us in our place:

> But could such dogmatical reasoners become sensible of the strange infirmities of human understanding, even in its most perfect state, and when most accurate and cautious in its determinations, such a reflection would naturally inspire them with more modesty and reserve, and diminish their fond opinion of themselves. . . . [I]f any of the learned be inclined . . . to haughtiness and obstinacy, a small tincture of Pyrrhonism might abate their pride, by showing them that the few advantages which they may have attained over their fellows are but inconsiderable, if compared with the universal perplexity and confusion which is inherent in human nature.[17]

I quote this passage because, although Hume's enormous influence on modern philosophy goes unquestioned by virtually all contemporary philosophers, and although many of Hume's ideas remain under lively discussion, seldom do scholars discuss what Hume himself thought was ultimately the good of his philosophical reflections. I suspect that Hume was right about the psychological effects of his philosophical reflections, though not about the desirability of those effects, nor about the truth of his doctrines.

Not everyone regarded the "perplexity and confusion which is inherent in human nature" as an edifying thing to behold. Thomas Reid commented thus on the arguments for philosophical skepticism:

> This opposition betwixt philosophy and common sense, is apt to have a very unhappy influence upon the philosopher himself. He sees human nature in an odd, unamiable, and mortifying light. He considers himself, and the rest of his

species, as born under a necessity of believing ten thousand absurdities and contradictions, and endowed with such a pittance of reason as is just sufficient to make this unhappy discovery: and this is all the fruit of his profound speculations. Such notions of human nature tend to slacken every nerve of the soul, to put every noble purpose and sentiment out of countenance, and spread a melancholy gloom over the face of things.[18]

A philosopher's first loyalty must be to reason: if skepticism is unequivocally supported by reason, then a philosopher, as such, must embrace it, and live with whatever unhappy consequences follow therefrom, including the belief that humans are generally irrational. This is why I say that, the more philosophically minded he is, the more uneasy the representationalist will feel in connection with the question of the rationality of his beliefs about the external world. Philosophy will never be satisfied with the sort of blindly instinctive beliefs Hume offered us; it inevitably seeks justification. I think, then, that I have offered a valuable service to philosophers, if only they will take me up on it—a *theoretical* defense of our ordinary, common sense beliefs, and with it a release from the problems to which Hume and Descartes introduced us.

Notes

1. Although a foundationalist need not hold that we lack reasons for our foundational beliefs, a foundationalist must think that it is *possible* to have a justified belief that one lacks reasons for. Since premises (8), (9), and (11) appear to be. necessary truths, if they are true at all, the argument can be adapted to show that this isn't even possible.

2. The term is from Alston, "Level Confusions in Epistemology."

3. This is what Fumerton calls "internal state internalism," as opposed to "access internalism" (*Metaepistemology*, 60-66). I have stated the principle in terms of the subject's "mental states" rather than in terms of his "internal states" in order to avoid begging questions about semantic externalism—I want to allow a semantic externalist, who thinks that what mental state one is in might depend upon external factors, to be an internalist about justification, provided he thinks that one's epistemic justification for a belief supervenes on what mental states one has. My claim in the text about the brain in the vat assumes that the BIV would also have the same mental states that you do; if not, then the verdict of same justification need not apply (though I think it does).

I note that the principle of internalism about justification, as I understand it, allows justification to depend upon a subject's total *history* of mental states, rather than just his current mental state; this is needed in order to account for the justification of beliefs that are in part based on memory (see my "The Problem of Memory Knowledge").

4. Prichard, 14.

5. Richard Fumerton has argued that, even when there *is* a logical connection between *P* and *Q*, I still need to have justification for believing that there is such a connection (*Metaepistemology*, 36; *Metaphysical and Epistemological Problems*, 38-52). However, see my "Fumerton's Principle of Inferential Justification" for a rebuttal.

6. Cf. my "Direct Realism and the Brain-in-a-Vat Argument," wherein I defend this same thesis but in a different way.

7. My point is not, of course, that one couldn't make an inference from the occurrence of certain sensory experiences to certain external facts, nor that such an inference would not be cogent. My point is that that is not how we know that there are external objects.

8. This is not exactly correct—something more than the logical possibility of one's being a brain in a vat is assumed, even by the skeptics. For it is logically contingent that I exist, but few brain-in-a-vat skeptics think "I don't exist" is a worthwhile skeptical scenario. What the skeptic wishes to rest his case on might better be described, "the logical possibility of my being a brain in a vat and everything appearing to me the way it does now."

9. See Vogel for a recent effort at this. It is not that I think the project hopeless, but I think it is far less clear how the indirect realist can make a case along these lines than it is how the *direct* realist can make his own case, and I think it would provide a less secure grounding for our perceptual knowledge. If I am supposed to believe there is a table here on the basis of the sort of consideration Vogel adduces, then, I think, I ought to be rather uncertain and tentative in my table claims.

10. Nozick (184-85) briefly discusses the matter of how to individuate belief-forming methods, at which point he suggests one constraint: if method A is indistinguishable, from the subject's point of view, from method B, then they should be considered instances of "the same method." This stricture also supports the conclusion that the brain in the vat uses the same belief-forming method that I do, when the brain tries to prove that it is not a BIV by holding up its supposed hands.

11. This is one formulation of the so-called "closure principle," widely used in formulations of the BIV argument. See Nozick, 204-11; Dretske, "Epistemic Operators"; and Audi, *Belief, Justification, and Knowledge*, 76-78, for criticisms of this principle. But see Klein, "Skepticism and Closure," 215-19, and Feldman, "In Defense of Closure" for responses to those criticisms.

Also note that the skeptic need not accept exactly principle (8); an alternative would be the principle, endorsed by Stroud (24-30), that if you know that *P*, and *your knowing P* is incompatible with *Q*, then you know (or are in a position to know) ~*Q*. But the latter is logically stronger than (8), so any criticism of (8) is a criticism of it.

12. Nozick (204-11) has shown this, though he thinks it is (8) that is false, and he doesn't see (7) as essential to the skeptic's argument. Garrett, however, has pointed out the importance of both the sensitivity requirement (7) and the closure principle (8) to the skeptic's case, as well as the conflict between them. My objection here essentially follows Garrett's.

13. Here, I have neglected to mention the method by which I formed the belief that ~*Q*. But this makes no difference to the argument. Perhaps my "method" here is "deduction from *P*," or perhaps it is whatever is the method by which I came to believe that *P*. Call my method, whatever it is, "M." The relevant point is that if I were to apply

M at a time when I was mistaken in believing *P*, I would still think that I wasn't mistaken in believing *P*.

14. This example is inspired by the skeptical scenario discussed by DeRose (22-23): "I'm an intelligent dog who's always incorrectly thinking he has hands." DeRose, understandably, finds this hypothesis ineffective in motivating skepticism.

15. Klein, "Skepticism and Closure," 215-19, suggests this as a possible way of defending the closure principle, though he is noncommittal on whether it is correct.

16. Descartes, *Meditations*, 17.

17. Hume, *Enquiry*, XII, part III. Hume sought to draw the same lesson from his skeptical arguments concerning induction (*Enquiry*, IV) and deductive reasoning (*Treatise*, I.IV.1). In both of the latter places, he seeks to establish that reason cannot justify, and so is not the cause of, our beliefs—allegedly demonstrating both that reason is impotent and that humans are not rational creatures. Note that Hume is not, in giving his skeptical arguments, trying to convince his reader to stop believing the things that are ostensibly under skeptical attack (see *Treatise*, I.IV.2, 187). He is trying to convince us to give up on rational justification.

18. Reid, 53. It is interesting to contrast Reid's and Hume's *attitudes* toward skeptical conclusions. I suggest that this is the central philosophical difference between the two. At first glance, there is not much difference between Hume's view that, for example, the practice of inductive inference is the effect of "custom" and the laws of association, and Reid's view that it is the effect of "the constitution of our nature"—except that Hume sees the conclusion as a welcome indictment of our cognitive imperfection, while Reid does not.

References

Adler, Mortimer J. *Ten Philosophical Mistakes*. New York: Macmillan, 1985.

Alston, William. "Has Foundationalism Been Refuted?" Pp. 39-56 in *Epistemic Justification*. Ithaca, N.Y.: Cornell University Press, 1989.

———. "Level Confusions in Epistemology." Pp. 153-71 in *Epistemic Justification*. Ithaca, N.Y.: Cornell University Press, 1989.

Aristotle. *The Basic Works of Aristotle*. Edited by Richard McKeon. New York: Random House, 1941.

Armstrong, David. *Perception and the Physical World*. London: Routledge & Kegan Paul, 1961.

Audi, Robert. *Belief, Justification, and Knowledge*. Belmont, Calif.: Wadsworth, 1988.

———. *The Structure of Justification*. Cambridge: Cambridge University Press, 1993.

Austin, John. *Sense and Sensibilia*. Oxford: Clarendon, 1962.

Barker, S. F. "Appearing and Appearances in Kant." Pp. 274-89 in *Kant Studies Today*. Edited by Lewis White Beck. LaSalle, Ill.: Open Court, 1969.

Bell, John S. "Bertlman's Socks and the Nature of Reality." Pp. 139-158 in *Speakable and Unspeakable in Quantum Mechanics*. Cambridge: Cambridge University Press, 1987.

Berkeley, George. *A Treatise Concerning the Principles of Human Knowledge* in *Principles, Dialogues, and Correspondence*. Indianapolis: Bobbs-Merrill, 1965. Referred to in the text as *Principles*.

———. *Three Dialogues between Hylas and Philonous* in *Principles, Dialogues, and Correspondence*. Indianapolis: Bobbs-Merrill, 1965. Referred to in the text as *Dialogues*.

Block, Ned. "On a Confusion about a Function of Consciousness." Pp. 375-415 in *The Nature of Consciousness*. Edited by Ned Block, Owen Flanagan, and Güven Güzeldere. Cambridge, Mass.: MIT Press, 1997.

BonJour, Laurence. *The Structure of Empirical Knowledge*. Cambridge, Mass.: Harvard University Press, 1985.

Burge, Tyler. "Content Preservation." *Philosophical Review* 102 (1993): 457-88.

Byrne, Alex, and David Hilbert. "Colors and Reflectances." Pp. 263-88 in *Readings on Color*. Vol. 1. Edited by Alex Byrne and David Hilbert. Cambridge, Mass.: MIT Press, 1997.

Chisholm, Roderick M. *Perceiving: A Philosophical Study.* Ithaca, N.Y.: Cornell University Press, 1957.

———. *Theory of Knowledge.* 2nd edition. Englewood Cliffs, N.J.: Prentice-Hall, 1977.

———. "The Problem of the Criterion." Pp. 61-75 in *The Foundations of Knowing.* Minneapolis, Minn.: University of Minnesota Press, 1982.

Dancy, Jonathan. "Arguments from Illusion." *Philosophical Quarterly* 45 (1995): 421-38.

Davidson, Donald. "A Coherence Theory of Truth and Knowledge." Pp. 120-38 in *Reading Rorty.* Edited by Alan Malachowski. Cambridge, Mass.: Basil Blackwell, 1990.

———. "Mental Events." Pp. 247-56 in *The Nature of Mind.* Edited by David Rosenthal. Oxford: Oxford University Press, 1991.

Dennett, Daniel. "Quining Qualia." Pp. 519-47 in *Mind and Cognition.* Edited by William Lycan. Cambridge, Mass.: Basil Blackwell, 1990.

———. *Consciousness Explained.* Boston: Little, Brown & Co., 1991.

DeRose, Keith. "Solving the Skeptical Problem." *Philosophical Review* 104 (1995): 1-52.

Descartes, René. *The Philosophical Writings of Descartes.* Edited by John Cottingham, Robert Stoothoff, and Dugald Murdoch. Cambridge: Cambridge University Press, 1984.

———. *Meditations on First Philosophy.* In *The Philosophical Writings of Descartes.* Vol. 2. Cambridge: Cambridge University Press, 1984.

Dretske, Fred. "Epistemic Operators." *Journal of Philosophy* 67 (1970): 1007-23.

———. "The Pragmatic Dimension of Knowledge." *Philosophical Studies* 40 (1981): 363-78.

Einstein, Albert. *Relativity: The Special and the General Theory.* New York: Bonanza Books, 1961.

Ellis, Albert. *Reason and Emotion in Psychotherapy.* New York: Carol Publishing Group, 1994.

Ellis, Albert, and Russell Grieger. *Handbook of Rational-Emotive Therapy.* Vol. 1. New York: Springer, 1977.

Evans, Gareth. *The Varieties of Reference.* Oxford: Clarendon, 1982.

Fales, Evan. *A Defense of the Given.* Lanham, Md.: Rowman & Littlefield, 1996.

Feldman, Richard. "In Defense of Closure." *Philosophical Quarterly* 45 (1995): 487-94.

Foley, Richard. "Epistemic Conservatism." *Philosophical Studies* 43 (1983): 165-82.

———. *Working without a Net.* New York: Oxford University Press, 1993.

Foley, Richard, and Richard Fumerton. "Davidson's Theism?" *Philosophical Studies* 48 (1985): 83-89.

Fumerton, Richard. *Metaphysical and Epistemological Problems of Perception.* Lincoln, Nebr.: University of Nebraska Press, 1985.

———. *Metaepistemology and Skepticism.* Lanham, Md.: Rowman & Littlefield, 1995.

Garrett, Bryan. "A Sceptical Tension." *Analysis* 59 (1999): 205-6.

Gettier, Edmund. "Is Justified True Belief Knowledge?" *Analysis* 23 (1963): 121-23.

Goldman, Alvin I. "What Is Justified Belief?" Pp. 1-23 in *Justification and Knowledge.*

Edited by George Pappas. Dordrecht: Reidel, 1979.

Haack, Susan. "Theories of Knowledge: An Analytic Framework." *Proceedings of the Aristotelian Society* 83 (1983): 143-57.

———. *Evidence and Inquiry*. Cambridge, Mass.: Blackwell, 1993.

Hardin, C. L. *Color for Philosophers*. Indianapolis: Hackett, 1988.

———. "Reinverting the Spectrum." Pp. 289-301 in *Readings on Color*. Vol. 1. Edited by Alex Byrne and David Hilbert. Cambridge, Mass.: MIT Press, 1997.

Hilbert, David. *Color and Color Perception: A Study in Anthropocentric Realism*. Stanford, Calif.: CSLI, 1987.

Huemer, Michael. Review of Evan Fales' *A Defense of the Given*. *Philosophical Review* 108 (1999): 128-30.

———. "The Problem of Memory Knowledge." *Pacific Philosophical Quarterly* 80 (1999): 346-57.

———. "Direct Realism and the Brain-in-a-Vat Argument." *Philosophy and Phenomenological Research* 61 (2000): 397-413.

———. "The Problem of Defeasible Justification." *Erkenntnis* 54 (2001): 375-97.

———. "Fumerton's Principle of Inferential Justification." *Journal of Philosophical Research*, forthcoming (2002).

Hume, David. *An Enquiry Concerning Human Understanding*. In *Enquiries Concerning Human Understanding and Concerning the Principles of Morals*. Edited by L. A. Selby-Bigge. Oxford: Clarendon, 1975.

———. *A Treatise of Human Nature*. Buffalo, N.Y.: Prometheus, 1992.

Hyman, John. "The Causal Theory of Perception." *Philosophical Quarterly* 42 (1992): 277-96.

Jackson, Frank. *Perception: A Representative Theory*. Cambridge: Cambridge University Press, 1977.

———. "Epiphenomenal Qualia." *Philosophical Quarterly* 32 (1982): 127-36.

Jacobs, Gerald. *Comparative Color Vision*. New York: Academic Press, 1981.

Jastrow, Joseph. *Fact and Fable in Psychology*. New York: Houghton, Mifflin, 1901.

Kant, Immanuel. *Prolegomena to any Future Metaphysics*. Edited by Lewis White Beck. Indianapolis: Bobbs-Merrill, 1950.

———. *Critique of Pure Reason*. Translated by Norman Kemp Smith. New York: St. Martin's Press, 1965.

Kelley, David. *The Evidence of the Senses*. Baton Rouge: Louisiana State University Press, 1986.

Klein, Peter. "A Proposed Definition of Propositional Knowledge." *Journal of Philosophy* 68 (1971): 471-82.

———. "Skepticism and Closure: Why the Evil Genius Argument Fails." *Philosophical Topics* 23 (1995): 213-36.

Kripke, Saul. *Naming and Necessity*. Cambridge, Mass.: Harvard University Press, 1980.

Langsam, Harold. "The Theory of Appearing Defended." *Philosophical Studies* 87 (1997): 33-59.

Lehrer, Keith. "Why Not Scepticism?" *Philosophical Forum* 2 (1971): 283-98.

Lehrer, Keith, and Thomas Paxson. "Knowledge: Undefeated Justified True Belief." *Journal of Philosophy* 66 (1969): 225-37.

Lewis, David. "Elusive Knowledge." *Australasian Journal of Philosophy* 74 (1996): 549-67.

Locke, John. *Essay Concerning Human Understanding*. Edited by P. H. Nidditch. Oxford: Clarendon, 1975.

McDowell, John. *Mind and World*. Cambridge, Mass.: Harvard University Press, 1994.

Moore, G. E. "Proof of an External World." *Proceedings of the British Academy* 25 (1939): 273-300.

———. "Hume's Theory Examined." Pp. 108-26 in *Some Main Problems of Philosophy*. London: Allen & Unwin, 1953.

———. "Moore's Paradox" Pp. 207-12 in *G. E. Moore: Selected Writings*. Edited by Thomas Baldwin. New York: Routledge, 1993.

Nozick, Robert. *Philosophical Explanations*. Cambridge: Cambridge University Press, 1981.

Oakley, I. T. "An Argument for Scepticism Concerning Justified Belief." *American Philosophical Quarterly* 13 (1976): 221-28.

Parfit, Derek. "Personal Identity." *Philosophical Review* 80 (1971): 3-27.

Peacocke, Christopher. *Sense and Content*. Oxford: Clarendon, 1983.

Peikoff, Leonard. *Objectivism: The Philosophy of Ayn Rand*. New York: Penguin, 1991.

Pitcher, George. *A Theory of Perception*. Princeton, N.J.: Princeton University Press, 1971.

Pollock, John L. "The Structure of Epistemic Justification." *American Philosophical Quarterly Monograph Series*, no. 4: *Studies in the Theory of Knowledge* (1970): 62-78.

———. *Contemporary Theories of Knowledge*. Totowa, N.J.: Rowman & Littlefield, 1986.

Price, H. H. *Perception*. London: Methuen, 1950.

Prichard, H. A. "Does Moral Philosophy Rest on a Mistake?" Pp. 1-17 in *Moral Obligation*. Oxford: Clarendon, 1949.

Putnam, Hilary. *Reason, Truth, and History*. Cambridge: Cambridge University Press, 1981.

Rand, Ayn. *Introduction to Objectivist Epistemology*. New York: Penguin Books, 1990.

Reid, Thomas. *Inquiry and Essays*. Edited by Ronald Beanblossom and Keith Lehrer. Indianapolis: Hackett, 1983.

Russell, Bertrand. *The Analysis of Matter*. New York: Harcourt, Brace, 1927.

———. *Human Knowledge: Its Scope and Limits*. New York: Simon and Schuster, 1948.

———. *The Problems of Philosophy*. New York: Oxford University Press, 1997.

Sacks, Oliver. *The Man Who Mistook His Wife for a Hat*. New York: Simon and Schuster, 1985.

Schilpp, Paul Arthur, ed. *The Philosophy of G. E. Moore*. London: Cambridge University Press, 1942.

Searle, John R. *Intentionality*. Cambridge: Cambridge University Press, 1983.

Sextus Empiricus. *Scepticism, Man, and God*. Edited by Philip Hallie. Middletown, Conn.: Wesleyan University Press, 1964.

Shoemaker, Sydney. "Persons and Their Pasts." *American Philosophical Quarterly* 7

(1970): 269-85.

———. "The Inverted Spectrum." *Journal of Philosophy* 79 (1982): 357-81.

Shope, Robert K. *The Analysis of Knowing: A Decade of Research.* Princeton, N.J.: Princeton University Press, 1983.

Steinbeck, John. *The Pearl.* New York: Viking Press, 1947.

Strawson, P. F. *The Bounds of Sense.* London: Methuen, 1966.

Stroud, Barry. *The Significance of Philosophical Scepticism.* Oxford: Clarendon, 1984.

Turnbull, H. W., ed. *The Correspondence of Isaac Newton.* Vol. 3. London: Cambridge University Press, 1961.

Tye, Michael. "Visual Qualia and Visual Content." Pp. 158-76 in *The Contents of Experience.* Edited by Tim Crane. Cambridge: Cambridge University Press, 1992.

Unger, Peter. *Ignorance: A Case for Scepticism.* Oxford: Clarendon, 1975.

Varela, Francisco, Adrian Palacios, and Timothy Goldsmith. "Color Vision of Birds." Pp. 77-98 in *Vision, Brain, and Behavior in Birds.* Edited by H. Philip Zeigler and Hans-Joachim Bischof. Cambridge, Mass.: MIT Press, 1993.

Vogel, Jonathan. "Cartesian Skepticism and Inference to the Best Explanation." *Journal of Philosophy* 87 (1990): 658-66.

Wittgenstein, Ludwig. *Philosophical Investigations.* New York: Macmillan, 1968.

Index

About the Author

Michael Huemer is assistant professor of philosophy at the University of Colorado at Boulder. He received his Ph.D. from Rutgers University and his B.A. from the University of California at Berkeley. This is his first book.

CPSIA information can be obtained
at www.ICGtesting.com
Printed in the USA
LVHW031722220119
604809LV00002B/314/P